A Castle with Many Rooms
The Story of the Middle Ages

by Lorene Lambert

A Castle with Many Rooms: The Story of the Middle Ages
© 2017 by Lorene Lambert

All rights reserved. However, we grant permission to make printed copies or use this work on multiple electronic devices for members of your immediate household. Quantity discounts are available for classroom and co-op use. Please contact us for details.

Cover Design: Sarah Shafer

ISBN 978-1-61634-383-5 printed
ISBN 978-1-61634-384-2 electronic download

Published by
Simply Charlotte Mason, LLC
930 New Hope Road #11-892
Lawrenceville, Georgia 30045
simplycharlottemason.com

Printed by PrintLogic, Inc.
Monroe, Georgia, USA

Contents

1. The Long Fall
   Glorious no longer, the Roman Empire exits the stage of history 5
2. Justinian the Great
   The legacy of Rome endures in Byzantium 13
3. King Arthur and the Saxons
   Facing invasion and ruin, the tribes of Britain unite under one leader 21
4. The Monastery
   In the Middle Ages, monks are the guardians of the written word 29
5. The Earliest Explorers
   An Irish monk and a band of Norsemen sail over the Atlantic's dark waters 37
6. Making a Nation
   The scattered tribes of the Franks unite under one true king. 45
7. The Scroll and the Stone
   Out of the deserts of Arabia, a new army arises. 51
8. Charles the Hammer
   The Franks face the armies of Islam at the Battle of Tours 59
9. Charlemagne
   A great king attempts to revive the Roman Empire 67
10. The Rushing North Wind
    The Vikings storm the shores of Europe. 77
11. The Meeting at Egbert's Stone
    A young king survives a swamp of despair 87
12. Cornstalks and Quetzal Feathers
    The Maya build cities and measure time in the jungles of America. 95
13. The Battle of Hastings
    William of Normandy becomes King of England 103
14. Feudalism
    The people of the Middle Ages arrange themselves into a pyramid. 113
15. The Way of the Warrior
    During the Middle Ages, warfare is bound by the rules of honor 119
16. The Cross Upon the Shield
    The knights of Europe crusade for the freedom of Jerusalem 127
17. Lionheart and Robin Hood
    As the crusades continue, England's king nearly loses his kingdom 135

18	Castles
	Fortresses of stone protect the lord and all his people *143*
19	The Great Charter
	For the first time, a written document limits the power of a king *151*
20	The Mongols
	Genghis Khan builds an empire on horseback. *159*
21	The Travels of Marco Polo
	A merchant from Venice explores the far reaches of the East *167*
22	Salt, Books, and Gold
	In Africa, all roads lead to the fabled city of Timbuktu *177*
23	A Fresh Breeze
	Giotto di Bondone transforms the art of painting *185*
24	Freedom Fighter
	In Switzerland, William Tell strikes a blow against tyranny. *193*
25	The Black Prince, the Black Death, and the White Knight of Orleans
	England and France fight the Hundred Years War. *199*
26	Conquerors of the Green Sea
	Prince Henry of Portugal unlocks the Age of Exploration. *209*
27	An Explosion of Words
	Johannes Gutenberg makes the wisdom of God and man available to everyone ..*217*
28	The Conquest of Constantinople
	One empire meets its end at the hands of another *225*
29	Rebirth
	The Renaissance fans the winds of change. *233*
30	Reformation
	With his pen and his hammer, Martin Luther seeks to change the Church *239*
31	Revolution
	Nicholas Copernicus invents a new universe *245*
32	One Thousand Years of History
	At the end of a long journey together, we bid farewell to the Castle. *253*

Endnotes 255
Bibliography. 261
Photo Credits 265
For Further Reading 267
Maps 273
Pronunciation Guide 285

Chapter One

The Long Fall

*Glorious no longer, the Roman Empire
exits the stage of history*

In 376 A.D. a host of people gathered on the northern bank of the Danube River, their faces turned to the south.

Today we know them as Goths, although that is not a name they used for themselves. In their own language, they were *Tervingi,* a word which meant "the forest people." Since ancient times, they had farmed the land in what is now Germany and eastern Europe, building small villages surrounded by fields of barley, wheat, and oats. But the Goths were not content with peacefully tilling the ground; they considered themselves to be warriors above all, and each man's worthiness among his fellow Goths was determined by the fearlessness with which he attacked his enemies in battle.

For all their warlike ways, however, the Goths were facing a foe far more ferocious. In the last half of the fourth century, the Huns, a tribe of fierce men astride swift and sturdy horses, had swept out of Asia like a mighty wind and plundered every Gothic village they could find. So dangerous were they that the Goths gave way before them, abandoned their homes, and fled, wandering west and south, until they had gathered on the Danube riverbank.

The Danube rises in the Black Forest of Germany and flows east for more than 1,700 miles until it empties into the Black Sea. It is broad and deep, the second-longest river in Europe, and in 376 A.D. it was the utmost frontier of the Roman Empire. Its smooth, rolling waters marked the truest sort of border: on the southern bank stood the mighty Roman Empire; to the north were the lands of the people whom the Romans called *Germani,* or Barbarians—the Goths among them.

The Romans considered the people of Germany to be "barbarian" because they thought that anyone who did not speak Latin was uncivilized. The people of ancient Greece had used the word *barbaros,* which meant "babbler," to refer to anyone who was not Greek, and the Romans had taken up both the word and the idea behind it. So to Roman minds, the Goths, in particular, were barbarian because they did not build cities or construct monuments or write their own history. To the Romans, it appeared that the Goths wished for nothing more than to die gloriously in battle; and from behind the safe walls of their strong empire, the Romans eyed the Goths with suspicion and fear.

The Danube River had always protected the northern edge of the empire. No bridges spanned its dark depths, making it difficult for an enemy to invade. If any were so bold as to try, the Roman soldiers guarding the frontier would fall upon them as they attempted to cross the river. The Danube was like a moat protecting a castle, keeping unwanted visitors out.

And for hundreds of years it had worked. The only barbarians who had been able to pass over the river successfully had been small, scattered family clans, who had quickly vanished into the vastness of the Roman Empire and become almost Roman themselves. No Gothic army had ever successfully invaded across the Danube.

Still, the Romans were wary of the menacing Goths, who so loved battle. They stationed soldiers at the frontier and trusted the river for protection; then they turned most of their attention to other problems.

And Rome, in 376, did indeed have other problems.

For over a thousand years, Rome had been master of the world. It had grown from a simple town, founded 600 years before the birth of Christ, to an enormous empire that ruled immense portions of Europe, Asia, and Africa. Its strong and disciplined army had conquered many lands, and its effective government had transformed them. When Rome conquered a people, it absorbed them into the empire, allowing them to live their lives under Roman protection and, eventually, become Roman citizens themselves. The empire built great cities, marvelous roads, towering aqueducts to carry water for many miles, and graceful bridges with strong, arched pillars. Within the empire, these conquered people lived for the most part in peace and safety, and in return they paid taxes, farmed crops that helped feed many of the empire's hungry mouths, and shepherded their flocks.

But there were problems, nevertheless. As time had gone by, Rome's love for order and civilization had darkened into a lust for wealth and idleness. The emperors, who in the empire's earlier days had ruled only as the "First Among Equals," now began to demand that the people worship them as *Dominus et Deus:* King and God. Of course, Rome had suffered the occasional bad emperor—men like Nero or Commodus—but the foolish wickedness of such men had been balanced by wiser leaders following after them. Now, though, a steady stream of weaker kings had occupied the throne. Instead of tending to the business of ruling, they had become lazy and more absorbed in pursuing luxury and pleasure. So more and more of the empire's daily life was conducted by town and city officials. Many of these leaders gave way to the temptations of greed and cruelty, taxing the people unfairly or punishing them harshly for the most minor of crimes.

Most importantly, the Empire was too large to be watched over from the throne in only one city. In 285, the emperor Diocletian (die-uh-CLEE-shun) had tried to solve this problem by splitting the empire into two halves, west and east, with the western capital in Rome and the eastern capital in Constantinople (con-stan-tih-NO-pull), which lies in what is now Turkey. But two capitals also meant two emperors, and as you might imagine, men of such power do not share that power easily.

And so in 376, when the host of Goths gathered on the Danube's banks, terrified of the encroaching Huns, the Rome from whom they sought protection was not quite the powerful, almighty Rome that it had been in the past.

The Goths sent messages to Emperor Valens (VAL-enz), who ruled the Eastern Roman Empire in Constantinople, requesting permission to cross the river and enter Roman lands peacefully. Although he may have paused at the idea of granting refuge to an enormous army of Goths, Valens nevertheless consented to give them entrance. They could come, he said, if they would agree to farm only vacant land, and if they would provide soldiers to serve in Rome's armies. The Goths quickly agreed and forded the river in safety. In allowing that crossing, however, Valens started in motion a toppling line of dominoes, a series of events that would eventually lead to the entire empire's downfall.

The Roman border, held unbroken for so long, had been breached. As this news made its way north, more and more Gothic clans, fleeing the Huns' terror, poured over the river. With Emperor Valens far away, the burden of dealing with all of these refugees fell upon the local Roman officials, and not all of them were equal to the task. Tax money was demanded, food supplies ran low, and insults were shouted from both sides. In just two years, the Goths decided that they had had enough and rebelled in open warfare against their Roman hosts.

Valens gathered up a portion of his army and marched west

to deal with the Gothic rebels, but in the meantime the Goths had been joined by many more of their kinsmen. On August 9, 378, the two forces met. Valens and his army were slaughtered on the battlefield.

Now the Goths knew something they hadn't known before: the mighty Roman army could be defeated in battle. The godlike emperor could be killed like any other man.

Freed from their awe of Roman power, the Goths began raiding deeper and deeper into the Empire, looting villages and towns. By 409, under the leadership of their war chief Alaric (AL-a-rik), they were laying siege to the city of Rome itself. The men of the city tried to appease him by offering a huge ransom of gold, but Alaric could not be deterred. In August of 410, the Goths entered Rome through one of its gates and pillaged the city for three days and nights.

It was the first time in more than 800 years that Rome had fallen to an enemy. The news spread like a rising tide, drowning all who heard it in shock and despair. Could it be true? Rome was known as "the Eternal City," blessed by God. How could it have been trampled under the boot of a heathen conqueror?

St. Jerome (juh-ROHM), a priest who had lived in Rome and devoted much of his life to translating the Bible into Latin, wrote of his terrible grief when he heard of the city's fall:

"Who could believe that Rome, built upon the conquest of the whole world, would fall to the ground? That the mother herself would become the tomb of her peoples?"

After humbling the Eternal City, the Goths departed, made their way north, and invaded Spain and Gaul, which today we know as France. There they established a kingdom of their own, the land of the Visigoths; we will meet them there again in a chapter to come.

But Rome was not to be spared further sorrow. The way had been shown; other barbarian tribes flooded into the empire from all directions. From Germany, another group of warriors, known as the Vandals, marched all the way through the Roman lands to seize the coast of North Africa. In 455 they launched their own attack against Rome and sacked the city again. Once more the news of Rome's humiliation spread through all the lands that had once bowed low before it.

Meanwhile, pressing ever closer were the Huns, the Asian nomads who struck such fear in the hearts of the Goths. By 400 A.D. they had built a giant empire that stretched from the Alps to the shores of the Caspian Sea. In 434 the Huns gained a new king, whose name you may already know: Attila (uh-TILL-uh). One historian, writing several hundred years later, described Attila the Hun as "a man born into the world to shake the nations, the scourge of all lands." With Attila leading them, the Huns stormed through both halves of the old Roman Empire, winning immense sums of gold from the king of the Eastern Empire in Constantinople, before turning to attack Rome in the west. As the Huns rode toward them, the Roman citizens cowered in fear, certain that the end of the world was at hand.

Rome was rescued from Attila's wrath, though not through any valiant effort on the part of her people. Before Attila could reach the city, he received word that Rome and all the countryside around it were suffering from terrible famine and sickness. Not wishing to risk the health of his soldiers, he turned aside to the north, burning and looting as he went.

Rome—wonder of the world, queen of cities, throne of the Roman Empire—was no longer any of those things. The nobles abandoned the city and fled to the town of Ravenna, which, being situated in the midst of a large marshy swamp, was easier to defend. Without any true or honorable way to determine who should be emperor, what power there was became more and more centered on the army. If a general felt that he had enough men to back him, he would march into Ravenna, kill whoever was currently on the throne, and declare himself King and God, though of course such behavior was neither godly nor kinglike. Over the course of its last seventy-three years, the Western Roman Empire had twenty-four emperors, and twenty of them were murdered while on the throne.

In 476 then, that precarious throne was occupied by a young man called Romulus Augustulus (ROM-yoo-lus ah-GUST-uh-lus), the "little Caesar." He was only a boy, really, left wearing the emperor's crown when his father, one of those very generals who had briefly seized control, had been forced to flee for his life.

But there was another who wanted that crown, as it seems there always must be. His name was Odoacer (OH-doh-AY-ser), and though a member of the Roman army, he was no Roman. History does not tell us the nature of his ancestry, but he was most likely a Goth or, perhaps, even a Hun.

At the head of his own army, he approached Ravenna, and once he had secured the city, he demanded that Romulus Augustulus surrender the throne and, with it, the title of emperor. The boy, with no other choice before him, agreed. And with that, Odoacer became king.

But king of what? Rome was no longer ruled by Romans. In fact, it no longer ruled anything at all. Devastated by centuries of weak emperors and barbarian invasions, Rome had lost its empire. The city stood alone amidst the dusty memories of its past glory.

The Roman Empire had been the fortress that kept the world stable and secure; when the empire ended, the era we think of as ancient times ended. But a new world would emerge from the dust of the empire's collapse. On Rome's shattered foundation, a majestic castle would rise—a castle of many kingdoms, its rooms filled with splendor and pageantry, sorrow and joy. That is the story that lies before us in the chapters to come: the long and rich tale of the Middle Ages.

Chapter Two

Justinian the Great

The legacy of Rome endures in Byzantium

Mighty Rome was no more. But as you may remember, the empire had been divided in two many years before. Though the city of Rome had fallen, and the western half of the empire with it, in the east the empire continued, centered on its magnificent capital: Constantinople.

At its beginning, 600 years or so before the birth of Christ, Constantinople had been nothing more than a modest Greek town called Byzantium (buh-ZAN-tee-um). But while the town may have been humble, its location was not. It stood on a triangle of land that jutted out into the Bosphorus Strait, a gleaming ribbon of water that was the gateway between Europe and Asia.

If you spin your globe and find the Mediterranean Sea, follow it eastward, past Greece and the Aegean Sea and into the smaller Sea of Marmara. Do you see a little further east the deep waters of the Black Sea? Only a thin bridge of land separates the Black Sea from the Sea of Marmara, and that neck of land, in turn, is divided by a narrow channel: the Strait of Bosphorus. This tiny opening is the only meeting place between the Black Sea and the Mediterranean where a ship could sail from the shores of western Asia to the far reaches of Europe. There, perched like a watchtower above the Bosphorus Strait, sat Byzantium. Whoever controlled the town also controlled the Strait, and therefore, all of the ships traveling back and forth between Europe and Asia.

Of course, such an important spot would not go unclaimed by the power that was Rome, and so in 324 A.D., the great emperor Constantine declared that Byzantium would be the site of a grand new capital, a wondrous city modeled after Rome itself. When he died in 337, the city was given his name, Constantinople.

After the empire was divided, Constantinople remained its eastern capital, the only Roman capital now that Rome itself had fallen. The city was immensely strong: the Bosphorus Strait protected its southern and eastern ramparts, and a deep inlet called the Golden Horn guarded it to the north. Any attacker would have no choice but to approach from the west, and there the emperors had caused a huge wall to be built, three layers deep. Within such a dauntless fortress, the kings of Constantinople felt safe from any enemy.

And yet on an afternoon in January of 532, heavy columns of black smoke rose over the city's center. Citizens cowered in their houses, their doors barred, listening fearfully as bands of armed men ran howling through the streets, striking down anyone they could find. In the palace, the emperor sat hunched on his throne, his face in his hands, his wife by his side, his last few loyal advisors huddled nearby. Constantinople was burning, but it had come under no attack from without. The proud city had been brought to its knees by its own people.

And it had all started with a game.

Of course, people have cheered and shouted at sporting events for thousands of years, and the Romans of Constantinople were no different. They had even built their own arena, just like the stadium where you might go to watch a baseball game—a large, open oval with rows and rows of tiered seats. In Constantinople this arena was called the Hippodrome; many years later a visiting knight described it like this:

> *Now there was another wonderful sight in another part of the city, for near the Palace was a place which was called the Games of the Emperor. That place was a full crossbow shot and a half long and nearly one wide. Around this place were fully thirty or forty steps where the [people of the city] used to climb up to watch the games. And above these steps was a very tasteful and noble box where the emperor and the empress used to sit when there were games with the other important men and ladies.*

Games of all sorts happened at the Hippodrome, but the most beloved sport by far was chariot racing.

In those days, chariot races were wild, dangerous events. As many as twelve four-horse teams would race around the Hippodrome's narrow oval track, and collisions and injuries happened in every race. The racers were divided into two teams, the Blues and the Greens. Spectators wore their team's colors and cheered madly for their favorites to win. At times the followers of the two different teams would clash in bloody brawls during and after the races, their skirmishes spilling out into the city streets and often ending with men lying dead, still dressed in blue or green.

The races had been popular in Constantinople for hundreds of years. But the brutal fights grew worse, with more and more people dying. On January 10, 532, a huge riot flared up at the races, with Blues and Greens falling viciously upon one another. The violence threatened to consume the entire city; and so at last, the emperor decided that something must be done.

This emperor was named Justinian (jus-TIN-ee-un). He had come to the throne in 527 as co-ruler with his uncle, Justin; when Justin died a few months later, Justinian became sole ruler in Constantinople. Though his uncle had provided him with an excellent education in law, history, and religion, Justinian had been born into a humble family, and many of the nobles in the Byzantine court looked down their noses at him despite the fact that he sat upon the throne. Ignoring their sneers, the new emperor had set about improving the lives of his people and the fortunes of the empire. He worked tirelessly; in fact, he became known as "the king who never sleeps."

Justinian's foremost goal was to reconquer all the lands of the western empire that had been lost to the Goths and Vandals, and to do this he had chosen as general of his armies a famous warrior named Belisarius (bell-ih-SAR-ee-us). He had appointed other advisors as well, including a clever man, John of Cappadocia (cap-uh-DOH-shee-uh), to be his tax collector. John's chief duty was to raise the money needed for Belisarius' wars against the barbarians.

Confident that all the lost Roman territory would be regained, Justinian had then turned his hand to a new project: gathering all of Roman law into one book. As you might imagine, an empire as long-lived as Rome's would issue many laws over the years, all of them written in dozens of different places and scattered widely, and often outdated or contradictory. Justinian sent out a team of ten lawyers to track down every Roman law. They were to eliminate any laws that were unnecessary and rewrite the remaining ones so that they agreed with one another. It was an enormous task, but Justinian kept close watch on their progress, prodding them forward.

Justinian's works were not always popular, though, with the people of Constantinople. The wars against the barbarians were very expensive, and John of Cappadocia continually levied new taxes in order to pay for them. The code of law that Justinian's lawyers were writing was all to the good, but in the meantime the emperor made it very clear that his will and his word were absolute. He would not bow to the wishes of the nobility or to the whims of popular opinion. The nobles muttered amongst themselves, Who is this son of commoners to reign over us?

Their unrest was caused not only by Justinian's humble background. They also objected to his wife, Theodora (thee-uh-DOR-uh). Justinian had married her in 525, before he had become king; she had been an actress and circus performer, and thus, a most unsuitable bride. Justinian was able to wed her only after his uncle passed a law allowing marriage between people of different classes, rich and poor. Though years had passed and Theodora conducted herself with dignity, the nobles could hardly believe that such a lady should be their empress. Even worse, from their point of view, was the trust that Justinian seemed to place in her; she was always the first of his advisors.

So there was already tension in the city that winter day in 532 when the fighting erupted at the chariot races. Justinian, who was a devoted fan of the Blues, nevertheless showed himself to be a fair judge. He commanded that the ringleaders of the riot, Blues and Greens alike, be arrested and executed.

However, on the day of the executions, two of the condemned men escaped and fled to a nearby church for refuge, only steps ahead of Justinian's soldiers. Not willing to attack a church, the soldiers surrounded the building and put it under heavy guard. An angry mob gathered, muttering and then shouting for the men to be pardoned.

That afternoon, as another round of races began in the Hippodrome, the restless, maddened crowd bellowed insults at Justinian as he sat above them in the emperor's box. The entire stadium rang with their shouts, until someone lifted up the cry of "Nika!" (NIE-kuh).

This word was the cheer used by the fans to spur their favorite charioteer on to victory. It meant "Win!" or "Conquer!" But on this day, as evening descended, the shouts of "Nika!" seemed to unite the crowd into a frenzy of anger, all directed at Justinian. The swarm of enraged citizens broke out of the

Hippodrome, surging forward to pound on the gates of the palace next door.

Justinian barricaded himself behind the palace walls, watching helplessly as the crazed mob set fire to the city. Finally, he tried to pacify them by dismissing the unpopular tax minister, John of Cappadocia, but they were not satisfied. The riots, and the fires, grew and spread.

For five days the horde laid siege to the palace. Many of Constantinople's noblemen, who had always looked down upon Justinian and who chafed against his new laws, urged the crowd into greater heights of madness and encouraged them to demand a new emperor.

When they named as emperor a young man called Hypatius (hi-PAY-shee-us), a nephew of a long-dead former emperor, Justinian fell into despair. He could see no good end to all of this and decided that his only course must be to give up his crown and flee the city. His last few remaining loyal councilors reluctantly agreed and made their own plans to leave.

But then, as Justinian contemplated the sad end to all his achievements, a voice stopped him. It was his wife, the empress Theodora. As she stood beside him, listening to the din outside the palace walls, she said to him, "One who has been a king and worn the crown can never endure its loss. I do not wish to live to see the day that I am not greeted as 'Queen.' " She paused for a moment as the shouts outside grew in rage and fervor, then she added, "Imperial purple is a fine color for a burial shroud."

A grim thought, perhaps, but Justinian found courage in it. He rallied and sent for his finest warrior, the general Belisarius, and presented to him a plan—a dreadful but necessary plan—to end the violent riot.

By this time, most of the mob had returned to the Hippodrome, where they were carrying out a crowning of Hypatius as emperor. The army, led by Belisarius himself, surrounded the stadium and blocked all its entrances, trapping the crowd inside. And then, as the Greek historian Theophanes (thee-OFF-uh-neez) tells us, "In the end, not one of the citizens, either of the Greens or of the Blues, who were in the Hippodrome, survived."

Over thirty thousand people died, and the riot died with them. Peace was restored, but at what great cost—so many killed and the beautiful city left almost entirely a smoking ruin!

But now Justinian was free. He ordered Hypatius executed and the noblemen who had supported the riot exiled. With no one to oppose him, he set to work.

First, he rebuilt the city. Its most beautiful church, a lovely building called the Hagia Sophia (ha-GHEE-ah so-FEE-ah), which means "Holy Wisdom," had collapsed completely. Justinian commanded that it be reconstructed as magnificently as possible. When it was finished, it boasted the largest dome in the world, with polished floors of stone from Egypt and Syria and columns taken from an ancient temple in Turkey. It was a wonder of the world, and still is today. Along with the church, Justinian also rebuilt the Hippodrome, but no races were held there for many, many years.

The law code was completed as well, and just as the Hagia Sophia still stands, so too does the Code of Justinian. His greatest concern was that the law be the same within the borders of the Byzantine Empire, so that all citizens could trust it as fair. Through all of the centuries that have passed between Justinian's time and our own, his laws have been used as a foundation for the law code of many nations. In fact, the men who devised the Constitution of the United States used Justinian's Code as a guide. Justinian's portrait hangs in the Capitol building in Washington, D.C., as a tribute to his part in creating the principles that underlie American law.

Justinian was the humble son of a commoner, and he married a lady whom many saw as far beneath him. He fled before the mob and almost surrendered his crown, but in the end, he is remembered in history not for those failures but for his mighty accomplishments and is known to this day as Justinian the Great.

Chapter Three

King Arthur and the Saxons

Facing invasion and ruin, the tribes of Britain unite under one leader

In the year 410 a letter arrived in Rome addressed to the current emperor, Honorius (huh-NOR-ee-us). Within its battered cover, it held an urgent plea from the citizens of the island that the Romans called Britannia, or Britain: We are threatened with invasion! You must help us!

But in those first few years of the fifth century, Rome was confronted by that same threat. As we have seen, the empire teetered on the edge of ruin with Goths, Vandals, and Huns pressing on every side. The emperors had begun to call back Rome's soldiers from the far-flung edges of the empire, and by 410 there were no longer any Roman legions left in Britain. Freed from the shadow of Rome's looming power, Britain's enemies gazed upon her green shores and soft hills with greedy eyes.

And so the Britons sent a cry for help to the Romans: Come back! Protect us!

But it was not to be. Honorius faced his own doom, for the Goths and their war chief Alaric were at that moment marching toward Rome. The emperor dictated a response to his scribes to be sent to every city and town in Britain:

"Vestrum est, Britanni, vos ipsos defendere."

Which, if we translate from the Latin, says something like this: It is your own task, Britons, to defend yourselves.

How distraught the Britons must have been when they received this reply! Defend themselves? The people of Britain had not been concerned with matters of war for hundreds of years. They had depended on the Roman legions for that. Britain's shores had been guarded by stout garrisons and a fleet of sleek Roman ships; the northern border had been secured by a large wall, built by the Roman emperor Hadrian (HAY-dree-un), to hold back the fierce tribes that lived in the rocky wilderness to the north. Safe from harm, the Britons lived in comfortable homes behind solid stone ramparts. They had learned the ways of Rome and filled their towns with Roman luxuries: hot baths, soft woolen carpets, intricate mosaic floors, shining copper coins inscribed with the head of the emperor.

But now the Romans had departed; the garrisons were deserted, Hadrian's wall unmanned, and the Britons were alone. They must find a way to defend themselves, because the Saxons were coming!

If you will look at your globe and find the island of Britain, you will see that it lies but a short distance across the North Sea from the northern plains of Germany, home in those early days of the Middle Ages to a group of formidable warriors called the Saxons. They had long looked toward the west and Britain's misty green isle, for their own homeland was shrinking, overrun by the same Goths and Huns who threatened Rome. For hundreds of years Saxon ships had cruised along the coasts of Britain like hungry sharks, but legions of hardened Roman troops had kept them from attempting anything more than lightning-quick raids. Now the guards were gone and the Saxons set sail once more, this time not to raid and then vanish back over the sea, but to invade and stay forever.

The warriors came first, attacking the towns and farms in the southern and eastern areas of the island. The Britons who lived there were forced to flee, for to remain meant either death or slavery under Saxon overlords. Then around the year 430, when the native Britons had been sufficiently subdued, the warriors sent for their families. A wave of Saxon immigrants swept over the shores of Britain, and they were soon joined by others: Jutes and Angles from Jutland, which is the peninsula that is called Denmark now.

For the next hundred years or so, the invaders contented themselves with carving out little kingdoms in what was once Roman Britannia. Even today the names of many British counties preserve the memories of this invasion: Sussex (South Saxons), Wessex (West Saxons), East Anglia (the Angles), Middlesex (the Middle Saxons). In fact, the very name "England" comes from an old word that means "land of the Angles."

Yet you might be surprised to learn that these Saxons and Angles were not always unwelcome. Even the Romans themselves had sometimes invited roving bands of Saxons to come to the shores of Britannia and help fight off other enemies. This the Saxons had always been willing to do, for a price. Such warriors-for-hire are called *mercenaries*—men who fight not for a king, or for love of country, but for gold. Even with the Romans gone, the practice of hiring Saxon mercenaries did not fade, and this would eventually lead both to the downfall of the Britons and also to the rise of one of their greatest legends.

That story starts with a man named Vortigern (VOR-ti-jern), a powerful chief among the Britons, so powerful, in fact, that much later the writers of Britain's history would refer to him as a king. The lands that he governed were under constant attack from the wild tribes of men from the north of Britain's isle, the Picts and the Scots, and in an effort to drive them back behind Hadrian's Wall, Vortigern decided to hire some help. He sent a message across the North Sea to a pair of Saxon warriors named Hengist (HEN-jist) and Horsa (HOR-sah).

Saxon legends tell us that these men were brothers,

ferocious fighters who accepted Vortigern's invitation to come and join the Britons in battle against the Scots. They arrived in three ships and settled peacefully in Kent, in the southeastern corner of Britain. For a while all was well; Vortigern took Hengist's daughter Rowena as his bride and showered his new Saxon in-laws with weapons, clothing, food, and gold. But Kent was a lovely place, hilly and green and much to be desired, and the two brothers hatched a plot to secure all of Kent for themselves. They suggested to Vortigern that his enemies could be defeated entirely if only more of their Saxon countrymen could be brought into the fight. "For," Hengist said, "the people of my country are strong, warlike, and robust." Vortigern agreed, and so Hengist and Horsa invited more and more of their Saxon kin to join them in Britain. Soon the Saxons in Kent were so numerous that Vortigern could no longer supply their needs, and he grew afraid. You are too many, he told them. You must fend for yourselves now. We need your help no longer. Go back home.

I suspect that you can imagine the Saxons' response. They had no desire to return to the cold plains of their homeland. They refused to leave; indeed, they turned their attack upon Vortigern himself.

So battle was joined between the Britons and the Saxons. Four times Vortigern's army, led by his son Vortimer (VOR-ti-mer), clashed with the Saxons in Kent. The war between them waxed and waned like a tide—sometimes the Saxons pushed forward, sometimes they were forced back. Finally, during one of these battles, in the year 455, Horsa was killed and the Saxons driven all the way back to the sea.

A short time passed as both sides took a breath, and then Hengist sent to Vortigern an offer of peace. In order to celebrate the end of their warring, Hengist ordered a great feast prepared, to which all of Vortigern's nobles were invited. But there was treachery afoot, most literally afoot, for Hengist directed every one of his warriors to conceal a sharp knife beneath the sole of his left foot. Then in the midst of the feast, when each Briton had eaten his fill and was heavy with food and wine, Hengist cried out, "Nima der saxa!" ("Take out the sword!")

At once, his men drew their blades, fell upon the helpless Britons, and killed them all. They spared only Vortigern, bundling him roughly in chains and casting him into a damp prison cell until he ransomed his own life by giving the Saxons large swaths of British land.

Now all seemed grim and hopeless for the Britons. Enemies threatened them on all sides: Hengist pushing from the south and east, Saxons and Angles raiding inward from their little kingdoms along the coasts, and wild Picts and Scottish tribes striking down from the north. Who could save them?

It is from this time, a time of fear and despair deep in the shadows of the earliest Middle Ages, that Britain's greatest legend arose. How much of his story is truth and how much fable and myth is a question lost in those same shadows, but the echoes of his name still resound, reaching even your ears as you sit and read this book in the 21st century. After all, who has not heard of the wondrous deeds and mighty works of King Arthur?

Who he was for certain has never been determined, for this is the time in history that is sometimes known as the Dark Ages, not because the sun did not shine just as brightly on Britain's gentle hills then as it does now, but because so few written records have survived. What remains are the folktales, the stories told over and over by the people of the land until at last they are written down by a scholar or a churchman many years after the events that they describe have faded into the past.

This is the case with Arthur. The earliest stories seem to tell us a tale that goes something like this.

When Vortigern had ransomed himself from the treacherous Saxons by giving them much of his own land, the battle lines were drawn once again between Saxon and Briton.

Vortigern had failed to defend his people, so the Britons looked to a new leader, a man who may have had roots in Rome, may have been Roman himself, and who was well-versed in the disciplined ways of the Roman legions. This commander rallied the Britons and their leaders and led them into war against the Saxons. One of the earliest histories of Britain, a book called the *Historia Brittonum*, describes it:

> At that time, the Saxons grew strong by virtue of their large number and increased in power in Britain. Hengist having died, however, his son Octha crossed from the northern part of Britain to the kingdom of Kent and from him are descended the kings of Kent. Then Arthur along with the kings of Britain fought against them in those days, but Arthur himself was the military commander.

Through battle after battle, the Britons with Arthur as their captain struggled to beat the Saxons back, even as more and more Saxon ships, filled with warriors, landed on the southern coast and claimed it for themselves as the Kingdom of the South Saxons, a name later shortened to Sussex and still used in England today. Sometimes the Britons prevailed and sometimes they fled before the Saxon charge, but always both armies returned to fight another day.

Finally in about the year 485, on a hilltop called Mount Badon, Arthur and his Britons won a great victory. The *Historia Brittonum* tells us that "the twelfth battle (against the Saxons) was on Mount Badon in which there fell in one day 960 men from one charge by Arthur; and no one struck them down except Arthur himself, and in all the wars he emerged as victor." Another old, old history book tells about "the Battle of Badon, in which Arthur carried the Cross of our Lord Jesus Christ for three days and three nights upon his shoulders [or shield] and the Britons were the victors."

The complete story of the Battle of Badon Hill is lost and

only these few scraps remain, but they were enough to fuel the legend of Arthur, the great leader who preserved his people from the rampaging Saxons. As the centuries went by, the story of Arthur grew into something ever more grand. He became a king who wielded a mighty, magical sword called Excalibur; who ruled over the blessed realm of Camelot, where his virtuous knights sat at the Round Table; and who married the beautiful lady Guinevere (GWEN-eh-veer).

The stories say too that in his last battle, when he lay mortally wounded on the field, he was carried away to the mystical island of Avalon, and there he sleeps still, to awaken again when Britain has need of him.

In truth, the Britons needed him even after Mount Badon was won. For though the Saxons were thrown back and a few years of peace descended, it did not last. In 511 or so, the legends say, Arthur was killed at the Battle of Camlann, not by the Saxons but by Britons jealous of his power. And the Saxon conquest continued, so that by the year 600, the Britons' kingdoms had become almost entirely the domain of their invaders.

But even as the history of England marched forward under a Saxon banner, leaving the Britons behind, Arthur was not forgotten. As the people of Britain told and retold his stories, they made Arthur their best example of a noble, virtuous king. Though he existed in the shadowy past, before England was truly England, he still lives on today as the story-book illustration of what an Englishman ought to be.

Chapter Four

The Monastery

In the Middle Ages, monks are the guardians of the written word

Sometime around the year 700, Eadfrith (EED-frith) of Lindisfarne (LIND-es-farn) dipped a goose-quill pen into a small jar of coal-black ink. On the slanted surface of the tall bench before him was stretched a smooth sheet of *vellum*, which is a kind of parchment made from the skin of a calf. At his elbow lay a book, a copy of the Bible opened to the Gospel of Matthew. With ink in his pen and a prayer in his heart, Eadfrith began to copy the holy words onto the blank, pale page.

Around him, the *scriptorium* was silent. It was a room set aside solely for the purpose of copying books, with dark wooden walls and light falling in shafts through tall, narrow windows. Others were there as well, carefully tracing words; the only sound was the scratch of their pens' tips across the vellum. They were all dressed alike, in rough grayish-white, woolen robes; and even though Eadfrith was their leader, he was attired just as plainly. They were monks, after all, these men, and each of them had promised, when he had entered the monastery here at Lindisfarne, to live as simply as possible.

Ruins of Lindisfarne Priory

The word *monk* means "single" or "alone," someone who has chosen to withdraw from the world and dedicate his life to the service of God. A monastery is a building, or often a whole group of buildings, where the monks live and work. During the Middle Ages a monastery was a world in itself, because everything that the monks might need was contained within its walls. The monks sewed their own clothes with wool spun from their own sheep. They grew their own food in the walled gardens and rolling fields that surrounded the monastery. They tended vineyards, milked cows, and baked bread. It was in this way, by removing any need to be out in the world, that they felt they could draw closer to God.

Lindisfarne was perched atop a tiny island off Britain's northeast coast. It was a lonely spot, reachable only at low tide when the ocean waves retreated and a visitor could scramble across the mudflats that separated the island from the mainland shore. But though it was lonely, it was not alone. It was part of a network of monasteries that spread throughout all of Europe during the Middle Ages.

Of course, the idea of removing yourself from the world in order to draw closer to God was not a new notion. Even in the earliest days of the Christian church there had been people who had retreated out into the desert to live completely alone, spending their days in fasting and prayer. They were called *hermits*. But as time went by, the hermits began to attract *disciples,* or followers, people fascinated by the hermits' lives and teachings. Soon the attention of their followers came to rest mostly on the hermits themselves, rather than on the God that they served. And so, seeking a better way, people who wanted to devote themselves to God began to gather together in communities, in contrast to the lone hermits. There they could still serve God, but also blend together as a whole group who felt the same way.

The idea of "sameness" was important to the monks, for if they were all the same, none could stand out from the rest. They were equal in their humility. At each monastery the monks dressed alike; ate the same food at long, common tables; and prayed and worshiped at the same time. Everyone's life in the monastery was governed by the same set of rules.

Many of these rules were established by a man named Benedict, who had written them down around the year 529. Benedict lived in Italy; as a young man, his parents had sent him to Rome to study the ancient books there, but he had found the city too wild and wicked for his taste and had fled to the mountains south of Rome. On a hilltop called Monte Cassino, he had destroyed a temple dedicated to the Roman god of light, Apollo, and built in its place a large, many-windowed monastery. As other monks came to join him there, he had written down his rules for a peaceful and godly life: pray and work. Benedict declared, "He who labors as he prays lifts his heart to God with his hands."

The Rule of Benedict decreed that monks should divide their days into three parts: working, whether for the good of the monastery or for the good of mankind; sleeping, each monk in a small, bare room which was called a *cell;* and praying, which Benedict thought of as the "work of God." Eight times a day, beginning in the dark hours before dawn and then every three hours until evening, the monks would gather in the monastery chapel to sing, usually from the Psalms, and pray. Then for the other hours of the day they would work, either doing the chores that were necessary to keep the monastery running, serving the people who lived in the countryside nearby, or studying the Bible and the monastery's other books.

Benedict's Rule spread quickly; its ideas seemed to promise an orderly and peaceful community, and many monasteries adopted it as their own. In this way life within a monastery was remarkably similar across Europe, whether it was Monte Cassino in the warm hills of Italy or Lindisfarne on its cool, fog-bound island far to the north.

The leader of the monastery, its head monk, was called the *abbot.* Since most monasteries were quite large communities, with many people, animals, and crops dependent on the abbot's leadership, he usually had a second-in-command, who was called the *prior.* There were also monks in charge of the various parts of the monastery's day: the *lector* read the Bible lesson during church services; the *cantor* led the choir; and the *sacrist,* like a librarian, was responsible for all the books. When a young person came to join the monastery, he would swear a vow before the abbot to dedicate his life to God, to give up all his worldly possessions, and to obey the rules of the monastery.

As the Middle Ages went on, many of the monasteries became enormously wealthy. They owned large swaths of land; often the people who lived nearby would work the land for free, for they believed that the only way to true salvation was through the Church, and devoting some of their time to farming the monastery's land would give God cause to look kindly upon them. For the same reason, every family in the area would bring gifts of money and food to the monastery, usually on holidays or feast days, as a way of gaining favor with God.

In return for the people's devotion, the monks in the monastery sought for ways to help them. They called this *charity,* a word that means "love," and indeed this was a way to show the love of God to the people. Benedict himself said, in his Rule, that a monk should reach out to the people he meets: "He should first show them in deeds rather than words all that is good and holy." Those living nearby knew that they could always come to the monastery if they were sick or hungry; the monks would give them the best medical care that they could, and the monastery kitchen always offered meals freely.

There were other sorts of charity as well. The monastery was known to be a place of refuge, where weary travelers could stop for the night in safety. Orphans often found homes within the monastery's walls, where they were cared for and taught a trade so that they could make their way in the world when they had grown. The monasteries also almost always included a school, where boys could come and learn to read and write.

Along with charity, the monks also followed another calling: missionary work. They believed strongly that they must bring the Word of God to the people who had not yet heard it. Especially in the early years of the Middle Ages, this was a dangerous calling indeed. Bandits and scoundrels lurked on the roadways, and much of northern Europe still worshiped its old pagan gods and was not eager to part with them. The monks would travel on foot, often alone, trusting God to protect them and establishing new monasteries wherever they went.

As the monasteries spread through all of Europe, they brought with them not only the Word of God but also the written words of men. One of the most important labors that the monastery undertook was scholarship. Every monastery appointed some monks to be scribes, specially trained in the copying and preserving of books. A monastery needed many books: the books of the Bible, of course, but also music books for the choir, books of theology by great Christian thinkers of the past, books about prayer, books to direct church services, books about history, books about faraway lands and long journeys, and the monastery's rule books. There were also piles of record books, since the monastery usually kept a listing of every birth, death, and marriage in the countryside round about it, as well as accounts of any interesting or important historical events.

All of these books were made by the monks themselves. They would prepare the parchment, mix the inks, copy the words onto the pages, and paint the illustrations to accompany the words. They even made the books' covers out of leather or wood; sometimes, if it was a special book, it would be beautifully decorated with gold and jewels. These books were one of the monasteries' most important accomplishments. With their copying and preserving, they saved many books that would otherwise have been lost forever and kept many records of history that could be found nowhere else. Most of all, by copying the books, the monks kept the light of learning and education alive in many places that might otherwise have been very dark.

In the scriptorium at Lindisfarne, this was the work of Eadfrith, as he carefully transferred the words of the Gospel of Matthew onto the blank page. He wrote in Latin, which was the language of the Bible in those days. He would pray each word as he formed it, because like every scribe, Eadfrith believed that copying the Scriptures was a way to worship God. With each page he finished, he set aside the black ink; brought out his vivid, colored pigments; and decorated the page with beautiful designs—scrolls and flowers, tiny animals and musical instruments, little pictures of men and angels. These lovely decorations were called *illuminations,* and Eadfrith planned to create four beautifully illuminated books, one for each Gospel: Matthew, Mark, Luke, and John. They would come to be called the Lindisfarne Gospels, and we shall see them again in just a few chapters.

Scholars, missionaries, doctors, teachers, farmers. The monks of the Middle Ages were all of these things, but most of all they were humble followers of their Rule. The life of the monastery was not an easy one, but many men nevertheless passed through its gate to live behind its walls and devote their lives to God.

Chapter Five

The Earliest Explorers

*An Irish monk and a band of Norsemen
sail over the Atlantic's dark waters*

On the southwestern tip of Ireland, a thin finger of land stretches out into the cold Atlantic Ocean, pointing toward the gray horizon. The 3,200-foot summit of Mt. Brandon rises above the waves as they pound the rocky shore; at its topmost peak crouch the ruins of a small, beehive-shaped chapel. Here, the legends say, began one of the most remarkable journeys of the Middle Ages, a seven-year voyage undertaken by a stalwart Irish monk named Brendan of Clonfert, whom later centuries would celebrate as Brendan the Navigator.

He was born in the year 484 and given into the service of the Church on his first birthday. He lived all of his childhood in monasteries, educated by monks, and when he was 28 years old, he was ordained as a priest himself. And more than just a priest, a traveler. For the rest of his life he sailed all around the islands that surrounded Ireland, spreading the gospel of Christ and founding monasteries for the service of God.

One of these was at the foot of Mt. Brandon, a place called *Seana Cill,* "the old church." It was there, in the church's tiny chapel atop the mountain, that Brendan gazed at the stormy sea and decided to sail into the unknown. He had been told by a fellow monk of an island out there somewhere, an island that resembled the lost Garden of Eden.

Such a journey could not be taken lightly, even for so experienced a sailor. He gathered a small crew of other monks, possibly as many as fourteen, who were willing to brave the ocean alongside him. Together they constructed a particular kind of Irish boat, a *currach* (KUH-ruhk), still built in Ireland to this day. It was made by crafting a wooden framework, covering it with leather hides, and then sealing all the seams with tar. They erected a mast with a small square sail in the center and, after devoting twenty days to prayer and fasting, set off.

Model of St. Brendan's Currach

There is no way to know how they must have felt as Mt. Brandon sank below the horizon behind them. Perhaps they were afraid, perhaps eager to make their way to Paradise, but surely they could never have known what wonders awaited them.

The legends of that journey tell of fantastic sights: crystal pillars floating serenely on the surface of the sea; an island filled with sheep the size of bulls; birds coursing overhead and shouting down the words of the Psalms; an island inhabited by fearsome giants who hurled globs of molten stone. Several times they encountered sea monsters, and one of the enormous beasts even raised their little boat upon its back. Eventually, the currach landed on a beautiful shore veiled in fog with thick stands of trees and flowers and groves of fruit. Was this Eden? Brendan and his crew could not be sure, but for a long time they camped there, eating their fill and resting from their voyage. Then warned by an angel to return to their home, they set sail back the way they had come, beaching their currach on Ireland's coast seven years after they had departed.

No sooner had they landed than the story began to spread, from monk to monk and village to village, throughout all of Ireland and further still. Brendan was revered for his courage and his remarkable voyage; people flocked to visit him until the day he died in 577, when he had reached the grand old age of ninety-three.

What are we to make of such a tale? Fire giants and talking birds sound more like fairytales than history! It is very hard to know if the story I have just told you is the one that Brendan himself shared. His account of the journey was never written down in his lifetime; in fact, three hundred years passed before another monk took the trouble to record the *Navigatio sancti Brendani abbatis,* the "Voyage of Saint Brendan the Abbot." By that time the story had become a marvelous legend.

So is it just a tale? Brendan certainly existed; there is no doubt at all about the fact of his life and his constant travels throughout Ireland. Did he also travel far out into the ocean? And if he did, where was that foggy, fruitful green shore that he discovered?

The Norsemen, whom we'll meet in just a moment, thought they knew. Their sagas—their long histories—tell us clearly that the furthest shore, far beyond Iceland and Greenland, the shore, in fact, of North America itself, was known to them as "Irland it

Mikla," which means "The Greater Ireland."

Could Brendan have sailed all the way to North America in his little open boat? If we think about it, we can start to see that some of those legendary sights could be matched to actual places in the North Atlantic. The crystal pillars could be icebergs; the talking birds could have been nesting seabirds off the coast of Greenland, their cries and squawks carried by the wind. The sea monsters might have been whales. And the fire giant could very well have been the eruption of one of Iceland's active volcanoes.

Despite this, skeptics scoffed for many years: no one could cross the Atlantic on a tiny leather boat! But in 1976 a writer and adventurer named Tim Severin decided to put the question to the test. With four friends, he built his own currach in the same way that Brendan would have. Setting off from the foot of Mt. Brendan, he made the same journey, passing Greenland and Iceland, the ocean's currents carrying him to the shore of Newfoundland in Canada. His journey proved beyond doubt that, 1,600 years before, Brendan the Navigator could very well have done the same thing.

And if he did, he would have been the first European to set foot on North American land, 900 years before Christopher Columbus.

There were others who followed in Brendan's wake. They were the Norsemen—the men from the North—who came from the lands that today we call Scandinavia: Denmark, Sweden, and Norway. Aboard their marvelous longships, the Norsemen felt no fear of the deep, forbidding ocean. They ranged far from the shores of their homelands, out into the north Atlantic to harvest the vast schools of fish that roamed in those waters.

In their wanderings, the Norsemen had discovered the island of Iceland and made it a colony, dotting it with sturdy settlements and snug farms. The weather was often dark and bitterly cold, but such a harsh environment only seemed to make these hardy people stronger.

Among their number was one Erik Thorvaldson (TOR-wuhl-suhn), a giant of a man who had come to Iceland when he was only ten years old; his father had been exiled to the island from Norway for the crime of murder. This Erik was much more commonly known among his neighbors as Erik the Red, both for his flowing red hair and bristling red beard and also for his fiery temper. In fact, the fate of his father soon overtook Erik as well, and because he had killed a man while in the grip of a towering rage, he found himself banished from Iceland for three years.

No matter. Erik knew where to find more land, free land, far beyond the horizon. Years before, one of Iceland's fishermen had been blown far off course by a wild winter storm and had returned full of tales of white cliffs and green fields and gray rock rising out of the western ocean. Turning his back on Iceland with an angry mutter, Erik set sail in about the year 982, determined to find these unknown shores.

And find them he did. You can follow his voyage yourself if you will locate Iceland on your globe and sail your fingertip straight west across the sea until you bump up against an enormous, icy island, just as Erik did.

Greenland.

It is, in fact, the largest island in the world, and only its fringes are habitable. The interior is entirely cloaked with a massive sheet of ice. Erik steered around its western tip and then up the western coast until he found a region that seemed protected and ice-free, perhaps even suitable for farming. He made a note of it and sailed on.

For the three years of his exile he explored all around this land, naming everything he found after himself: Erik's Island, Erik's Valley, Erik's Inlet. In all, he navigated over 6,000 miles of sea water, an impressive feat indeed.

When the time of his banishment had expired, he returned to Iceland and took up his plow and spade, planning to return to his life as a farmer. But it was not to be. His temper betrayed him once again, and he entered into a vicious feud with his neighbor. When he was sentenced to banishment a second time, he decided that he would leave Iceland forever.

He was not so hotheaded that he ignored the dangers of attempting to build a life all by himself on the ice-rimmed shores of Greenland. To survive, he needed others. So cannily, he began to boast of the wonders of this huge island he had explored. It was filled with game, he declared to anyone who would listen, seals, moose, bear, walrus, more fish than anyone could ever net and eat. All of this awaited the brave souls who would sail with him westward. In fact, it was Erik who gave the island the alluring name of "Greenland," in an attempt to suggest that it was more hospitable and warm than frigid Iceland.

Erik's scheming succeeded. When he sailed away from Iceland for the last time, twenty-four ships and seven hundred people accompanied him. Though storms and hardship caused some to turn back, in the summer of 986 Erik the Red and four hundred former Icelanders settled on the southern coast of Greenland and set about carving farmland out of the frozen hillsides.

The settlement flourished. Eventually it grew to more than 5,000 inhabitants, of whom the chiefest was Erik himself.

Erik had, of course, brought his family along with him. Among his four children was one son, a young man named Leif Erikson. Though Leif had been born in Iceland, he grew up amid the wild hills and rocky inlets of Greenland. When he reached manhood, Leif began to chart a very different course from his father.

He assembled a crew and voyaged all the way back to Norway in the year 999. There he learned the ways of Christianity and became a follower of Christ. Determined to bring this new truth back to his people in Greenland, who had never heard it, he set sail for home. But a fearsome storm erupted from the east and the savage winds blew him past Greenland, far to the west. Though the sky was still thick with the storm's wind and rain, Leif could discern land on the western horizon, stretching to the north and south as far as the eye could see, green with "self-sown fields of wheat, and grapevines." Vinland, Leif called it. The Land of Vines.

Astonishing though this find was, it was not, to Leif, totally unexpected. Several years before, a merchant and fisherman named Bjarni Herjolfsson (BYAR-nee HER-yolf-suhn) made the claim that he had discovered a vast land in the far west. Surely this was it.

When the storm had emptied itself out, Leif and his men sailed back to Iceland. There he sought out Bjarni Herjolfsson, bought from him his ship, and gathered a new, larger crew. Full of excitement he went to his father, Erik, and made a request: Would Erik be willing to come along as the leader of the expedition? His experience as an explorer would surely be valuable.

Though he was an old man by this time, Erik was indeed willing. But as he made his way toward the ship, ready to embark, his horse stumbled and Erik fell, injuring his leg. Shaken, he sent his son off alone. The Icelandic sagas tell us that he said, "It was not meant for me to discover other lands than that in which we now live. We shall sail together no more."

And that was true. Leif departed, and Erik limped back to his farm. An illness soon took hold of him and, in his weakened state, he died. His son, venturing off into the west, never again saw his father alive.

After Leif and his crew had anchored their ship in one of Vinland's sheltered coves, they built huts to live in and a stable for the few cows that they had brought along. The land around them seemed incredibly rich—meadows of deep grass for the cattle, thick forests with trees soaring into the sky, salmon almost as big as a man teeming in the cold ocean waters just offshore.

They decided to stay for the winter, and when spring came they sailed back to Greenland with the holds of their ship stuffed with good things: grapes, timber, smoked fish.

Despite these treasures, Leif never returned to Vinland. His father was dead; he assumed leadership of his family and settled down on his farm in Greenland to grow crops and to tell his neighbors about his faith in Jesus Christ. In the years that followed, other Norsemen occasionally sailed to Vinland's shores to bring back timber and fish, but none of them stayed for longer than a few weeks. They had met the native people who lived there, and these meetings had not been friendly. The idea of building a permanent Norse settlement in Vinland seems to have faded away and with it, the memory of Leif's voyage there.

But hundreds of years later, the remains of Leif's little town were found in Newfoundland, in Canada, proving without a doubt that these Greenlanders had successfully settled in North America. It would be five hundred more years before Christopher Columbus would turn his face toward the horizon and sail off into the west, into the New World.

Chapter Six

Making a Nation

*The scattered tribes of the Franks
unite under one true king*

If you look at a map of the world and find the Danube River, winding east toward the Black Sea, you will see to the west another of Europe's great rivers: the Rhine. It flows down out of the lofty Alps and makes its way north through Germany and the Netherlands until it empties into the icy, wind-whipped waters of the North Sea. South and west of the Rhine lie the modern-day countries of Switzerland, Belgium, and France, the land that in the days of the Roman Empire was known as Gaul.

In those days several tribes of tall, fair-haired warriors lived along the eastern banks of the Rhine. They were proud men, said to have been descended from the defenders of ancient Troy, and their name, the Franks, came from an old, old word which meant "a thrown spear." They were another of the people that the Romans called *Germani,* or barbarians, and like the Goths, they sought to cross the river.

As Rome's power weakened, they did just that. The Franks pushed further and further west, establishing little strongholds for themselves throughout Gaul. Each Frankish tribe was ruled by its own chief, and they often fell to squabbling among themselves, with each chieftain seeking to wrest power away from his neighbor. But sometimes a greater enemy would appear, for Gaul at this time in history was home to a patchwork host of different peoples. If some outsider arose to threaten the Franks as a whole, the various Frankish rulers would lay aside their quarrels and join together to defeat the menace and then, often as not, return to their homes and immediately take up arms against one another.

As time went by, a certain Frankish chief, Childeric (CHIL-der-ick), gathered enough power and collected enough land that he began to call himself a king; in fact, he wore a signet ring made of solid gold with an inscription that read *CHILDIRICI REGIS,* which means "of Childeric the king." Making such a proud claim meant that Childeric was often in conflict with both his neighbors and his enemies, neither of whom wished to acknowledge his right to that claim, and so he spent much of his reign fighting battles.

Childeric always rode into war with his son by his side. This young man, whose name was Clovis, had seen firsthand the strength which resulted when the Franks fought together, united, instead of against one another. If they would only remain united permanently, all of Gaul could be theirs! But welding the separate, quarrelsome tribes into one people was a fearsome task, a seemingly impossible task, for not one of the Frankish chiefs would ever willingly agree to submit to any of the others. It would require a heart of iron and a stern fist to accomplish; and as it turned out, Clovis had both.

Childeric died in the year 481, when Clovis was just fifteen years old. Despite his youth, the prince immediately donned his father's crown and assumed leadership of his tribe, the Salian Franks. They ruled a portion of Gaul that had been formally given to Clovis' grandfather by the Romans, and indeed, the Salian Franks had often joined the Romans in battle. You might remember from our first chapter that the Romans' great enemies, the Goths, had marched north after sacking Rome itself. They had carved for themselves a kingdom in the southernmost parts of Gaul, but the Romans still guarded Gaul—the last tiny remnant of their once mighty empire—and fought desperately to prevent the Goths from pushing any further north. In this, the Salian Franks had aided the Gaulish Roman legions. They were allies against the common enemy.

Clovis, though, looked doubtfully upon the Roman troops. He knew that he would never be able to persuade the Franks to unite under his leadership while the Roman banner flew in Gaul. As long as the smallest spark of Roman power still smoldered, the various tribes would always look to the Romans for leadership against the Goths or against the Huns to the east. If Clovis wanted to rule over all of Gaul, he would have to rid Gaul of the Romans. To do that, he would have to convince the other Franks to come together under his leadership.

In the year that Clovis became king, Roman Gaul was ruled by a military leader named Syagrius (si-AY-gree-uhs), who bore the title *magister militum:* "Master of the Soldiers." He controlled five of Gaul's strong cities and ruled from one of them, a place called Soissons (swah-SON). Syagrius had occupied a difficult position for many years, trying to maintain Roman power in Gaul even as the empire withered away and Rome itself collapsed. We can only imagine his dismay when, in 486, he received a message from Clovis, bearing a formal challenge and naming a time and a place for battle.

Syagrius had no choice but to respond, and on the appointed day his legions marched out to the battlefield to face rank upon rank of grim Frankish warriors, each man gripping a spear and a thick, double-bladed battle-axe. Clovis had managed to gather several Frankish tribes and create a sizable army.

Not all of them, though. One Frankish chieftain, a man named Chararic (CHAR-uh-rick), brought his forces to the battlefield but then kept them back from the fight, commanding them to stand still and watch until the battle was over. He planned to then ally himself with the winner, whether it be Childeric or the Romans under Syagrius.

He did not have to wait long for a result. The battle that day was short; the Romans were quickly and thoroughly defeated.

Friendless now, Syagrius fled to his old adversaries, the Goths, taking refuge with them in one of their largest towns. But Clovis realized that his victory over Rome could not be complete without the head of the *magister militum,* and so he sent a blunt threat to the Goths: Give him up or I will bring war upon you. Fearing the Franks' growing power, the Goths bound Syagrius and handed him over to Clovis to be executed.

With Syagrius' death, Roman Gaul fell entirely into Clovis' grasp and his realm was now suddenly doubled in size. But that was not sufficient for Clovis. He wanted nothing less than all of Gaul, and so within just a few years, he brought all of the other Frankish tribes under his control. Some he attacked without mercy; one of the first to fall before him was the faithless Chararic. Some surrendered to him willingly, when he promised them safety and reward. Some met him in battle after a formal challenge and were defeated. But one way or another, every Frankish chief eventually bowed his knee to Clovis.

Still, even as king over all the Franks, Clovis was not without enemies. Other tribes—the Burgundians, the Allemani, and the Goths in the south—still lived and fought in Gaul, and Clovis continually strove for ways to gain the advantage over them.

With the Burgundians, he decided to seek alliance rather than battle, for he had met the youngest Burgundian princess, a lady named Clotilde (cloh-TILD), and determined at once that she should be his wife. He sent a message saying as much to her uncle, Gundobad, an evil man who had killed the poor girl's mother and father. Gundobad wanted very much to refuse, for he would have liked to give her in marriage to someone who would benefit him. But his greed was overshadowed by his fear of Clovis' power, and so, reluctantly, he permitted Clotilde to leave his court and travel into the lands of the Franks. She and Clovis were married as soon as she arrived.

Clotilde was a devout follower of Christianity, and her dearest wish was for her husband to join her in faith. For many years he resisted; he scoffed when Clotilde insisted on baptizing their children. But tradition tells us that one day his mind was changed. He had ridden into war against the Allemani and his men were failing badly, falling back before the enemy's determined charge. A Frankish historian, writing a few years after Clovis' death, tells us the story:

> Clovis took to wife Clotilde, daughter of the Burgundians and a Christian. The queen unceasingly urged the king to acknowledge the true God, and forsake idols. But he could not in any wise be brought until war broke out with the Alamani. The two armies were in battle and there was great slaughter. Clovis' army was near to utter destruction. He raised his eyes to heaven, saying, Jesus Christ, if thou shalt grant me victory over these enemies, I will believe in thee and be baptized in thy name.

The tide of the battle shifted and Clovis emerged victorious. As he had promised, he returned to his home and was baptized as a Christian along with thousands of his fellow Franks. Confident that it was his newfound God who had given him success against the Allemani, Clovis turned his attention to the Franks' last remaining obstacle, the Goths. In 507 he marched his army to face them at a place called Poitiers (PWAH-tee-ay), a city in central Gaul, where at last he defeated and killed their leader. The Goths were forced to retreat, back further and further, until they were removed from Gaul entirely. They contented themselves with re-establishing their kingdom far to the south in the land of Spain. We will see them again, there, in just a chapter or two.

As for Clovis, he had secured all of Gaul for himself and his Franks, just as he had planned all those years ago when he had been given his father's crown at the young age of fifteen. The Franks were no longer a collection of scattered, individual tribes; they were now truly a nation, sharing lands and king.

Nation is a difficult word to define. How does a group of people grow into nationhood? The Franks had always held certain things in common: they came from the same regions on the east bank of the Rhine River; they spoke the same language; they shared many of the same traditions; they had descended from the same ancestors. But under Clovis the various tribes began to think of themselves not as members of individual tribes but as Franks. The old tribal divisions disappeared. And when a group of people begin to view themselves as a whole and the land they live in as their shared country, they have become a nation. In our Castle of the Middle Ages, the Franks were creating their own room, separate and distinct.

Clovis recognized that the Frankish nation needed a central capital city. So he moved his court and his family to a town in the center of Gaul, formerly a Roman place called Lutetia Parisiorum (loo-TET-see-uh pa-REE-see-or-um), which had been well equipped by the Roman legions with baths, temples, theaters, and markets. The Franks shortened its name to Paris, and Clovis made it his capital in 508. From that year forward, it would grow into one of the world's greatest cities, and Gaul itself would take on a new name: France, land of the Franks.

Just a few years later, in 511, Clovis died. He left behind a people that would endure as the nation of France. Even today the French people look back to Clovis as the founder of their country, the first in a long line of kings that would stretch forward into modern times.

Chapter Seven

The Scroll and the Stone

*Out of the deserts of Arabia,
a new army arises*

Imagine a traveler in the year 600 leaving the comforts and splendor of Constantinople and journeying into the east. He shares the road with caravans of heavily-laden donkeys and camels; perhaps he strikes up a conversation with the animals' merchant masters as they ride along astride shaggy horses. Eventually, if our traveler continues straight eastward, he will pass the fringes of the Byzantine empire and enter into the land of Persia, the place that is in our modern day the nation of Iran. The Persians are a mighty people, ruled by a family of kings called the Sassanids (suh-SAW-nids). Their power stretches beyond their own borders into an empire that includes all the land between Syria on the coast of the Mediterranean Sea and India far to the east. Their kings live in domed palaces, their cities sparkle with magnificent art and enormous libraries stuffed with books and scrolls, and their caravans bulge with a wealth of goods—silk and woolen carpets, soft tanned leather, and lustrous pearls from the Persian Gulf. Persia is a wonder to behold.

But our traveler is a Byzantine, and thus, to him, Persia is the enemy. For in addition to all of her wealth, Persia also possesses a fearsome army, equal in every way to the armies of

Constantinople. Like two bulls caged in the same pasture, the Persians and the Byzantines clashed over and over again. In the year 600 the two empires had been at war with each other, off and on, for more than two hundred years.

Unwilling to enter the lands of his enemies, our traveler turns instead to the south. He joins a group of wandering camel merchants and makes his way down into Arabia.

It is a dry, dusty road he follows, for although Arabia is a peninsula surrounded by water—the Red Sea to the west, the Arabian Sea southward, the Persian Gulf in the east—the land itself is an arid desert. A flat carpet of sand unrolls as far as the eye can see, pounded by relentless heat, occasionally rippled by outcroppings of bare rock and once in a while the green trees of an oasis.

The people who live in this harsh place spare very little thought for the wars of the empires to the north. They are mostly concerned with finding food and water. Some of them are nomads, wandering here and there across the desert, seeking hidden springs and patches of grass for their flocks. The rest live in the towns that have grown up wherever there is a reliable well. The townspeople make their living by farming the nearby land or working as merchants. But whether nomads or townsfolk, the people of Arabia depend on each other, for there is no other way to survive in the desert. Their lives are bound together in tight-knit families called clans. Groups of related clans are called tribes, and the headmen of the different tribes provide leadership for all of Arabia. There is no king.

As you might well imagine, our traveler will find no huge cities either, nothing to match Constantinople or Rome. But there is the town of Mecca, a settlement in western Arabia, positioned at the crossroads of three major caravan routes. It bustles with a marketplace where merchants trade leather, cloth, and camel butter. Its inns overflow with worshipers who come to Mecca to visit Arabia's most revered shrine, a square structure called the Kaaba (KAH-bah) which shelters 360 idols, each representing a day of the year. Embedded into one of the Kaaba's walls is a black stone that was said to have fallen from heaven, making the place so sacred that tradition forbids any warfare or violence within twenty miles of the shrine. With its marketplace and its intriguing Kaaba, Mecca is an interesting town, and our traveler might decide to break his journey there.

But if he does, he will no doubt be disappointed. For a flood had swept through Mecca that spring and damaged the Kaaba. The shrine is in disrepair; the idols are broken and the black stone has fallen. After spending just a day or two, our traveler will depart, wandering north again toward his home in Constantinople.

But let's stay behind in Mecca. Something is about to happen here that will ultimately change the world.

The merchants who ruled in Mecca were not content to leave the Kaaba broken down. Over the next few years, they rebuilt the walls and repaired all 360 idols; all that was left to do was restore the sacred black stone to its place. But which clan among all the people of Mecca was most worthy to set the stone back into the wall? No one could agree, and the arguments grew fierce and heated until finally the leaders of the clans agreed that the next man who entered the city gate would make the decision.

That man was Muhammad, a merchant who was married to one of Mecca's most wealthy ladies. When the city's leaders demanded that he solve the argument, he thought for a while and then proposed an honorable solution: the stone would be placed on a cloth, the elders from each of the clans would raise the cloth together, and then Muhammad himself would set the stone into place. Everyone recognized the fairness of this plan, and Muhammad was praised for his wisdom.

Muhammad had not always held a place of honor among the people of Mecca. He had been born into one of the city's poorest clans, and his parents had both died by the time he was six years old, leaving him an orphan in the care of his uncle. He was required to earn his keep in the clan by traveling far abroad with his uncle's merchant caravans.

When he was twenty-five years old, and still poor, he agreed to lead a caravan for a wealthy widow named Khadija (KHAH-dee-juh). He took her camels all the way north to Syria and sold the goods from their packs for a huge profit; when he returned, the widow suggested that the two of them should marry. Muhammad agreed, even though she was fifteen years older than he. They had a long and seemingly happy marriage, for while she lived, Muhammad took no other wife, which was unusual among the clans of Arabia in those days.

Like everyone else in Mecca, Muhammad worshiped Arabia's pagan gods. He sought to gain their favor by spending one month of every year praying, giving food to those who were hungry, and walking around the Kaaba seven times each day. As the years went by, he began to go out alone during this month of service to pray in a cave outside the city.

In the year 610, tradition tells us, Muhammad was praying in the cave when he fell asleep. A dream came to him then, a vision of an angel offering him a scroll and commanding him to read it. Three times Muhammad asked, "What shall I read?" Finally he accepted the scroll and read its words. Then in his dream the angel left him and he awoke.

At first Muhammad was frightened, afraid that he was going mad. He ran back to his home and told Khadija everything he had seen. She comforted him and urged him to continue to pray. The next day Muhammad saw the angel again, who this time gave him an additional message: he, Muhammad, was a prophet, and he must take the angel's words to the rest of his people.

For three years after these dreams, Muhammad spoke of them only to his wife, a friend named Abu Bakr (AH-boo BECK-er), and a few of his relatives. But in 613 he began to urge his message upon all of the people of Mecca. He told them that they must forsake all of their pagan gods, because there was only one god, the creator of all, whose name was Allah. They must give to the poor, live good and righteous lives, and serve Allah only.

At first his listeners were inclined to scoff at this. They already knew Allah, who was merely one of the many gods worshiped in Arabia. But Muhammad insisted upon Allah alone, and gradually more and more people began to hear and follow him. Most of these followers were the poor and weak; the wealthy leaders of Mecca were not so eager to embrace Muhammad's message that they must live humbly and give much of their wealth away. They viewed Muhammad with suspicion, afraid that he would lead his followers into a rebellion against them. Soon Muhammad's followers were being attacked in alleyways, pushed out of Mecca, or refused water from the town's well. Many of them fled, going north to another of Arabia's larger settlements, the town of Medina (meh-DEE-nah).

Muhammad, meanwhile, was sad and alone, for his wife Khadija had died and he had received no more messages from the angel. But he continued to dream, and he believed that Allah was revealing his commands to him through those dreams. One night the dreams told him something new: Allah would allow those who were being harmed and driven away to fight back.

By now almost all of Muhammad's followers were gone from Mecca. When the clan leaders of the city heard that Muhammad's followers were now free to fight, they determined that they must be rid of him once and for all. They chose one man from each clan, forming a group of assassins who planned to surround the house where Muhammad was staying, bring him out, and kill him.

So in the dark of an autumn night in the year 622, with the house watched and death waiting for him in the morning, Muhammad climbed out of a back window, his friend Abu Bakr by his side. They swiftly made their way north to Medina where many of Muhammad's followers awaited them. This flight is known as "The Hegira," which means "the migration." It is the beginning of what came to be called the Islamic era.

Islam means "submission." To follow Muhammad's teaching is to submit completely and without question to the worship of Allah, and the ones who do so are called Muslims, "those who submit." As time went on, the Muslims became the most powerful group in Medina, and although he did not claim the title, Muhammad became a sort of king. Soon the rule of Islam would expand much further.

In 630 Muhammad and the Muslims of Medina attacked Mecca. The clans of Mecca had continued to seek Muhammad's life; they had killed many of his followers and captured and destroyed his caravans. So in obedience to the revelation that the Muslims could defend themselves, Muhammad formed his people into an army 10,000 strong, marched south, and overthrew Mecca. On that same day Muhammad went to the Kaaba and, picking up a stick from the ground, knocked down every one of the 360 idols. From that time forward, the Kaaba became the center of Muslim worship and Mecca the capital of the Islamic religion.

Many of the surrounding tribes and clans saw the conquest of Mecca as a sign of Allah's power and began to honor Muhammad as a prophet. Within just a few years, the Muslims had conquered the whole of Arabia. Muhammad set up his government in Medina and ruled the peninsula from there. But it was a short reign; in 632 he was struck down by an infection and died.

Islam, however, did not die with him. Muhammad had united all of Arabia's tribes under one government and one religion, something that had never happened there before. Determined that they should continue on the path that their prophet had shown them, Muhammad's friend Abu Bakr ordered all of Muhammad's teaching recorded into a single book, which

Muslims today call the Quran (kuh-RAHN). It established five responsibilities which every Muslim must fulfill if he wishes to please Allah: faith in Allah alone; prayer five times every day; gifts to the poor; fasts for one month out of the year; and once in his lifetime, a pilgrimage to Mecca, to the Kaaba.

With the Quran in one hand and a sword in the other, the Muslims began to look beyond their sandy peninsula, firm in their belief that Allah wanted them to spread the message of Islam as far as possible by any means possible. Abu Bakr became their leader; he was called the *caliph,* which means "successor." He in turn was followed by others, all friends or relatives of Muhammad, and under their leadership the armies of Islam marched out of Arabia. They conquered their once-mighty neighbors, the Persians; they gained control of huge portions of what had been the Byzantine empire; they overthrew the small kingdoms of northern Africa. By 650 they controlled most of the land around the Mediterranean Sea, and they had marched through Persia all the way east into India. Their armies moved like the wind; and in the seventh century, the people of Europe began to hear the distant thunder of the Islamic storm. They gazed fearfully toward the east; it seemed to them as if the Muslims had come out of nowhere to threaten the entire world.

Perhaps so. For the Quran urged them onward to unlimited conquest, and it seemed that none would stand before them.

But one would and did. We will meet him in the next chapter.

Chapter Eight

Charles the Hammer

*The Franks face the armies of Islam
at the Battle of Tours*

If we think of the Middle Ages as a castle formed of many different rooms, then we might imagine the followers of Muhammad as a fire ignited on Arabia's barren hearth, its smoke billowing outward and filling chamber after chamber. By the end of the seventh century, the Muslim armies had conquered eastward all the way across Persia into India, northward through Turkey toward Constantinople, and westward across the Mediterranean Sea into North Africa. The lands under the rule of Islam were known as the Caliphate, because as you might remember, after the death of Muhammad the Muslim rulers were called *caliphs*.

In the year 711 the Muslim commander in North Africa was a man named Tariq-ibn-Ziyad (TAR-ick ih-bin zee-AD). He was a *Berber*, a man born into a tribe of nomads that wandered the north African deserts. Though he had once been a slave, his skills as a soldier had earned him his freedom, along with command of the Muslim army. When all of North Africa had been brought into the Caliphate, Tariq turned his eyes and ambition north toward the kingdom of the Visigoths.

Do you remember the Goths? When we saw them last, they

had been driven out of Gaul by Clovis and the Franks and forced to re-establish themselves in the lands that the Romans had called Hispania; today we know it as Spain. They had become Christian and had built many churches as well as strong, well-fortressed cities and towns. But they struggled to hold their kingdom together. Their kings had always been chosen by vote; the most powerful noblemen in the land would settle upon a suitable candidate and give him the crown. Unfortunately, a dying ruler of Hispania would often wish, as kings do, to leave his crown to his son, his own heir, rather than let the nobles determine who among them was worthy to be the next king. Arguments and even open warfare were the result, and the throne of Hispania wobbled dangerously this way and that. From his headquarters in North Africa, Tariq observed the quarreling Goths and saw an opportunity for conquest.

To understand what happened next, you must take a moment and study a map of the Mediterranean Sea. Fanciful students have often thought that the Mediterranean is shaped rather like a flying duck with its head outstretched toward the west and the Atlantic Ocean. If you look at the very tip of the duck's bill, you will see the place where Africa and Europe meet, as the peninsula of Spain reaches down and almost touches the sandy beaches of Africa. There stands the Rock of Gibraltar, a shining wedge of pale gray limestone that rears up into an enormous cliff. It stands guard over the narrow channel of seawater that marks the entrance to the Mediterranean Sea. In ancient times it was one of the Pillars of Hercules, the boundary of the known world. Throughout history this immense promontory has been an important fortress, for whoever controlled the Rock controlled the gateway in and out of the Sea.

On the opposite shore lies an African city, Tangiers, and it was here that Tariq gathered his army. The looming cliff must have been a constant reminder of Hispania's tantalizing nearness; he lacked only a way to ferry his soldiers across the water. Now in 711 a way opened for him.

There was, you see, near Tangiers a Gothic stronghold unconquered by the Muslims. Its ruler, a nobleman named Julian, harbored a deep and lasting hatred for the current Gothic king, Roderic. He also possessed a fleet of merchant ships, and so he proposed a treaty: if his fortress were spared from any further Muslim attack, he would secretly transport Tariq's army to Hispania under Roderic's very nose. Tariq was quick to agree to these terms. On April 29, 711, a Muslim army landed at Gibraltar aboard Julian's ships.

It was an army composed of seven thousand Berber horseman and five thousand foot soldiers, all of them willing to take up the sword for Islam. As they assembled there in the shadow of the mighty cliff, with all of Hispania, and thus all of Europe, standing like an open gate before them, Tariq placed himself at their head and shouted these words:

> *Oh my warriors, whither would you flee? Behind you is the sea, before you, the enemy. You have left now only the hope of your courage and your constancy… Your enemy is before you, protected by an innumerable army; he has men in abundance, but you, as your only aid, have your own swords, and, as your only chance for life, such chance as you can snatch from the hands of your enemy.*

With this challenge ringing in their ears, Tariq's warriors began to make their way inland, burning and looting as they went. After overcoming the shock of their sudden arrival, Roderic hastily gathered an army to meet them, but it was for naught. A few months later, on July 19, Tariq's Berbers smashed the Goths at the Battle of Guadalete. In one day Roderic and almost every other Gothic nobleman were killed, all the great families of the Goths were left leaderless, and the Goths were, for the most part, wiped out from the pages of history.

Hispania was no more; it became instead the Islamic

province of al-Andalus (AL AN-dah-LOOS), with Tariq-ibn-Zayid as its governor. And the majestic, enormous rock, the starting point of his conquest, was renamed "Jebal-tariq" (JEH-bull TAR-ick), the mountain of Tariq, a word that eventually evolved into our modern name for that place, Gibraltar.

The smoke arising from Hispania's defeat did not go unnoticed. While the Muslims rejoiced in the expansion of their empire, far to the north the Franks recoiled in dismay. How easily the Goths had been defeated! Surely the Franks themselves were in mortal danger should the armies of Islam continue to press forward!

At such a time as this, frightened people usually look to their kings, but the Franks had little reason to do so. Clovis had been a strong and mighty king, but after his death the Frankish lands had been divided among his four sons, and as the years had passed that division had continued. Rather than thriving under one strong ruler, the Franks struggled along with four who were, as you can imagine, constantly at war with one another. The years of squabbling had weakened the power of the kings and strengthened instead the Frankish noblemen, the counts and dukes. Indeed, in each of the four kingdoms of France, the real power lay not with the king but with his chief steward, a nobleman bearing the title "Mayor of the Palace." He was the one who controlled the royal treasury and made the decisions regarding the kingdom, while the king concerned himself with little more than the daily combing of his long beard and the menu for his luncheon—so much so, that these kings were called *rois faineants,* which means "the do-nothing kings."

Finally in 680 Pepin the Second, who was the Mayor of the Palace for Austrasia (au-STRAY-zha), one of the four Frankish kingdoms, decided that he'd had enough. He managed to collect enough men to form an army and then, with the army behind him, persuaded the other three kingdoms to recognize him as their mayor. He did not go so far as to call himself King Pepin, but he took the title *Dux Francorum,* Duke of all the Franks, and conducted himself in every way as if he wore a crown.

After he died in 714 his son Charles assumed the position of Mayor of Austrasia. For the next four years he battled the other three kingdoms until at last they submitted and bestowed on him the same title they had given his father: Duke of all the Franks. Only then did he turn his eyes to the south, to al-Andalus, to the attack that he knew was coming.

The long years of warfare had hardened Charles into a seasoned general. From afar he studied the tactics and strengths of the Muslim army, and he came to believe that only professional soldiers could defend his people from the inevitable invasion.

At this time in history very few kingdoms in the world provided themselves with what we would call a *standing army:* a large group of trained men who do not disband after a battle but instead live and work full-time as soldiers, ready at any moment to go to war. When Rome fell, her standing armies fell too; during the Middle Ages, if a king needed an army he would have to call upon his people—farmers, herdsmen, merchants—to lay aside their usual lives and come fight for him. Sometimes he might even force them to do so, an action that was called *conscription.*

But frightened, untrained, conscripted men would never stand against the sweeping wildfire that was the Muslim horsemen. Charles needed something better, soldiers who were steady and ready for battle. So with an eye to the south, he began to quietly build and train his army.

Meanwhile in al-Andalus, the Muslims were restless. Tariq-ibn-Zayid had been succeeded as governor by a new leader, Abd-al-Rahman Al Ghafiqi (ABD-al-RAH-man al gah-FEE-kee), and the Muslim army in al-Andalus had grown to more than 60,000 men. By 732 Abd-al-Rahman felt prepared to lead his army in a full-scale invasion of France.

Crossing the border into Frankish lands, the Muslims

marched northward, effortlessly smashing any resistance that they found in southern France. So easy was their advance that the army soon split apart, with large raiding parties moving off to plunder the defenseless towns and farms while the main body of soldiers continued swiftly onward. Their goal was Tours, a city in central France which was the location of the Abbey of Saint Martin of Tours, one of the richest monasteries in Europe.

Charles' moment had come. He collected his army, perhaps as many as 30,000 men strong, and made his way south. He moved stealthily, avoiding the main roads, hoping to catch the Muslims off-guard. But he also urged his soldiers to march at the greatest possible speed, because he knew that by the time the Muslims reached Tours, his army must already be in position to meet them on a battleground of his own choosing.

In a river valley south of Tours, he found just the right place: a high, sloping, wooded plain. The slope would give his men the high ground, which is always an advantage in battle, and the trees would slow the Muslim horsemen and thus protect his soldiers from being overrun. Charles arranged his army into a *phalanx,* a large square with the men standing shoulder to shoulder in a solid mass. Then he settled down to wait.

When Abd-al-Rahman and the Muslims arrived, they were astonished to find an army of Franks poised for battle. Abd-al-Rahman must have been dismayed, for he knew that his soldiers were fighting at a huge disadvantage if they had to charge uphill through the trees. But turning back and refusing to fight held little appeal; after all, they were so close to Tours with all of its gleaming gold, and Abd-al-Rahman knew that Charles' army was outnumbered by his own. He trusted, as well, in the might of his horsemen, each of them armed with a sword and a long spear. So he set up his camp and sat down to wait too; he sent out messengers to gather all the fragments of his army that were elsewhere, raiding the countryside.

For seven days the two men and their soldiers faced each

other, the Franks up on their hillside and the Muslims down below. Neither of them wanted to be the first to attack; Abd-al-Rahman still did not have his full army collected, and Charles had no desire to leave the high ground. But the battle could not be postponed forever, and Abd-al-Rahman especially needed to hurry things along. The nights were growing piercingly cold; his Muslim soldiers were not dressed for the freezing temperatures, unlike the Franks who were well wrapped up in layers of fur and wool.

So finally on the seventh day, Abd-al-Rahman sent his horsemen forward, up the hill, in wave after wave of attack. But the Franks did not fall back before them; each assault was met with a determined defense and the phalanx did not break apart.

A few of the Muslims managed to fight their way into the square, pushing toward Charles himself; they hoped to end the battle quickly by killing the Frankish leader. But Charles' personal bodyguard protected him, and they slew the attackers before they could accomplish their deadly goal.

Meanwhile, with the phalanx holding, Charles put into action the second part of his battle plan. He sent scouts into the Muslim camp with orders to free any prisoners, steal or burn the Muslims' supply carts, and generally cause as much trouble as possible. When the smoke of the supply carts' burning rose into the air, some of the Muslim soldiers realized that their camp, and thus all of their plunder, was in danger. A large portion of Abd-al-Rahman's army broke off from the battle and raced back toward the camp. This, in turn, caused alarm and confusion. The Muslims began to fear that the battle was lost and their fellow soldiers were fleeing; they moved backward into a full-scale retreat, and as they did, Abd-al-Rahman was left unprotected. He was engulfed by the Franks and killed.

The next day brought no new attack from the Muslims. The Franks feared that they were circling around for an ambush. Finally scouts were dispatched to spy out the Muslim camp, and they discovered that during the night the Muslims had disappeared. Over the next few weeks, the leaderless army retreated all the way back into al-Andalus.

As the news of this victory spread, Charles acquired a new nickname, Martel (mar-TELL), from the Latin word that means "hammer." In the Battle of Tours he displayed all the qualities that made him a truly great general: he studied his enemy closely, chose the best battle plan possible, and inspired his army to stand firm in the face of repeated attacks from an enemy superior in both numbers and weapons.

Had his men failed, had they fallen back before the Muslim attack, the history that you are reading would no doubt have been very different. After all, the armies of Islam would not have been content with merely looting the city of Tours; after vanquishing Hispania, they stood balanced in the doorway, and they might very well have continued onward, conquering France and northward from there until all of Europe became part of a great Islamic caliphate.

But Charles Martel and the Battle of Tours closed the gate and barred the door. Islam would continue to grow and conquer, but it would not do so in Europe. From this point on, the armies of Islam never again invaded north of Spain.

The Battle of Tours, then, is one of history's great hinges—a place where, if the door had swung the other way, the world as we know it would be greatly changed. And indeed, this victory is remembered to this day at breakfast tables all over France. For after the battle was over and the Muslims had retreated, Frankish bakers invented a soft, flaky pastry shaped into a crescent, the symbol of Islam, to be eaten in celebration. The next time that you bite into a warm, buttery *croissant,* perhaps you also will remember Charles the Hammer and the door that slammed shut at the Battle of Tours.

Chapter Nine

Charlemagne

*A great king attempts to revive
the Roman Empire*

On Christmas Day in the year 800, crowds thronged the square in front of the church of St. Peter in the very heart of Rome. They had gathered, it was true, to celebrate Christ's birth, but they also craned their necks and jostled one another to catch a glimpse of an earthly king as he made his way up the broad steps of the church, his sons at his side. This was Charles, king of the Franks and grandson of Charles Martel, a man so great in power and deeds that he was better known as Carolus Magnus—Charles the Great—or in the language of the Franks, Charlemagne (SHAR-luh-main). He had come to Rome for only the second time in his life at the urgent invitation of the pope, Leo III.

He was draped, none too comfortably, in the long tunic and purple robe of a Roman nobleman. He preferred to dress as a Frankish commoner—a woolen cloak, linen shirt, and leather vest with a sword strapped at his hip—but Pope Leo had requested that he wear the more luxurious Roman robes, and Charlemagne had found it impossible to refuse. It was, after all, Christmas, and within the church crowds of worshipers had joined together to celebrate the holiday. Surely such an occasion called for fancier clothing.

Inside the church the glow of a thousand candles illuminated the arched ceilings, the richly painted walls, and the golden altar where Leo stood. Charlemagne knelt at the pope's feet, bowing his head in prayer. But as he did, Leo in turn drew something out from beneath his robes: a crown. Lifting it high so that all could see, he brought it down squarely upon Charlemagne's bent head.

As one, the people in the church cried out, "Long life and victory to the mighty Charles, the great and peaceful emperor of Rome, crowned of God!" The church shook with their voices, as the waiting crowds outside took up the shout as well.

Long life and victory to the emperor of Rome!

Charlemagne rose to his feet in startled surprise. The Pope knelt before him, acclaiming him as emperor.

This was not the Christmas celebration that Charlemagne had been expecting! In fact, as the Frankish historian Einhard (INE-hard) would later write, "At first, he was far from wanting this. He made it clear that he would not have entered the cathedral that day at all, although it was the greatest of all the festivals of the Church, if he had known in advance what the Pope was planning to do."

And why had the Pope done this extraordinary thing? There had been no emperor in Rome for three hundred years, since the city had fallen to the Goths. What remained of Rome's vast empire was centered in Byzantium with its capital and throne at Constantinople. When people thought of Rome, they thought of the Byzantine empire.

But Leo had his reasons. Just two years before, the Byzantine ruler, a young man named Constantine VI, had been overthrown by his own mother. She now reigned in Constantinople, calling herself the Empress Irene, but many questioned whether she could truly be considered the Queen. She had, after all, stolen the throne from the rightful ruler, even if he were very young. For Leo, and many others, Irene's actions presented an opportunity to pry the idea of Rome—the Rome that represented civilization, order, and tradition—away from Constantinople.

Leo also harbored other, more personal, reasons for crowning Charlemagne. He owed the Frankish king a great debt, for just the year before, in 799, Leo's enemies had viciously attacked him and he had been forced to flee the city and scramble all the way north to Charlemagne's kingdom in France. Charlemagne had provided him with soldiers to escort him back to Rome, and the sight of all those stern-faced Frankish warriors had made the message clear to Leo's enemies: any further attacks upon Leo would bring Charlemagne's wrath down on their heads.

Is it any wonder, then, that Leo should wish to make Charlemagne's power all the more secure? But to crown him before the altar in St. Peter's church was a bold move! How could this Frankish king be considered an emperor of Rome?

Charlemagne's life had begun as the son of a man called Pepin the Short, who was himself the younger son of Charles Martel. Like his father before him, Pepin had been Mayor of the Palace for the Franks, ruling the people while a man named Childeric III, who was king in name only, sat upon the Frankish throne. But in the year 751, Pepin sent a message to the pope in Rome asking a simple question: "Is it proper for the Franks to have as their king a man who does not actually possess any royal power?" No, the pope replied. The one who holds the power should be the one wearing the crown.

With the pope's written approval in hand, Pepin forced Childeric to give up his throne and move into a monastery. Then to no one's surprise, the Frankish noblemen elected Pepin as their new ruler, and in 754 the pope traveled all the way from Rome to France to anoint Pepin as King of the Franks. This was the first time that a pope of the Roman Church performed the crowning of a civil king.

Pepin died in 768. He left behind a large kingdom composed of not only France but also much of the land that today we know as Belgium, the Netherlands, and Germany. According to their law and their long tradition, the Franks then gave the crown and the kingdom to both of Pepin's two sons: Charlemagne, the elder, and his younger brother Carloman (CAR-lo-man).

A single kingdom ruled by two kings is never really at peace. Charlemagne took control of the outer regions of the kingdom, and Carloman the inner, but the two brothers disagreed about almost everything. Should they ally with the neighboring peoples or go to war and seek to conquer them? Who were France's friends? Who were her enemies? Which noblemen should be promoted and which ignored? In none of these questions could the brothers find agreement. Eventually, no doubt, they would have ended up at war with each other, fighting for the throne, but in 771 Carloman died.

With his brother gone, Charlemagne was now the sole King of the Franks. From his palace in Aachen (AH-ken), a city in Germany, he looked out upon his vast realm and was grieved by what he saw. The Franks were returning to the ways of their barbarian forefathers, neglecting the Church and abandoning learning and scholarship. The peoples who lived along the northern and eastern borders of his kingdom were pagans who knew nothing of Christianity. And to the south the Roman Church herself was locked in a long battle for land and power with the kingdom of Lombard in northern Italy. In every direction there was peril and discord, problems that only a strong king could solve.

Charlemagne determined to be that king. He would bring all of Europe under one crown, his own, and he would bring the Word of God to the pagans. Europe would have one ruler and one faith. In pursuit of that goal, Charlemagne spent much of the next thirty years in the saddle, fighting battle after battle.

Driven by his devotion to the Church, Charles turned his attention first to the Lombards. They were descendants of a Gothic tribe who had traveled south after the fall of Rome and become Christian. By 569 they had captured all of northern Italy and established a kingdom there, with each of their kings wearing the Iron Crown of Lombardy, a magnificent circlet of jeweled gold bound with an iron band that was said to have come from one of the nails used at Christ's crucifixion. Since those early years of the Middle Ages, the Iron Crown would be used thirty-four times to crown a king of Italy, all the way up into the nineteenth century. It is one of Italy's great treasures, and you can see it for yourself if you should ever happen to travel to the city of Milan where the crown is displayed in a cathedral there.

The Iron Crown of Lombardy

Christian or no, the Lombards often found themselves in conflict with the Church in Rome. In 772 they attacked several cities over which the Church claimed governorship and took them for themselves. As soon as this news reached him, Charlemagne marched south over the towering mountains of the Alps and besieged the Lombards within their own capital. By the spring of 774, the Lombards were desperate to surrender, and in order to save their lives, they offered up their kingdom. Charlemagne demanded that each of the Lombardy noblemen bow before him in submission, and he had himself crowned with the Iron Crown as king of Italy.

The war with the Lombards was only the beginning of Charlemagne's battles. He had sworn that he would bring under his rule all of the pagan peoples that lived on the borders of his empire: the Avars in Hungary, the Slavs in central Europe, and especially the Saxons in the north, in Germany—the same Saxons whose kinsman had conquered Britain. To do this he would have to engage in almost constant warfare. Again and again he rode out against the pagans until he had forced them to either accept him as king, and Christianity as their faith, or stand with their old ways and die. It was a harsh choice that he offered them, and many refused to submit and were killed at his hand, but in the end he built an empire in the name of Christianity that encompassed almost every corner of Europe.

Several constant companions rode with Charlemagne during those years: his sons, who commanded the army along with their father; his bodyguard, a band of skillful soldiers who had pledged to die in his service; and most of all, his sword.

In those days, before guns and cannons changed warfare forever, a king's sword was much more than a pretty decoration. Charlemagne's sword was constantly at his side or in his fist. He called it "Joyeuse" (JWAY-oos), which means "joyful," and it quickly entered into the realm of legend. Stories were told of the sword's brilliant golden hilt, which could blind the king's enemies, or its flashing blade, which changed color "thirty times a day."

Once, the sword was struck from the king's hand and disappeared into the turmoil of the battlefield. Charlemagne shouted out that he would give a mighty reward to any man who could retrieve the sword. When finally one of his soldiers found it and brought it back to him, the grateful king planted the sword into the hillside and announced, "Here will be built an estate of which you will be the lord and master, and your descendants will take the name of my wonderful sword: Joyeuse." Today the town of Joyeuse, France, is said to have been founded on that spot in honor of the king's sword. The sword itself survived for centuries after Charlemagne's death as the coronation sword for the kings of France. It rests now in the most famous of all French museums, the Louvre, in Paris.

By 800, when Charlemagne entered into the church of St. Peter in Rome on that Christmas morning, he was already a great king ruling over a vast empire. But he had never sought the formal title of emperor. Why then did Leo choose to give him an emperor's crown, and why did Charlemagne accept it?

For the Church's part, it may well be that Leo felt the need to tie Charlemagne's immense power more tightly to the Roman Church; from the beginning, Charlemagne's realm was called the Holy Roman Empire. It was also, perhaps, a way to make Europe, with all of its different peoples, more like Rome—more unified, more civilized. But for Charlemagne, the title of "Holy Roman emperor" seems to have meant security and peace for the lands under his control, in much the same way that the Romans brought peace to the world of their time. It was, at times, a brutal peace, for Charlemagne demanded submission to his authority in the same way that the Romans did: obey or die. But nevertheless, Charlemagne truly sought to raise his people up out of paganism and ignorance.

To do this he made every effort to increase the education of all people within the empire. He greatly admired learning; he insisted that all of his children and grandchildren be well-educated, and he ordered schools to be established throughout his realm. He directed his scholars to seek out as many ancient texts as they could find and to copy and preserve them. He also studied, himself, hiring teachers to instruct him in grammar, logic, arithmetic, and astronomy. And that is all the more astounding when we consider that Charlemagne was never able to learn to write, though he tried throughout his life and even kept a practice tablet under the pillow on his bed.

Charlemagne also reformed the empire's money, so everyone was using the same types of coins and no one could be cheated in the markets and shops. He repaired the old Roman roads, so travel became easier and safer; and he encouraged better farming methods out in the countryside, so more food could be grown. In every way he could think of, he tried to make his people's lives better.

By the year 813, Charlemagne's health was starting to fail. Einhard the historian gives us a description of the old king:

> *He was heavily built, sturdy, and of considerable stature, although not exceptionally so, since his height was seven times the length of his own foot. He had a round head, large and lively eyes, a slightly larger nose than usual, white but still attractive hair, a bright and cheerful expression, a short and fat neck, and he enjoyed good health, except for the fevers that affected him in the last few years of his life. Toward the end, he dragged one leg. Even then, he stubbornly did what he wanted and refused to listen to doctors, indeed he detested them, because they wanted to persuade him to stop eating roast meat, as was his wont, and to be content with boiled meat.*

After a lifetime spent in battle, Charles was ready to lay down his sword. He called his son Louis to his court and crowned him with his own hands as the next Holy Roman emperor. Late that winter he fell ill. As Einhard tells us,

> *He died January twenty-eighth, the seventh day from the time that he took to his bed, at nine o'clock in the morning, after partaking of the Holy Communion, in the seventy-second year of his age and the forty-seventh of his reign.*

Charlemagne's realm did not endure; it was divided up by his grandsons. For most of the Middle Ages, the Holy Roman Empire was, as historians like to joke, neither "holy" nor

"Roman" nor an "empire." It became a collection of hundreds of "kingdoms" and city-states in the midst of Europe, as if our Castle contained in its center an enormous room divided into many tiny chambers. Each little territory within the empire was ruled by a powerful duke or prince. These noblemen would choose an emperor from among their number by vote, but he was required to pay them large sums of gold and land to stay in power, so for the most part, each was weaker than the one before. Still, it was not until the seventeenth and eighteenth centuries that the Holy Roman Empire disappeared completely, becoming instead the Europe we know now with separate modern nations like Germany, Austria, and Italy.

It was Charlemagne who began it. Through his schools, the people of Europe began to value the knowledge of writing and reading; through his standardizing of the money, trade became easier and Europe became more prosperous; through his insistence on Christianity as a common faith, the many tribes and peoples of Europe began to develop a common mind and culture and to think of themselves as one. Though he saw himself as a warrior for his kingdom and for the Church, over the years he has come to be seen instead as a father: Charlemagne, the father of Europe itself.

Chapter Ten

The Rushing North Wind

The Vikings storm the shores of Europe

One chilly autumn morning in 1879, two brothers trudged across the fields of Gokstad (GOCK-stad), their father's farm deep in the countryside of Norway. The harvest was over for the year, the winter chores were still far in the offing, and so with nothing better to do, the boys set out to investigate the strange mound of stiff blue clay that rose up, large and brooding, in the midst of the farm's barley crop. It had been there as long as anyone could remember, an unnatural hill known to the people thereabout as King's Mound. Local legends boasted that it was stuffed with treasure, and the brothers had decided to climb up, dig down into it, and see what they could find.

Their breath rose in frosty puffs as they struggled to shovel and lift the heavy clay. It was cold, difficult work; perhaps they were tiring of it and beginning to think longingly of the warm fireplace back in the farmhouse when one of their spades struck something in the ground with a ringing crack. All thought of the cold forgotten, they dug furiously, first with the spades and then, more carefully, with their gloved hands until they had uncovered a slim, graceful curve of planked wood, the prow of a ship buried there in the clay.

Word of the brothers' discovery quickly spread. By February it had reached the ears of a man named Nicolay Nicolaysen (NICK-oh-LIE NICK-oh-LIE-sin), who was at that time Norway's first official archaeologist. Hurrying to the farm, he ordered all digging stopped. Then when spring arrived and the frozen ground began to thaw, he set up camp right there in the field and took charge of the excavation himself.

Little by little the ship was freed from its prison. And with every inch that was uncovered, Nicolay grew more astonished. Never had he seen a ship like this: seventy-six-and-a-half feet long, built entirely of thin oak planks, each overlapping the one beneath, with a tall prow at each end. Along the bottom of its hull ran a *keel*, which is the long, straight beam around which a ship is built, fifty-eight feet long and constructed of a single piece of solid oak. He could only imagine the giant tree from which it had been cut!

The Gokstad Viking Ship

Along each side lay sixteen oar-holes, and above them hung the remnants of thirty-two round wooden shields painted alternately yellow and black. A large oaken *rudder*—a square board which was used to steer the ship—was attached to the stern. And inside the hull were oars, tubs for food and kegs for water, and the remains of an immense square sail, forty feet across, made of tightly-woven wool. All of this and more were perfectly preserved by the waterproof clay in which the ship had been buried. For Nicolay, it was the greatest archaeological discovery in Norway's history: an intact Viking longship, the like of which had not been seen in the world for almost a thousand years. Newspapers in every European country published joyful reports of the Gokstad Ship, as it was called, trumpeting its treasures and musing over its mystery: Why had such a huge vessel been buried in the earth? Every story was illustrated with photographs of the sleekly curved prow.

And yet . . .

A thousand years before, a glimpse of that same curved prow, appearing on the sea's horizon like a lifted spear, would have provoked not joy but terror and despair. The longships were dreaded and feared, and the Vikings who sailed them were called "the demon Norsemen."

You have met the Norsemen already when we traveled to Greenland and beyond with Erik the Red and his son Leif Erikson. But while those explorers piloted their longships across the stormy Atlantic in search of unknown lands, many of their kinsman set sail with a far different goal in mind: plunder. In their language they called themselves *vikings,* voyagers, and they were going "a-viking," to raid and to loot the vulnerable towns of Europe. To their victims they were a vicious storm that seemed to have come out of a clear sky to rain down destruction. One Irish monk, who was driven from his home by Viking attacks, described them like this:

> *The swollen North Wind ravages us—piteous to see—*
> *Learned grammarians and holy priests,*
> *For the rushing North Wind spares no persons*
> *Lacerating us with his cruel beak.*

The longships made the raids possible. In the earliest years of the Middle Ages, before the longship was invented, the Norsemen were simply farmers and merchants, a northern offshoot of the same people that produced the Goths and Vandals who conquered Rome. They had settled into Scandinavia—the modern nations of Denmark, Norway, and Sweden—and begun to build farms and towns, but even then, in the centuries before the longship, they were fearless travelers. Eager to find new markets for their goods—woolen cloth, furs, and beautiful amber beads—Norse merchants ventured out in small, squat trading boats along the coasts of western Europe. When they returned, they brought back with them, along with Europe's glass, wine, spices, and silk, reports of unguarded monasteries and unwalled cities.

And so sometime in the middle of the eighth century, Viking ship-builders began to craft a new kind of ship, the fastest sailing vessel the world had ever seen. The Gokstad Ship shows us how it was done. After the long keel beam was laid down, overlapping planks of oak were nailed together and then tied to the ship's ribs with long, braided cords made of animal hair or spruce tree roots. This made the ship flexible, so it could bend and twist in the heaving waves without breaking apart, while at the same time the keel kept the ship stable and afloat. The joints were stuffed with tar and cloth until the ship was watertight. A tall mast was attached in the midst, with a hinge at its bottom so that it could be raised or lowered, and the square sail was hung from a strong oak crossbeam.

The huge sail and streamlined hull gave the ship tremendous speed, and yet it rode lightly on the waves. It could weather the most dreadful storm, flying easily over the ocean abyss, but it could also float gently up a river as shallow as three feet deep. With these marvelous ships, the Norsemen would become Vikings.

Early in the morning of June 8, 793, the monks at

Lindisfarne awoke to the frantic clanging of the chapel's bells. They stumbled out into the pale light of dawn and looked toward the sea, only to be confronted by a sight that no one in Europe had ever beheld until that moment: a fleet of longships. Each one was packed with as many as a hundred men, some of them pulling hard on the oars. As the monks watched, scarcely believing their eyes, the ships were driven right up onto the beach. In an instant the sailors erupted out of the ships and stormed up the steep hillside, bristling with swords and battle-axes. The monks turned to flee and hide, but for many of them, it was too late. The Vikings fell upon them, killing most and binding the rest to take as slaves. Then they looted the monastery, gathering up the golden candlesticks and rich chalices, the silver crosses and elaborately gilded statues. They ripped the jeweled covers from the Gospels that Eadfrith had so carefully copied ninety years earlier and scattered the vellum pages across the Scriptorium's floor. Then with all of Lindisfarne's treasures piled into the hulls of the longships, they sailed away back to Scandinavia.

This raid was the beginning of the Viking's reign of terror, and it caused a wave of shock throughout Europe. Who were these dreadful pirates who would dare to attack a holy monastery? Alcuin, a scholar in Charlemagne's court at that time, lamented:

> *Never before has such terror appeared in Britain as we have now suffered from a pagan race… The heathens poured out the blood of saints around the altar, and trampled on the bodies of saints in the temple of God, like dung in the streets.*

Their success at Lindisfarne put wind in the Vikings' sails. They began to range further and further, aiming for larger, richer targets. Their ships' shallow keels enabled them to sail up almost any river, which meant that all of Europe was within their reach. They cruised up the Thames River and attacked London. They sailed up the Seine and besieged Paris, refusing to leave until the king, Charlemagne's grandson, paid them off with almost 6,000 pounds of gold and silver. They ventured far to the east across the Black and Caspian Seas into the Byzantine empire, and south across the Mediterranean Sea and along the shores of North Africa. Many historians believe that they traveled all the way to Baghdad, the center of the Islamic empire. Deep in the hull of the Gokstad Ship, Nicolay Nicolaysen and his team of archaeologists found the bones of two peacocks, proof of the Vikings' long reach.

Everywhere they went, they raided. Their swift, silent ships gave little warning of their approach; they could land on a beach and swarm into a nearby town, taking whatever they wanted and burning the rest. By the time a cry went out and help arrived, the Vikings would be gone. No other ships could possibly pursue the speeding longships, and, in any case, the Vikings rarely left anyone alive to give chase.

Europe tried to defend itself. Powerful noblemen erected castles where farmers and townsfolk could take shelter during a Viking raid. Towers were built along the coastlines to keep watch and sound the alarm at the first sight of a square sail. But despite this, to most of Europe's people the Vikings seemed like shadowy, unknowable, unstoppable demons.

Looking back on them from our vantage point here in the twenty-first century, we can know them a little better. While they left behind few written records, archaeology and history have lightened the shadows; the Vikings were cruel and greedy raiders, truly, but they were also more than that.

In the beginning the lands of Scandinavia were divided into many small kingdoms, each with its own ruler. These men were often at war with one another, for as you well know from your study of history, every small king harbors deep in his heart the wish to be a much bigger king.

In order to make that wish come true, a king would keep around him a troop of warriors, his *thanes,* who pledged him their loyalty. In return, the king would reward his soldiers with any spoils from a battle, often in the form of gold or silver arm-rings. In fact, in some old, old poems, the king is called a "ring-giver."

Just below the kings in rank and power were the *jarls*—in English we would use the word "earls." These were warriors who had gained wealth and power through raiding and conquering, and who kept, in turn, their own bands of soldiers. Both the kings and the jarls owned huge estates in the countryside where tenant farmers worked the land in return for a share in the harvests.

Most of the people were freemen, who were called *karls*. Many karls were farmers who owned their own land, but some were also merchants, fishermen, or fur trappers. Karls often pledged their loyalty to a nearby jarl, who might call upon them to join him when he sailed off on a viking raid.

All of these—kings, jarls, and karls—depended on the service of *thralls,* the slaves who were owned by their masters just as if they were cows or horses. They labored in the fields and workshops and kitchens, most of them captured during raids and brought back to Scandinavia to serve until they died. Most of them were not mistreated, because the Vikings considered it rude and uncivilized to be cruel to a slave, but nevertheless, thralls had no more rights or freedom than did the village goats.

Once or twice a year, the karls would leave their farms and workshops and gather together in an assembly called a *Thing*. They would meet outdoors, usually on a hilltop, where they would make laws, settle disputes between neighbors, and pass judgment on any lawbreakers. The Thing was usually led by a local jarl, who would call for a vote when the debate on each question had finally slowed. The karls would vote by rattling their weapons in support; the louder the rattle, the greater the vote. The Things were one of the earliest forms of modern *democracy,* where the people vote for the laws that affect them rather than merely obeying the decrees of a leader.

The Vikings were not ruled merely by democracy. They also followed an ancient, pagan religion. They believed in hundreds of gods and goddesses, all of them dwelling in a mystical land called Asgard where Odin (OH-din) ruled from the giant hall of Valhalla (vahl-HAL-la). A Viking warrior believed that if he were to fall in battle, a beautiful goddess called a Valkyrie (VAHL-keer-ee) would come for him and deliver him to Valhalla, there to feast forever in glory and honor among the gods. To protect themselves, nevertheless, most Vikings wore a carving of a hammer around their necks, the symbol of Thor, the god of storms. Thor was so revered, in fact, that "Thor's Day," which has become our Thursday, was the day of the week upon which great feasts were held and important meetings were conducted.

More than anything else—more than silver and gold, more than safety, even more than Valhalla—the Viking warriors sought fame. They prized fearlessness and daring, because they lived in a cold, harsh world, and their myths taught them that a man could win immortality; he could be remembered after death. Among the Vikings, fame and glory were the very highest virtues, and there could be no better end than a glorious death in battle. The story of a valiant fight would be retold around the fire for years to come. The most honored kings were the ones who could lead their followers to glory aboard the longships; when a king died, he was entombed inside his ship, so he could continue to go a-viking after death. This was the answer to the mystery of the Gokstad ship; it was buried because it was the final resting place of a king, a testament to the daring raids and fierce battles that had filled his life.

An old Viking poem says this:

Cattle die,
Kinsmen die,
Each man dies himself,

*But one thing
will never die,
the fame that he has earned.*

    For nearly three hundred years, from 793 to 1066, the Vikings pursued plunder, glory, and fame. Eventually though, the age of the longships faded away. The rushing north wind was tamed by its own success; the great kings of Scandinavia grew more concerned with ruling than with raiding, and the young men found, as time went past, that it was easier and more profitable to stay at home as farmers or craftsmen. Their pagan religion faded too, as monks brought the message of Christianity to the far northern reaches of Europe, and the fierce longing for fame and a glorious death in battle was replaced by the Christian virtues of patience, mercy, and diligence.

    Of course, some of the Vikings sailed away from Scandinavia with no intention of returning. They were bent on finding new land for themselves, whether it be far in the unknown west, like Erik the Red, or somewhere rather closer. We will see them again in the chapters to come.

Chapter Eleven

The Meeting at Egbert's Stone

A young king survives a swamp of despair

When we last saw the people of Britain, they were divided into several groups: the Britons, who had lived long upon the island under Roman government; the Saxons, who had conquered them; and the wild tribes of the north, the Picts and the Scots. As the years passed the Saxons had gradually absorbed the Britons until they were blended into one people, Anglo-Saxons, with the land divided into four kingdoms: Mercia (MER-se-ah), East Anglia, Northumbria, and Wessex. Like their Frankish neighbors to the south, the Saxon kings tended to squabble with one another, vying for land and power; but let an enemy appear and they would band together to present a united front against the threat.

In 865 however, the greatest threat they had ever faced came sailing over the North Sea: an enormous fleet of Viking longships. The history written during those times, a book titled *The Anglo-Saxon Chronicle,* calls them "the Great Heathen Army."

The Vikings had been raiding Britain and the rest of Europe for more than fifty years. Kings and jarls had taken shiploads of treasure back to Scandinavia, showering their followers with rich rewards and enlarging their own power. By the middle of the ninth century, Viking kings in Denmark, Norway, and Sweden had begun to establish those lands as single kingdoms, and they were looking to extend their reach. The fleet that attacked Britain in 865 was no raiding party sent to loot and burn and then return to Scandinavia; led by a powerful Viking prince named Ivar (EE-var) the Boneless, its purpose was conquest. The Saxons, who had once been invaders themselves, now faced an overwhelming invasion.

Against this menacing army were arrayed the four Anglo-Saxon kingdoms. East Anglia fell at once, for its king was weak and surrendered to the Vikings, hoping to save himself and his people by offering the invaders food and horses. It did him little good, however, since the Vikings took his offered help and then killed him anyway. The invasion flowed onward; after conquering Northumbria in 867, the Vikings turned toward Mercia. The frightened Mercian king appealed for help to Ethelred, the king of Wessex, and the combined army of Mercia and Wessex battled the Vikings to a standstill. But no clear victory was achieved, and desperate to get rid of them, the king of Mercia offered the Vikings a fortune in gold and silver. They accepted this and retreated back into East Anglia.

Of course, they were not content to stay there. Soon enough the Vikings returned to Mercia, forced the king into exile, and put a puppet ruler of their own choice on his throne. The kingdom of Northumbria was given over to Viking warriors, who took the abandoned Saxon farms for themselves. Of all the Saxon kingdoms, only Wessex stood unconquered, facing the Vikings alone.

Ethelred, king of Wessex, died in 871. He left a young son as his heir, who by all rights should have been king after him, but Ethelred knew that a kingdom under the threat of Viking swords could not be ruled by a child. So in the weeks before his death, he had declared that his crown must go to his brother, Alfred, who was 21 years old that year.

Alfred had never imagined that he might one day be king. He was the youngest of four brothers in his family and had always assumed that they and their sons would occupy the throne. As a young man, he had devoted himself to studying books rather than warfare; he learned several languages and memorized long passages of literature and philosophy. Once, in fact, he won a beautiful book of poetry by memorizing every poem within it. He had traveled, too, in his youth to Ireland and France and even all the way south to Rome; he was often ill and he found strength and healing in visiting these places. Alfred was a scholar and philosopher, not a warrior.

But when the Vikings threatened to overwhelm the Saxon kingdoms, Alfred abandoned his books and papers and picked up his sword. He rode at his brother's side in every battle; he was Ethelred's most trusted commander. And so when the king died and Alfred was crowned in his place, the people of Wessex were willing to put their trust in him.

Less than four months after Alfred's coronation, the Vikings invaded Wessex. The new king led his army out to meet them, but he was soundly defeated. Desperate, Alfred paid them a great ransom in silver coins to persuade them to leave. Even as he watched them sail away down the Thames River, he knew they would be back.

Sure enough, in 876, with a new leader named Guthrum, the Viking army crossed the border into Wessex and seized one of the towns. Alfred acted quickly; he brought in his men under the cover of night and surrounded the town. But all of his attacks were turned back; finally, frustrated, he decided to negotiate a peace agreement, a *treaty*. The two armies exchanged *hostages,* which are men who agree to hand themselves over to the enemy as a guarantee that the treaty between two armies will be kept. The Vikings swore, on a ring decorated with the hammer of their beloved god Thor, that they would honor the treaty. But instead, late that night they killed the men of Wessex who had volunteered as hostages and slipped away to the seacoast. There they planned to board their ships and launch another attack.

Alfred pursued them; with his own ships, he managed to block the Viking vessels so they could not set to sea. Stranded, Guthrum had no choice but to retreat from Wessex. The people rejoiced, but Alfred strengthened his guard.

The Vikings would be back. He knew it.

The year darkened into winter, and Alfred welcomed the snow and ice, which he hoped would keep Guthrum at bay. He settled into his royal fortress at Chippenham, enjoying the Christmas feasts and the start of a new year. But perhaps he should have remembered that the pagan Vikings, who were well-acquainted with snow and cold, had no reason to respect the celebration of Christ's birth. In a whip-swift attack on the night of January 6, they overwhelmed Chippenham's defenses. The king barely escaped with his life. He ran, with only the clothes on his back and a few of his followers, into a nearby swamp.

Guthrum moved his entire army into Chippenham, and then with the fortress as their base, the Vikings rampaged through Wessex. Alfred's people were forced to surrender or to flee. For weeks Alfred and his men remained hidden in the swamp, shivering in the sharp cold, begging the local farmers for food, clean water, dry firewood, and shelter.

It was the lowest point that a king could reach: his people conquered, his army scattered, his enemy feasting at his own table in his own fortress. But such dark times allow the true light of a man's character to shine. Alfred did not give in to despair; he did not rage at his men for failing to defend Chippenham; and he did not complain about his terrible circumstances and demand that someone bring him hot food and warm blankets. His years of study as a young man had taught Alfred the virtues of a truly Christian king: he should seek humility rather than power. He must live only to serve his people, to watch over them, and in difficult times, to suffer with them.

An old story shows us Alfred's humble spirit:

Once, Alfred crept out of the swamp, hungry, cold, and weary. He knocked on the door of a simple cottage and asked the peasant woman there if he might have a bite to eat. She eyed this dirty, ragged stranger with alarm, but his face was kind, and so she agreed.

"Sit here by the fire and warm yourself," she said.

She had been baking cakes on the hot stones of the hearth, and as she turned away to tend to other chores, she asked Alfred to watch them and turn them when they were golden brown.

Alfred sat to do as he was bid, but his mind soon wandered, his face growing sad and stern as he thought about the terrible struggle he faced. Before his unseeing eyes, the cakes baked darker and darker until they were little more than smoking coals.

The peasant woman, rushing back to the fire at the smell of smoke, turned to Alfred and rebuked him roundly. "You lazy bones! How could you have failed at such a simple task?"

Little did she know that she was scolding the king himself. Alfred did not correct her or punish her for speaking so sharply; he apologized quietly, and soon, after warming himself, he slipped back into the swamp to rejoin his men in their dismal camp.

As winter began to tilt toward spring, Alfred marched his little band of loyal soldiers—*thanes,* such men were called—to Athelney (ATH-el-nee), an island in the midst of the swamp where lay the ruins of an ancient fortress. While his men repaired it and forged new weapons for themselves, Alfred sent out messages to every nearby town: on the seventh week after Easter, he said, meet me at Egbert's Stone.

The first week of May, then, found Alfred and his thanes

riding toward the meeting place. Historians are not sure exactly where or what it was—perhaps a landmark boulder or a standing stone left over from deep in the past. But in any case, when Alfred arrived, he was met by three thousand men of Wessex. Three thousand who had not fled! Three thousand who were willing to fight the Viking invaders.

Two days later the army of Wessex met Guthrum and the Vikings in a savage battle that lasted an entire day.

> *Fighting ferociously, forming a dense shield-wall against the whole army of the Pagans, and striving long and bravely... at last [Alfred] gained the victory. He overthrew the Pagans with great slaughter, and smiting the fugitives, he pursued them as far as the fortress [of Chippenham].*

At Chippenham Alfred and his army laid siege to the fortress and refused to let anyone in or out. After fourteen days without food or water, the Vikings, starved and weak, surrendered. As always, they promised that they would retreat from Alfred's kingdom, a promise that they had failed to keep in the past. But this time they had been thoroughly defeated and Alfred believed them. He knew, though, that despite this victory, he would never have a large enough army to drive the Vikings completely from Britain's shores. So he proposed a new peace treaty: the Vikings would leave Wessex, he and the Vikings would split the kingdom of Mercia, and Guthrum would be baptized as a Christian.

In the space of a mere six months, Alfred had gone from a fugitive huddling in a swamp to the most powerful king in Britain. Yet in spite of this rapid rise in power, he remained the virtuous man who had humbly apologized for burning a peasant woman's cakes.

For the first time in many years, the people of Wessex could live in peace. Alfred was determined to keep it that way. Guthrum and his army had been defeated, but some new, equally fearsome

Viking warlord might arise and threaten the peace. Alfred began at once to organize a defense for Wessex unlike anything that Britain had ever seen.

First he divided his thanes into groups and put the groups into a rotation: one group would be on alert and ready to respond with the greatest possible speed should Wessex be attacked, while the others would return to their homes and tend to their families and farms. Then he built *burhs,* which were fortresses, each with a tower and a defensive wall. Every burh was connected to all the others with a network of roads, which allowed an army to move quickly against any invaders; they were often built along rivers, with a fortified bridge that could block Viking ships from passing through. The food and supplies for each burh were provided by the landowner on whose property it had been built. This system was not always popular with the noblemen of Wessex, who objected to spending their gold for such a purpose, but Alfred insisted that every man do his part.

Because he believed that a king must lead by example, Alfred gave away much of his own wealth for the good of the kingdom. As king, of course, he owned many miles of rich farmland. Every year Alfred gave away half of the profits from his estates: to his loyal thanes, to the skilled craftsmen who were working on his building projects, to the poor. Most of the rest of his wealth was spent encouraging education; like Charlemagne, whom he admired, Alfred built schools and monasteries and brought in monks and teachers from all over Europe. He was concerned that his people learn to think rightly, so he hired translators to take the most "needful books" and translate them from Latin into the Anglo-Saxon language. Tradition says that the king felt so strongly about the importance of this project that he did some of the translation work himself.

Alfred spent the rest of his life defending his kingdom— the Vikings did arise to attack him again, but he once again repelled them—and rebuilding the damage done by the Viking wars. He grew in power and influence, and by the end of his days his papers and coins were referring to him as "the king of the English." Following his example, his sons and grandsons would go on to unite all of the kingdoms of Britain, both Anglo-Saxon and Viking, into the nation of England.

A thousand years after Alfred's reign, one of England's greatest writers, Charles Dickens, described him this way:

> *The noble king, who in his single person, possessed all the Saxon virtues. Whom misfortune could not subdue, whom prosperity could not spoil, whose perseverance, nothing could shake. Who was hopeful in defeat, and generous in success. Who loved justice, freedom, truth and knowledge.*

When we consider his life, with his courageous battles against the Vikings, his wisdom in defending and building his kingdom, and his dedication to learning and to virtue, we can well understand why Alfred is the only king of England to be known as "the Great."

Chapter Twelve

Cornstalks and Quetzal Feathers

*The Maya build cities and measure time
in the jungles of America*

Deep in the wilderness of Central America, the forests drape themselves over the rolling crests of steep-sided mountains. The clouds drift through the tree-tops and the branches drip with dew-beaded moss. In the stillness, the only movement is a flash of brilliant green as a graceful, long-tailed bird darts from tree to tree. This is the quetzal (KET-sal), the sacred bird of the Maya (MY-yuh).

As Rome faded and the Middle Ages blossomed in Europe, while Charlemagne built his empire and the Vikings raided the monasteries of England, Central America was the kingdom of the Maya. As a people, they made these jungles their home for more than 1500 years before disappearing into the shadows of history. They left behind marvels: enormous stepped pyramids, mysterious hieroglyphs, and complex stone calendars to measure different kinds of time.

The Maya did not create an empire. Instead, they carved hundreds of cities out of the jungle, each ruled by its own king. He was believed to have been sent by the gods, to be the voice of the gods on earth; and like the ancient Egyptians, the Maya thought that when a king died, he became a god himself. The king was so special that when he left the halls of his great stone palace to walk among the commoners, two of his servants would walk before him holding a cloth over his face, so no unworthy person could meet the king's eyes.

The Maya worshiped a multitude of gods, all of them attached to some aspect of the natural world that pressed so closely upon them: there was Itzamna (eat-SAHM-na), the god of the sun; Bolon Tzacab (BOO-lun TSAH-cob), the god of storms; and Chaac (CHOCK), the rain god, whose lightning axe could strike the clouds and produce a thundering downpour. To honor them the Maya constructed temples, "the god houses," and raised them far above the everyday life of the city by placing them atop large pyramids. A temple could only be reached by climbing hundreds of stairs built into its pyramid's side.

Because the Maya so revered and feared their gods, the priests possessed enormous power. A Mayan king would never attempt to go to war or choose a new member of his council without first consulting his priests, and he would humbly submit to their advice. The priests kept the city and its people in good favor with the gods; they were the ones who scaled the pyramids, entered the dark temples, and performed there the sacrifices that the gods demanded. But the priests' power came at the price of heavy burdens, because the Mayan people believed that they were responsible for making the rain fall, preventing famine and earthquakes, and predicting the future.

The priests also watched the stars. The Maya were skilled astronomers and mathematicians and kept detailed measurements of the movements of the sun and moon, the stars and the planets. Venus was especially honored; they tracked it carefully and planned their wars so battle would begin just as the planet appeared in the morning sky. Festivals and ceremonies were scheduled according to the positions of the stars, which made some days lucky and others not. And perhaps most importantly, the Mayan astronomers created calendars.

The calendar of the Maya was a complicated set of interlocking wheels. There were actually two calendars, separate and yet running alongside each other. One was based on the sun and had eighteen months of twenty days each, with an additional five days, special but very unlucky, to bring the total to the 365 that make up a year. The other calendar was devoted to the Mayan gods with 260 individually-named days. Every 52 years the two calendars would come together and restart their cycles on the same day. This was a momentous event called the Festival of New Fire. All of the household fires would be put out, and all old, worn-out tools and pots would be thrown away. When the sun dawned the next day, the fires would be re-lit, and the people would celebrate the new beginning.

The Maya also kept a third calendar, the Long Count, to show the whole stretch of their history. The Long Count started on the date that we would call August 11, 3114 B.C., which the Maya believed was the day that the earth was created, and ended on December 21, 2012. There were, strangely enough, some people in our modern world who looked at the Mayan Long Count and thought that perhaps, just before Christmas in 2012, the world was going to come to an end. Of course, as we can clearly see, it did not. Instead, the descendants of the Maya who still live in Central America today simply started the calendar again, a new Long Count.

It might seem strange to us, this use of three different calendars to keep track of time. But the Maya are not alone in this. Even today in China people follow the familiar 12-month, January to December cycle, but they add alongside a calendar based on the moon's phases, which determines the dates of holidays and festivals. Jews and Muslims do the same.

While the Mayan priests concerned themselves with tending the calendar and pleasing the gods, the king had other duties. He was not only the ambassador to the gods for his people; he was also the people's war chief. Though every Mayan

simplycharlottemason.com 97

city had a group of full-time guards who lived at the palace and a larger group of part-time warriors who would come out to battle at the king's command, the ruler alone was the battlefield general and the captain of the guard. With the aid of his priests, he decided when and how each war would be fought. And warfare was a continual part of Mayan life; each city-state often battled the others, because there was a constant need for captives to be slaves for the construction of the massive stone palaces and temples and to be sacrifices to the gods within those temple walls. The Mayan gods demanded blood; in fact, in order to plead for victory in battle, the king would have to offer his own blood to the gods by cutting his finger or nose or piercing his tongue and letting the blood drip out.

Sometimes as an alternative to war, the king might invite a neighboring city to come and play a game. Each city was equipped with a ball court, usually somewhere near the temples and the king's palace. Long and rectangular and smoothly paved with stone, the court was bounded on both sides by steep, slanted platforms where the spectators would sit. Using only their elbows, knees, hips and shoulders, players would try to bounce a rubber ball through a stone hoop set high on the walls of the court. This was hard to do; so difficult, in fact, that if one of the players managed it, the game was over then and there. The victors would celebrate, but the losers would meet the same fate that would doom them if they were captured on the battlefield: slavery or sacrifice.

When he wasn't at war or watching a ball game, the king was aided in the governing of the city by a council of noblemen, who set themselves apart from the common people with their clothing and appearance. A Mayan nobleman would wear a beautifully-woven cloak or a headdress decorated with hundreds of quetzal feathers. The headdress was a sign of wealth and power, because it was forbidden to kill the sacred quetzal bird; the beautiful green feathers could only be acquired, one by one, through capturing the birds, carefully plucking their tails, and then letting them go. Therefore, the more important a man might be, the taller and wider his headdress.

Goal Hoop on a Mayan Ball Court

The noble families of the Maya placed high value on symbols of status and beauty. It was considered a mark of the gods' high favor if a person were cross-eyed, so a noble Mayan mother might tie a little figurine into her baby's hair to dangle in front of his eyes until they were permanently crossed. She might also bind a board across the child's forehead to flatten it and thus make the little one all the more beautiful. High-born warriors filed their teeth into fearsome points, and their noble mothers and sisters often drilled holes into their teeth and filled them with decorations made from jade, turquoise, or crystal. A large nose was most attractive, so many noble men and women used creams and paints to emphasize their noses and make them look bigger.

An ordinary Mayan person would not have attempted these sorts of beauty treatments. It was actually a crime for a commoner to wear the clothing or symbols of a nobleman. And of course, as is often the case throughout history, the common people had no time for such pursuits; they spent their days working hard, many of them as farmers. They lived outside the city in small stone or mud huts usually raised up on platforms as protection from floods. They cleared fields with simple tools made of wood, shell, or stone, and planted them with an abundance of different crops.

The jungle provided plenty of sunshine and rain. The Maya grew beans and squash, chile peppers and avocados. They harvested cotton seeds and sunflower kernels to make cooking oil. They farmed some crops which could be found only in the Americas, delicious things like tomatoes, sweet potatoes, and papaya. And, of course, they gathered cacao beans.

Can you imagine a world without chocolate—no candy bars or peppermint patties or mugs of hot cocoa on a cold winter day? That was the unfortunate fate for most of the world in the Middle Ages. The only ones who were enjoying the fruit of the cacao tree were the people of Central America. The cacao beans were plucked from the trees and roasted in a clay oven, then ground up into a paste and mixed with water and chile peppers and honey. The mixture was poured back and forth, from one pot to another, until it made a foamy, spicy, delicious drink, which only the noblemen and the king were allowed to enjoy. It was so prized that it was called "the drink of the gods."

Despite the sweet luxury of chocolate, the most important crop on a Mayan farm was not the cacao tree. It was *maize*, the plant that we have come to know in modern times as corn. The Maya filled fields and fields with it and ate it at every meal, as a porridge for breakfast or ground up and made into tortillas. It was roasted and stewed, baked into cakes, and popped as a snack. Corn was so important to the Maya that they worshiped a god of maize.

Harvesting corn, drinking chocolate, and weaving beautiful headdresses from the tail feathers of the quetzal bird, the Maya lived and prospered for centuries. But around the year 900 or so, they began to disappear. Many of the stone cities were deserted, left to the jungle which slowly swallowed them up until even the tallest pyramid disappeared into the great green belly of the forest. The cities vanished so completely that many of them were not uncovered again until modern times; and most archaeologists believe that more await discovery somewhere out there in the mountains of Guatemala or El Salvador.

Historians are not entirely sure what caused the Maya to decline. It may have been a famine or drought, which prevented the farmers from growing enough food. It might have been the constant warfare, and the destruction and enslavement that went with it. The cities may have been devastated by storms or earthquakes, or the people may have been scattered by the Aztec, another group of people who were rising to power in Central America as the Maya were declining. Perhaps it was a combination of all of these things. Much of Mayan history is lost, overgrown by the jungle or trampled by conquerors.

You may be wondering then, how it is that we know anything about them—the kings, the calendars, the gods, the ball games. Fortunately, the cities tell their tales when archaeologists uncover them because the Maya left behind their words in stone inscriptions and in books, all of them written in a system of intriguing little pictures that are called *glyphs*. The Maya used more than 700 glyphs in all, some to represent sounds and some to represent entire words. Among the peoples who lived in Central America, the Maya were the only ones to develop a complete writing system.

The priests handled most of the reading and writing. Like the monks in the scriptorium at Lindisfarne, they would mix up their ink from charcoal and water and dip into it with a quill pen made from the tail feather of a turkey. But a Mayan book, which was called a *codex,* looked very different from a European manuscript. The priests would draw closely-spaced lines of glyphs on long sheets of soft bark, which had been coated with a bright white, chalky paste. When the ink dried, the pages were folded up like a fan to make a book and stored within the king's palace. Untold hundreds of them were probably written over the centuries, but sadly most have been lost, and now only three remain intact.

Nevertheless, with those three and with the many glyphs carved into stone statues and temple walls, we can read a little bit of the story of the Maya. We can gaze at their many-stepped pyramids and imposing palaces and wonder at their interlocking calendars and peer closely at the crowded glyphs along a stone wall. Perhaps we can imagine, also, the rustling fields of corn, the sweet scent of warm chocolate, and faintly in the distance, the haunting call of the quetzal.

Chapter Thirteen

The Battle of Hastings

William of Normandy becomes King of England

The town of Bayeux (BYE-you) rests in northern France, four miles inland from the rocky coastline and gray seas of the English Channel. Just out of sight to the north, across the water, lies England.

In the town's center, a great cathedral rears its mighty walls. It is built on ancient ground—a Roman temple once occupied this same land—but its fame hinges not on the building itself or where it stands but rather the relic that lies protected inside. For one of the chiefest treasures of the Middle Ages is sheltered there: a long strip of embroidered linen called the Bayeux Tapestry.

Sometime in the years between 1070 and 1080, a crew of skilled seamsters carefully sewed together nine long, narrow panels of linen to create a continuous strip two hundred and thirty feet long. Then using woolen yarn in vivid colors of orange, olive green, golden yellow, and blue, they began to tell a story, not with words but with pictures embroidered onto the cloth, a story that would eventually fill the entire 230-foot length. A story, I think you'll agree, that was and is important enough to be remembered in such a way. It is a story of two men, King Harold Godwinson, the Anglo-Saxon ruler of England, and William, Duke of Normandy, and the battle between them

simplycharlottemason.com 103

one autumn day in the year 1066. A story that begins right here in Bayeux with a shipwreck.

Two years before the battle, in 1064, Harold Godwinson boarded a ship and set out across the English Channel. He was not king of England just yet; he was merely a nobleman. The throne was occupied instead by one of the descendants of Alfred the Great, a godly man called Edward the Confessor. Edward had no son to succeed him as king, so he had promised the throne of England, after his death, to his cousin, William, the Duke of Normandy.

Normandy is the northernmost section of France, where the land faces England across the English Channel, and its name gives you a clue to its origins: "Normandy," land of the Northmen. It had been settled by wandering Vikings in the two hundred years before William's birth, and even though its people were supposed to owe some loyalty to the kings of France, it had always been an independent sort of place, a little kingdom of its own. William, the Duke of Normandy, was a powerful man.

So it was that Edward the Confessor sent Harold Godwinson to Normandy, for reasons that are lost in the shadows of history. Perhaps he wanted to confirm the promise he had made, that the English crown would one day belong to Duke William. If that is the case, it cannot have been a pleasant errand for Harold, who would, rightly, have feared that his own lands and power would disappear should William of Normandy ever become king of England. The Normans of France and the Anglo-Saxons of England had little love for one another; the Saxons still remembered well the Viking invasions of their island in the years of Alfred the Great.

In any case, whatever his errand may have been, Harold fell into trouble almost at once. His ship was overtaken by a wild wind in the channel and blown far off course, so that he was cast ashore on the desolate northern coast of France. A Norman count promptly scooped him up and delivered him as a prisoner to the town of Bayeux, there to await Duke William.

William was no fool. He recognized that his unwilling guest was a powerful Anglo-Saxon noble and thus a potential threat to his hopes for the English throne; so before he would let Harold return to England, William required him to swear an oath.

A prominent panel of the Bayeux Tapestry shows the scene: William, looking regal upon a throne-like chair, points with a gesture of command. Harold stands with his hands, palms flat, atop two chests most likely filled with holy relics to bear witness to the solemn nature of the oath. No one knows how this oath was worded or what exactly it promised, except that it required Harold to swear loyalty to William should he ever come to the throne of England.

The Bayeux Tapestry Scene of Harold Swearing the Oath before William

Only after the promise was made did William allow Harold to leave, and he arrived back in England shortly thereafter, no doubt fuming over the whole affair.

And so things might have remained. The promise might have faded away, a thing of no importance, except that two years later, in January of 1066, Edward the Confessor fell ill. His noblemen flocked to his bedside; they all heard him as he turned to Harold and asked him, weakly, to look after his queen and his people. Then, that very day, he died.

The noblemen, and certainly Harold himself, took from these words only one possible meaning: Edward wanted Harold, not William of Normandy, to be king after him. Just a few hours later, after burying Edward with all ceremony, they crowned Harold Godwinson king of England.

Harold was forty-three years old when he became king; he was regarded as a just and wise man. But like William, he was no fool, and he knew well enough that he would have to fight to keep his throne. Within England itself there were those who would oppose him, since he was not a son of the royal line. To the north, across the North Sea, the fierce Viking kings of Denmark and Sweden would surely see Edward's death as an invitation to attack. And most of all, William of Normandy had every expectation of being offered the throne of England himself, since Edward had promised it to him fifteen years before.

The old stories tell us that Duke William was out hunting when he heard the news: Edward the Confessor was dead and Harold crowned. Silent and shocked, he handed his long bow to a servant and stood for several minutes, unlacing his cloak and then lacing it up again, over and over, his face grim and eyes lost in thought. Then, still silent, he mounted his horse and rode back to his castle where he sat for a long while, his back against a stone pillar and his cloak drawn up over his face. When finally one of his closest friends dared to approach, he rose and said only four words.

"We go to England."

Of course, it's one thing to make such a bold statement, and another thing to actually see it through. William knew that he would never succeed in an invasion of England unless he had the support of all his noblemen, since it was the Norman nobles who would supply him with the soldiers, ships, and horses he needed. He called them together into a large assembly, explained his plans, and asked for their help. One of William's friends spoke up excitedly, shouting at the noblemen, "What are you waiting for? He is your master and requires your services. It is your duty to come forward with a good heart and honor your obligations!" But the noblemen only responded with shouts of their own, and the meeting broke up in a swirl of angry chaos.

William decided to try a different tactic. Instead of gathering the nobles together, he set out on horseback and visited each one of them personally. The noblemen found it much more difficult to refuse the duke when he stood there, face to face, with them, and each one of them agreed to supply him with ships or warriors. William had been sure to bring along a scribe, who carefully wrote down each nobleman's pledge so there could be no arguing later about who had agreed to send what.

For the next few months, thousands of trees fell throughout Normandy as William's carpenters began the long process of shipbuilding. Seven hundred ships would be needed to ferry William's army across the English Channel. They were not large or majestic; in fact, they were more like open boats, far smaller than the graceful longships of the Vikings. But they existed for one purpose only: to carry men and horses across the channel's open water, and for that, they were large enough.

Meanwhile, over in England Harold also prepared for war. Both he and his soldiers knew very well that William was coming. Then, in April a new urgency was added to their preparations: a streak of bearded light appeared in the night sky, a "fiery dragon." It was Halley's Comet, which appears every eighty-six years. To the people of England, it was a sign that something of huge importance was about to happen. The Bayeux Tapestry shows a crowd of Englishmen pointing upward in astonishment as the comet, tail trailing, soars overhead.

In June Harold summoned his army from every corner of

England, experienced warriors and humble peasants alike. The invasion could come at any time; so he placed twelve thousand men on the southern coastline, ready to pounce on William's forces the moment their ships appeared on the horizon. They waited and waited, eyes gazing out over the sea. They waited for weeks, but no enemy appeared.

It wasn't that William wanted to keep them waiting; he had every intention of invading and his fleet was completely assembled, but he could not set sail. A strong, persistent wind blew from the north all summer long, and William's ships could not cross the channel without a south wind to blow them onward. William paced and fumed upon the beach in Normandy, his useless ships rocking at anchor before him.

By September Harold began to breathe easier. The cold wind and the rough waters in the channel continued to make sailing impossible, and he suspected that William had missed his chance and that the invasion attempt would have to wait until the next spring. Many in Harold's army were growing restless after months of futile waiting; they were mostly farmers, after all, and they were needed at home to bring in the harvest. So on September 8 Harold dismissed his troops.

But alas! It was too soon, for just as Harold had returned to his fortress in London, he received a breathless, frantic messenger who came bearing terrible news: a fleet of Viking longships had landed in the north, poised to attack like a pack of wolves.

Harold had no choice. He recalled his army once more; many of them had only just arrived home and now were required to turn at once and travel back to the king's side. The Vikings had come ashore near the city of York, 190 miles to the north. The king and his army left London on September 19th, gathering more and more men along the way. They were able to march swiftly along the smooth roadway that the Romans had built hundreds of years before, and by the morning of September 25th, they had arrived at the bridge that led into the city of York.

A single Viking warrior stood there, determined to prevent the English army from entering the city. With awesome ferocity he fought the English back, killing forty of them. No one could get past him. Finally an English soldier found a large wooden tub on the riverbank and, slipping into the water aboard this makeshift raft, he was able to make his way under the bridge and spear the mighty Viking through the gaps in the bridge's planking.

Now the battle began in earnest and continued until sundown. The invading Viking force was killed or driven off, but at great cost. The English army had lost many soldiers, both wounded and killed. They returned to the city of York and rested there a week, trying to regain their strength. And so it was that on October 1st, as he sat down to dinner within York's sturdy walls, Harold received the worst of news: William of Normandy had landed on England's southern coast.

While Harold had been beating back the Vikings two hundred miles to the north, William and his army had been kneeling in prayer on the beaches of Normandy, pleading for a change in the wind. That very night a thunderstorm had pummeled them, and the next morning, the wind was blowing from the south. At once William had loaded his army onto the waiting ships and crossed the channel. They had scrambled ashore in England, weapons held ready, but no soldiers sprang forward to meet them. To their surprise, the coast seemed entirely deserted. They had no way of knowing that the English army was actually miles away.

They were marching south as fast as they could, but they were weary and much diminished from their fierce battle with the Vikings. Harold had sent out a message across the length and breadth of England: any man or boy who could fight should meet the king and his army at the "hoar-apple tree atop Calbec Hill," a well-known landmark a few miles north of the town of Hastings. On October 13th Harold and his army, about four thousand men, arrived at Calbec Hill, there to find about three thousand more Englishmen awaiting them, most of them peasants and farmers nervously clutching homemade axes or pitchforks.

William's army lay waiting six miles to the south. The next morning, in the gray light of dawn, the Normans marched forward to attack the English.

Harold's army was spread in a tight line across the top of Calbec Hill. He was using the defense that was called the "Shield Wall," similar to the phalanx that Charles Martel had used to defeat the Muslims at the Battle of Tours. It was a good plan, because it meant that William's army would have to attack uphill. The Normans were fighting on horseback, many of them, and the English were all afoot, but the Shield Wall could repel the horses if the English held firm.

At nine o'clock on October 14th, 1066, a Norman minstrel sounded the charge on his trumpet, and William's army surged upward in attack.

William planned to attack as he always did in any battle: archers first, then horsemen. But his archers were firing upward, and the Shield Wall defeated them, with many of the arrows falling short or bouncing harmlessly off the thick wood of the shields. In just a few minutes the archers had shot every arrow they possessed; normally they would have replenished their supply by seizing the arrows that the enemy had shot back at them. But the English army contained no archers that day, so the Normans were out of luck.

William had no choice but to send forward his horsemen, but again the Shield Wall and the uphill slope defeated them, and they were forced into retreat. Finally they attacked on foot, and soon both armies were engaged in a desperate struggle. As the battle stretched on into the hours after noon, a terrible rumor began to sweep the Norman army: William had been killed!

William's men began to panic, stumbling backward in wild

retreat. William knew he must act at once or the battle would be lost. He ripped off his helmet, shouting at the top of his lungs, "Look at me! I am alive and will conquer with God's help!"

The retreat stopped. William's men rallied around him and pressed forward once more. Thousands of soldiers on both sides had been killed or wounded, but neither Harold nor William was any closer to victory. Then, unexpectedly, William's army fell back once more into retreat. The Normans, writing later about this battle, claimed that this was a clever plan of William's, a false retreat to lure the English forward. And perhaps it was, for that is exactly what happened. Seeing their enemy fleeing, the English broke their Shield Wall and began to pursue after them. At once, the Normans turned and attacked once more and finally gained the top of Calbec Hill.

Now Harold knew the battle was lost. He continued to fight bravely, but with the Shield Wall gone there was nothing to protect his army. Once again the Norman arrows flew, "thicker than rain before the wind," and the English army fell before them. William caught his first glimpse of Harold, "fiercely hewing to pieces the Normans who were besetting him," and he sent twenty of his best warriors toward the English king. In the minutes that followed, Harold Godwinson, the last Anglo-Saxon king of England, was killed.

With their king dead, the English army was defeated, although the king's personal bodyguard refused to surrender and fought to the last man. As the sun sank behind the hill, the surviving peasants and farmers began to scatter. The Battle of Hastings was over.

William, Duke of Normandy, was now William the Conqueror, King of England. He was crowned in London on Christmas Day, 1066, in the same church where 877 years later his descendent, Queen Elizabeth II, would also be crowned.

William changed everything when he became ruler of England: laws, religion, language. He and his noblemen all spoke French, and Anglo-Saxon became the language of peasants and slaves. He brought a new system of government called "feudalism," which you will learn about in the next chapter, and he covered England with square Norman fortresses and giant Norman castles. But most of all, he ended the Anglo-Saxon line of kings. Though Alfred the Great had once defeated them, the Vikings conquered England after all in the person of a Norman king. England and its people were changed forever.

Chapter Fourteen

Feudalism

*The people of the Middle Ages
arrange themselves into a pyramid*

Have you ever built a pyramid out of blocks, perhaps when you were very small? Can you remember how that worked? It was different from building a tower, where you need only concern yourself with keeping the edges straight. To build a pyramid you would carefully construct each layer just a little smaller than the one below, until at the very top, you placed the final block. It's the same when children play "King of the Mountain": there's room at the top for only one.

In many ways the people who lived in the Middle Ages arranged their lives in the same way. Like a pyramid of blocks, the people were divided into layers with many on the bottom and just one at the top. They did this for the same reason that little children like to build pyramids: they do not topple over. A tower, where every layer is the same, might begin to crumble and fall as it gets taller and larger. But a pyramid will never fall; the pyramids of ancient Egypt have stood for thousands of years! Pyramids are stable shapes.

During the Middle Ages, stability was a very important virtue indeed.

More than anything else, medieval people valued order.

To them, an orderly world was the only world that made sense. They looked to the Church for their truth, and the Church taught them the truth of the Bible: that God had created, in just six days, an orderly universe—first light, then water and land, then plants and animals, and finally, as the climax of His creative work, man. Man was then given rulership over the lesser works that had been created before him. So, like layers in a pyramid, man stood above all the created world, while looking down upon him were God's angels and, supreme over all, God Himself sat on His heavenly throne. This kind of arrangement is called a *hierarchy*, a system in which people or groups are ranked above each other according to their power and authority.

To the people of the Middle Ages, God's order could be seen in every part of the created world, and the logic and rightness of that order was a blessing. It was a sign of God's goodness; He had made a world where things were intended to be sensible, logical, fair, and just. This knowledge offered the people comfort and certainty when their lives became difficult and full of disorder.

For there was much hardship in medieval life. Death was everywhere; people rarely reached the age of fifty. Many women died in childbirth and many men in warfare. Those who were spared such tragedies often lost their lives to illness, to bitterly cold winters, or to famine.

The spring of 1315 was cold and wet; the ground grew so muddy that it could not be plowed, and the seeds that should have been planted rotted in their sacks. With little harvest that year, the people quickly ran short of food, for as you can imagine, there were few ways during the Middle Ages to preserve meat and vegetables. People did the best that they could, gathering nuts and edible roots in the forests. But the next year was just as rainy and cold, and there was no food to be had. The weather warmed again in 1317, but there was no seed to be planted because every grain had been eaten. Not until 1325 were the tables once again set with enough food, and by then many, many people had died all across Europe.

For those who survived, the hardships often continued. Food might be scarce and difficult to come by. They might have to pay heavy taxes to a nearby nobleman or be forced to fight in his wars.

But despite their sorrows, the people did not blame these dreadful troubles on God. Rather, they saw mankind himself as the cause of all evils, and they sought to return the world to the perfect, ordered place that God intended it to be.

After the fall of Rome, and later with Charlemagne's death and the collapse of his empire, disorder filled almost every part of Europe. There was no one at the top of the pyramid, no one to keep things in line. Smaller, lesser kings would squabble and fight over scraps of power; the terrible Viking longships would swoop ashore, lighting wildfires of panic and terror; bandits haunted the roadways, which fell into disrepair. And so, gradually, a new sort of order began to develop; rather than look to a distant emperor for order and safety, the people of Europe turned instead to local noblemen, who reigned with absolute power on their own lands. They built fortresses to defend against the Vikings, hunted down and punished bandits, kept the roads through their lands in good repair, and provided land and crops to support the people; in return the people farmed the land and gave their service to the noblemen. Nowadays, when we look back at the Middle Ages, we call this organizational system *feudalism* or *the feudal system*. It lasted in Europe for almost 600 years, from the ninth to the fifteenth century, and it was entirely dependent on land and loyalty, on oaths between vassals and lords.

A *vassal* was a nobleman who made a pledge to another nobleman, the *lord*. The vassal would agree to supply the lord with soldiers and weapons, and in return, the lord would provide the vassal with protection and safety; supply the things he needed, such as food and clothing; and most importantly, give him a portion of his own land. The gifted land was called a *fief* (feef), and it is from this word, which is *feudum* in Latin, that we get the term "feudal." The vassal would receive all the profits from the fief's crops and herds; in return, he would fight the lord's battles at his command.

The pledge made between a vassal and a lord was cemented at a public ceremony, which was called a *commendation*. There, before an audience of other noblemen, the vassal would pay homage to the lord and bow in submission. He would swear to be faithful and loyal, a promise that was called an *oath of fealty*. The lord, after the vassal had made his oath, would vow in return to protect the vassal from enemies. Then he would bestow upon him the fief, the land that would support him and his family through the years to come.

As well as supplying soldiers, the vassal was also obliged to provide his lord with other sorts of aid. If the lord came to visit, the vassal was required to host him, and all those traveling with him, in the best possible style with feasting and deluxe accommodations. It could be a terrible burden if the lord arrived with all of his household in tow. William the Conquerer once came to spend Christmas with one of his vassals, and in three days of feasting, he and his household devoured 6,000 chickens, 1,000 rabbits, 90 boars, 50 peacocks, 200 geese, 10,000 eels, and thousands of eggs. If the lord was in need of advice, the vassal must travel to wherever the lord was holding his court and sit with the other vassals in a kind of council, passing judgment on captured thieves, for example, or deliberating on the question of whether the lord should press forward and attack his enemies.

And strange as it may seem, if the lord were in need of money, which he often was, he could call upon the vassal to supply it.

All of this may make it seem that being a vassal was more trouble than it was worth, but usually it was considered an excellent honor to be a vassal. Only noblemen were vassals; common people never took the oath of fealty. And the vassals often wielded immense power, especially those whose fiefs were large and wealthy. The oath of loyalty that bound a vassal to his lord was a tie of honorable duty, and fulfilling it well was a source of pride.

Every nobleman in the land, be he great or small, was vassal to the king. The king was the tip of the pyramid; all the land in the kingdom technically belonged to him alone, to be dispensed as fiefs to his loyal followers. Below the king, on the next level of the pyramid, were the mighty lords who were the personal vassals to the ruler; they had stood before the king in a commendation ceremony and given him their oaths of fealty to his face. These great men, in turn, were lords to lesser nobles, and so on down the levels of the pyramid until finally there were the minor vassals who had no vassals of their own.

But alas, in actual practice the system was not quite so neatly arranged. In fact, the uppermost vassals, rulers of huge fiefdoms that were like kingdoms in themselves, were often far more powerful than any king. And many noblemen pledged themselves as vassals to more than one lord, greedy for the bountiful harvests from fief after fief. All of these oaths of loyalty led to much anger and confusion, for it was often unclear to which lord the vassal owed his first and foremost allegiance. Messy arguments and outright war were often the result.

Of course, these noblemen and their tangled alliances were only a small fraction of the people who lived during the Middle Ages. Most people were common farmers and craftsmen; they owned no land and swore no oaths of fealty. They were just as dependent upon the feudal system as the greatest lord; however, rather than living at the top of the pyramid, they labored long and hard at the bottom.

Some of the common people were workers who were called *freemen*. These were farmers who paid a sum of money every year to a lord and, in return, were allowed to lean upon the lord for protection and plant their crops on a portion of the lord's land.

All of the profit from a freeman's harvest belonged to him; if he produced a bountiful harvest, he might be able to stash away part of his money in the hope of renting even more land the next year. If he did poorly, he was free to leave and take his service elsewhere, trying his luck on a different piece of land.

But there were many more who were not so free. They were called *serfs,* and unlike the freemen, they were bound to a specific lord's land and could never leave it. The lord provided his serfs with protection and with a small plot of land. The serfs were then required to labor without pay in the lord's fields, or in his stables or his mills or his mines, in any place on the fief or in the lord's house and its attached lands, which was known as the *manor.* Most of every week the serf would work for the lord and then scramble in the other day or two to grow food for his family on his little plot of land. Without his lord's permission, a serf could not marry or leave the manor or try some different job. He remained right where he was, often in the same house where he had been born, doing the same work until the day that he died.

Despite all of that, the serf was not a slave like the Viking thralls. The lord of the manor could not sell his serfs to some other lord or take away a serf's land.

Without the serfs to do all of the work, the feudal system would have collapsed completely. Instead, it flourished. Every person in Europe occupied his place in the great pyramid, knowing that when he died, his son would do the same and his son's son after him. In the midst of all the uncertainties of medieval life, the feudal pyramid remained, as stable as if it were built of stone.

Chapter Fifteen

The Way of the Warrior

During the Middle Ages, warfare is bound by the rules of honor

In southwest Japan the tall fortress of Fushimi (foo-shee-mee) Castle stood atop a green hill overlooking the city of Kyoto (kyoh-toh). The lord of Fushimi, Tokugawa Ieyasu (toh-koo-ga-wa ee-ay-ya-soo), gazed out at the city, watching the August sun gild the roofs and wondering if this might be his last day upon the earth. An army of forty thousand warriors was even then marching toward Fushimi with one purpose only: to kill him. The castle's garrison, two thousand men strong, had no hope of defeating them.

He turned to the captain of his forces, Torii Mototada (to-ree mo-toh-tah-dah). "We cannot hold out against them," he said. "We must retreat, while we can."

But Torii shook his head. "You will go, master, but I will stay. The men and I will defend the castle to our last breath, and in this way you will be able to escape."

Tokugawa bowed his head before such a display of selfless loyalty and both men wept, knowing that they would never meet again. Then, as his lord fled for his life, Torii called for ink and pen and wrote a final letter to his beloved son.

Do not mourn for me, he said:

I am resolved to make a stand within the castle and to die a quick death. It would not take much trouble to break through a part of their numbers and escape . . . But that is not the true meaning of being of a warrior, and it would be difficult to account as loyalty. Rather, I will stand off the forces of the entire country here, and, without even one one-hundredth of the men necessary to do so, and I will throw up a defense and die a resplendent death. . . . It is not the way of the warrior to be shamed and avoid death. It goes without saying that to sacrifice one's life for one's master is an unchanging principle.

Torii and his two thousand men held the attacking army at bay for ten days until, with the castle in flames around him, he could see that final defeat was only moments away. Enemy soldiers pressed forward through fire and smoke and falling beams in their eagerness to capture the valiant defender of Fushimi, but retreating to the highest balcony of the castle, Torii drew out his sword and took his own life. He would die rather than fall into their hands.

His death was not in vain. Torii's hopeless battle at Fushimi made it possible for Tokugawa to pull together an army, defeat his enemies once and for all, and so become the shogun, the lord not only of Fushimi but of all Japan.

A shogun was not a king but a military leader with his own private army of thousands of warriors. The shoguns dominated Japan for seven hundred years, from 1170 to 1868. Even though Japan had always been—and still is, in fact—ruled by an emperor, during the Middle Ages the emperor was merely a *figurehead*, much like the do-nothing Frankish kings whose power was really given over to the Mayors of the Palace. The emperors lived luxurious but empty lives in the palace at Kyoto; the shoguns set up their own governments elsewhere, which were called *bakufu* (bah-koo-foo): "tent headquarters." It was as if the shoguns were downplaying their own power, pretending to be humble military servants waiting patiently in their tents for orders from the great emperor in Kyoto. But everyone knew that the emperors were actually powerless and the true business of running the country was happening in the bakufu.

The shogun's power came from his lands and men. Just as the lords of Europe based their greatness on the size of their estates and the oaths of their vassals, so too did the shogun depend upon the loyalty pledged to him by the *daimyo* (die-mio), the landowners of Japan. When a shogun came to power, he would reward the loyalty of his followers by giving to them, daimyo and warrior alike, the lands that had once belonged to his enemies. The land would be farmed by peasants, just as it was by serfs in Europe. They would do the hard work of planting and cultivating in exchange for a share in the harvest and the daimyo's protection from battles and bandits.

This protection was provided by the daimyo's warriors, the *samurai* (sa-mur-eye).

Samurai were proud men, often following in the footsteps of a father or brother who had been samurai before them. They followed a strict code of conduct, the *bushido* (boo-shee-doh), which emphasized eight important virtues.

The samurai must always seek to do justice, act with great courage, and demonstrate mercy to the less fortunate.

He must be polite, honest, and loyal.

He must behave with self-control.

And most of all, he must always conduct himself with honor. A samurai's honor meant everything to him, because if his good name were lost, it could never be recovered. A samurai felt that "dishonor is like a scar on a tree, which time, instead of effacing, only helps to enlarge."

As the story of Torii Mototada shows us, a samurai would gladly give his life for his lord; like the Vikings, the samurai considered death in battle to be the ultimate honor. To be captured by the enemy was the deepest disgrace, and the samurai would fight to the death to avoid it. For these warriors the battlefield was governed by the rules of honor and duty. An enemy samurai must be treated with utmost respect, and the samurai must face him shoulder to shoulder with his lord, showing no fear. The samurai would fight with all of their skill to the utmost, for if the daimyo fell, so would his warriors. A samurai would never quit a battle, not while his lord was still standing.

If the daimyo's battles required other sorts of attack—ambush, assassination, sabotage—he could not ask such dishonorable actions of his samurai. He would have to rely on *ninja* instead: the secret spies who were not subject to the code of the bushido.

Sometimes a question of honor might be decided by a duel between two samurai. What a sight they must have been as they circled each other, two armored warriors with their swords drawn! Every samurai wielded a special sword called a *katana,* a "dispenser of enemies," with a long, curved, double-edged blade. He would slide it into his *obi,* a fabric sash tied around his waist, with the curved edge facing outward so that he could draw the sword and strike his enemy all in the same movement. Samurai also carried a short sword, a *wakizashi* (wa-kee-za-shee), tucked into the obi alongside the katana; by law in Japan only a samurai was allowed to wear both swords at once.

A samurai went into battle dressed in distinctive armor made of overlapping plates of metal and leather. The metal was brightly lacquered, often in a pattern that was unique to him. This was another matter of honor; he wanted to be easily identified on the battlefield, so that his brave deeds could be seen by others and remembered.

When the battle was over and the samurai returned to their wooden castles, they took bushido with them off the battlefield too. They combined the eight virtues of the Way of the Warrior with the religion of Zen Buddhism, which had come from India and which emphasized the importance of a calm and humble life. The samurai displayed their humility by valuing things that were simple or unadorned—houses with plain, wooden walls and unpainted floors, or gardens made only of rocks and boulders and carefully raked gravel. Instead of planting flowerbeds filled with extravagant blossoms, they employed bonsai masters, whose job it was to carefully select a maple or pine sapling and prune and shape it until it was a miniature version of a tree, planted in a shallow dish and set out in the garden for guests to admire. Many years of careful tending were needed to produce a single bonsai tree, and to the samurai, this practice reflected the discipline and duty that their devotion to the code of bushido required.

A Bonsai tree in training for more than 30 years

In our Castle of the Middle Ages, the room that might represent Japan would be exotically decorated, with katana swords and brightly-colored suits of armor, with serene stone gardens and tiny bonsai trees. But if we look more closely, we might see that the furniture scattered around the room is not so different after all. The feudalism that governed most of Europe in the Middle Ages ruled Japan as well, with the weak, distant king isolated in his palace and the powerful landowners ruling their fiefdoms like little kingdoms, guarded by skilled and loyal fighters, while the peasants sweated in the sun and shivered in the cold to work the fields and bring in the crops. And just as the samurai followed the bushido, the warriors of Europe also developed their own code of honor, the practice of *chivalry*.

The word *samurai* originally meant "one who serves." In much the same way, the warriors of Europe came to be called "knights," a title which comes from an old German word that means "servant," because they gave their service to the great lords in their castles in return for land and castles of their own.

Like the samurai, the knights valued discipline and duty. Much effort and self-sacrifice were required in order to become a knight. A boy might give himself into the service of an older knight when he was only seven years old. He would work as a *page,* learning to hunt and fight, to care for the horses and polish the armor, as well as to read and write. When he turned fifteen, he could become a *squire;* wearing his own armor now, he must practice the seven agilities of knighthood: riding, swimming, shooting a bow, climbing, wrestling, sword-fighting, and dancing. Finally at the age of 21, he would be ready for the *accolade:* the knighthood ceremony. He would spend the whole night before the ceremony kneeling in prayer in a chapel; when morning came, he would swear an oath of fealty and loyalty before his lord, who would tap him on both shoulders with the tip of a sword. Then the lord would present him with the sword and declare him a true knight.

On that day the newly-made knight would also dedicate himself to the code of chivalry. Originally this word came from the Frankish word *chevalier,* which simply meant a warrior on horseback, and indeed, at first the rules of chivalry were only concerned with the battlefield. But as time went on, the idea of chivalry broadened to include every part of the knight's life, in the same way that the bushido governed the samurai. And like the samurai, the knight was expected to behave always with loyalty, self-control, courage, perseverance, mercy, justice, and honor. He must swear, under the code of chivalry, to be a "hand of God," which meant that he would always protect the innocent and the poor and serve the Church whenever there was need. To fail in any of these virtues meant disgrace and, of course, dishonor.

For the sake of honor, knights could challenge each other in a kind of duel on horseback, a *joust*. There were no sleekly-curved katana swords here! Mounted on huge, armored warhorses, two knights would charge toward each other at full gallop, each man attempting to knock the other out of his saddle with a long wooden lance. Instead of brightly-lacquered armor, a knight would identify himself, both at the jousting tournament and on the battlefield, with his *coat of arms*. This was a special symbol or set of symbols that was painted on his shield, embroidered onto the surcoat that covered his armor, and stitched into the banner that was carried by his squire. In the joust a knight must show honor even in defeat, for if he lost the contest, he was obliged to yield up his armor, his horse, and his banner to the victor.

The knight astride his warhorse and the samurai contemplating his bonsai garden would each have had no idea that the other existed. Far, far to the east of Europe, beyond the huge expanse of China, Japan lay past a horizon that no European had yet crossed. But still these two warriors had much in common. Skilled on the battlefield, devoted to a code of loyalty and duty, enriched by the rewards of serving their wealthy masters, the knights of Europe and the samurai of Japan lived lives that were immeasurably different and yet, in many ways, exactly the same.

Chapter Sixteen

The Cross Upon the Shield

*The knights of Europe crusade
for the freedom of Jerusalem*

Suppose I were to ask you to draw a map of the world. Where would you start?

If I suggested that you begin by making a dot for the North Pole and then go outward from there, I think you would probably disagree! Instead you would get out a sheet of paper and draw the outline of your home country in the center, and then the neighboring nations and the oceans that surround your continent, and finally the other continents on the opposite side of the globe. You would do your best to get the shapes and sizes of the various countries correct; after all, Canada is larger than Cuba! You would want your map to be truthful, so someone could look at it and get an accurate picture of the earth's geography. As a *cartographer*—a person who creates maps—your goal is to represent the lands and seas that actually exist on the earth's surface.

But that worthy goal hasn't always been the case among cartographers. If we were to travel to Hereford, England, and visit the cathedral there, we would find, displayed in a specially-built museum room, a map of the world drawn during the Middle Ages. At first glance it seems an ordinary map with rivers and cities and mountains. We can make out Egypt and the Nile River, the land of Greece, the continent of Africa, Italy and the city of Rome, the Rock of Gibraltar—all things we might expect to see on any map of the world. But a closer look reveals that this map contains some very unusual features. Strangely enough, even though it was made by an Englishman, the island of Britain is shown way down at the bottom and far to the left. At the top, instead of Arctic ice and the North Pole, the mapmaker has drawn the gates of Paradise encircled with fire. The location of Noah's Ark is carefully marked, as well as the Garden of Eden off to one side. And in the center is drawn, instead of England or any part of Europe, a great, walled city with its name written above in fine red ink: Jerusalem.

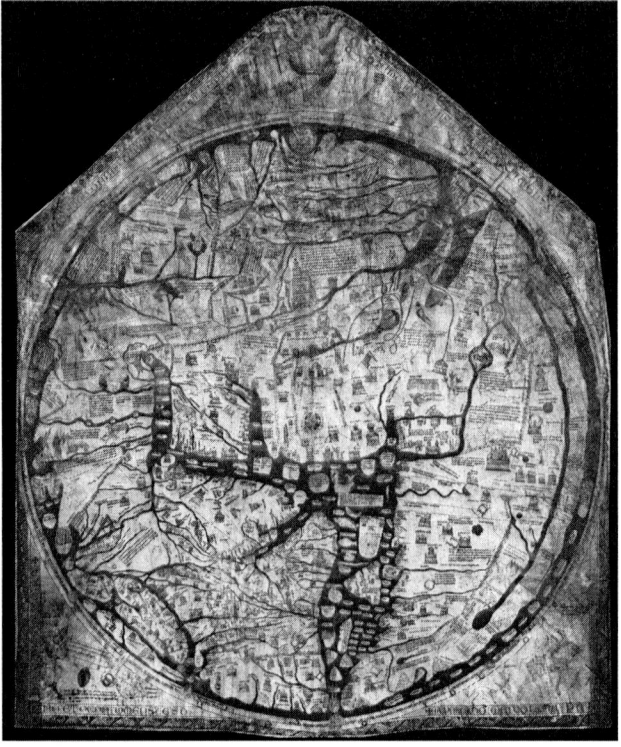

The Hereford Map

The mapmakers of the Middle Ages did not seek to represent the actual earth with mountains, rivers, cities, and roads drawn to their exact position and size. Instead, a map was meant to show the world as a story. It was not a guide to help you get from one place to another like a modern map would be. It was instead a guide for how to think about the world. The events of the Bible are part of the world's story, and so the cartographers of the Middle Ages put them on the map. The location of the Garden of Eden—people in the Middle Ages thought that it was far away at the very edge of the world—was just as important as the location of Rome, and so both things must be shown.

The fact that Jerusalem rests at the center of a medieval map tells us something about the significance of that city to the mind of the mapmaker. Jerusalem was the city of Christ; for the people of Christian Europe, no other place on earth could be deemed more important, and to place anything else at the center would be the height of disrespect. As the Middle Ages went on, many men would follow the mapmakers' lead and place Jerusalem at the heart of their dreams, quests, and fortunes.

This is the story of those quests, which became known as the Crusades. Jerusalem lay in the midst of Palestine, which was the Romans' name for the ancient land of Israel. Despite their long history in the city, which was the site of Solomon's Temple and the capital of their beloved king David, the Jews no longer controlled Jerusalem. They had been scattered far abroad in ancient times; during the Middle Ages, most Jews lived in little communities in different parts of Europe and Africa. A few still remained in Jerusalem, but the city was ruled by Muslims, who had taken it by force when they had swept out of Arabia in the eighth century.

Even before that conquest, since the days of the Roman Empire, Christians had been making *pilgrimages* to Palestine; a pilgrim is someone who journeys to a shrine or a holy place, and naturally, the holiest of all destinations was Jerusalem, where

Christ died and rose again. After the city fell to the Muslims, pilgrimages became more difficult, but many still made the effort. Some of the Muslim rulers were more tolerant than others and were willing to welcome the pilgrims, along with the money they brought to pay for food and shelter.

But in 1072 Jerusalem was conquered again, by the Seljuk (SEL-jook) Turks who had arisen out of their homeland north of the Caspian Sea, migrated into Persia, and then expanded their dominion westward through the peninsula that is called Asia Minor, modern-day Turkey. Pressing ever onward, they eventually built a large empire that included all of Palestine. The new Turkish rulers of Jerusalem had no interest in hosting Christian pilgrims; in fact, reports began to reach Europe of pilgrims who had been attacked and murdered, and pilgrimage roads blocked or destroyed.

For the Byzantine emperor, Alexius I (ah-LEX-ee-us), the Turks presented a grave threat. Turkish armies in Asia Minor were pushing against his borders, advancing nearer and nearer to Constantinople itself. In 1095 he made a request for help to the pope in Rome, who at that time was a man named Urban II. The pope saw in the emperor's plea an opportunity to finally bring the holy city of Jerusalem into Christian hands.

So in November of that year, the pope preached a fiery sermon pleading for Christians to rise up and fight for the freedom of Jerusalem. "Deus vult!" he shouted: God wills it! He commanded the warriors of Europe to arm themselves and to put the cross of Christ upon their shields as a badge of honor. He also made a promise to every man who answered his call:

> *Whoever for devotion alone, but not to gain honour or money, goes to Jerusalem to liberate the Church of God can substitute this journey for all penance.*

In offering *penance,* the pope was saying that those who went to battle for Jerusalem could receive a spiritual reward:

forgiveness for any sins that they had committed.

The ringing call to join the expedition echoed loudly across Europe. In response, thousands left their homes and lands to take up both the pope's offer of salvation and the Byzantine emperor's appeal for help. They painted bright red crosses on their shields and sewed them onto their cloaks to show that they were no ordinary army. They were fighting for God and for Jerusalem! And so, because the Latin word for cross is "crux," they were called *crusaders,* and their quests to rescue the city from its Muslim overlords became known as the Crusades.

The main crusader armies arrived in Constantinople in 1096. Alexius may have been a bit shocked at the huge number of men who had come in response to his plea, but he rose to the occasion. He offered the armies food and horses, as well as guides and servants; in return, the crusaders promised to hand over to him any lands that they recovered from the Turks. Then with banners flying and helmets gleaming, they marched off toward Jerusalem.

It took them two years to get there. They were an enormous group, and at first they moved slowly and awkwardly, the army stringing itself along the desert road like metal beads on a thin, dusty wire. The Turks were quick to attack any stragglers, and in the beginning the crusaders lost a great deal of men and supplies. But as the months dragged by, they learned to work together and to protect themselves as they traveled, and eventually they reached the city of Antioch, whose ruins lie today in Turkey near the border with Syria.

Here was their first great test: if they could take Antioch then perhaps they would also be successful at Jerusalem, for the two cities were much alike: large, surrounded by a fearsome wall, and guarded by a strong force of Muslim Turks. With winter coming on, the crusaders settled into siege around the city. They suffered cold and starvation all through the winter and spring; they were able to break into the city and secure it, but the

Muslims still held the fortress that towered over the city walls. By June they were out of food, and some of the leaders began to mutter that the crusade was hopeless and all was lost. But just in time, one of the army's priests was visited by a dream in which he held in his hands a piece of the Holy Lance, the spear that had pierced Christ's side at His crucifixion. The dream showed him exactly where he must dig in order to recover this holy relic, and perhaps not surprisingly, that very morning it was found. A new energy and excitement swept through the army. Though they had lost all but a few hundred of their horses, they mounted for battle and charged the Muslim fortress one last time. On June 28, 1098, on their final attempt, the crusader army overcame the Muslim defenses and took full control of the fortress. Antioch was theirs.

Now tempers began to flair. Some of the leaders wished to stay at Antioch and strengthen their position there. But others insisted that the army must fulfill its true purpose and march southward at once. Eventually most of the knights agreed with this second group, and one year later, in June of 1099, the crusaders finally arrived outside the gates of Jerusalem. Many of them fell to their knees, weeping at the sight of the city they had journeyed so far to reach. But there was little time for joy or celebration; they had no water and little food, the hot sun was beating down, and both men and horses were suffering.

So several groups of knights were sent out toward the Mediterranean Sea to find wood wherever they could. These foraging parties brought back four hundred logs, as well as all the timber from a fleet of ships that they had discovered and seized. With these supplies the crusaders were able to build the only weapon that could defeat the walls of Jerusalem: siege towers.

A siege tower is like a little house on wheels, a very tall and narrow little house. Within its walls are platforms and ladders, which allow the soldiers packed inside to climb upward as the tower is rolled forward against a city's wall. Then they can burst out of the door at the top of the tower, overwhelm the wall's defenders, and fight their way down to open the city gates from the inside so the rest of the army can enter.

If the siege towers were successful, the city would fall and the Muslims knew it. They flung burning pots of oil as the towers were pushed forward, and soon one of them was cloaked in flames. But after two hours of intense battle, the other tower reached the wall and the fighters inside surged out over the top and down into the city. By the end of that day, the crusaders had killed all of the city's defenders; they were the victors in Jerusalem.

Most of them returned home then, eager to see their lands and families again. But not all. They had marched as one in the name of Christ, but with the victory came the temptation for each man to grasp power for himself. Over the next ten years, some of the crusaders made themselves kings and princes, not only of Jerusalem but also all of the land up and down the coast of Palestine along the Mediterranean Sea. They grew rich marketing the Muslims' trading goods to the cities of Venice and Genoa (JEN-ah-wah), in Italy, who in turn packed the hulls of their ships with spices, pearls, and silken rugs and sailed north to sell all of these luxuries to the merchants of Europe. The crusader kings—of Antioch, Jerusalem, and the rest—established treaties of peace with their Muslim neighbors, but since they were vastly outnumbered by those same Muslims, they built enormous castles, as well, to guard their little realms from attack. Then with the Holy Land around Jerusalem secure, they invited the pilgrims to return. Over the next fifty years, thousands of Europeans would make the pilgrimage to Palestine and back.

So Jerusalem rested securely in Christian hands. Pope Urban's call had been answered, and Alexius' plea for help had met with astonishing success. Muslim and Christian lived side by side, and all seemed well. The crusaders thought that they had achieved a peace for Jerusalem that would last for centuries, a peace that God had willed.

But they were wrong. This was only the First Crusade; there would be more to come.

Artist's Rendering of the Krak des Chevaliers Crusader Castle

Chapter Seventeen

Lionheart and Robin Hood

*As the crusades continue,
England's king nearly loses his kingdom*

The First Crusade had ended and an uneasy peace lay over the crusader kingdoms. Pilgrims shuffled along the dusty paths toward Jerusalem, and the merchant ships of Venice and Genoa sailed endlessly back and forth between Europe and the ports of Palestine. The crusaders themselves lived richly behind their castle walls. Their Muslim neighbors were quiet, but they had not forgotten the blood that had been spilled in Jerusalem by the crusaders' swords.

In December of 1144 the Muslims struck back. An army of Turks from the city of Aleppo (ah-LEP-po) attacked the Crusader kingdom of Edessa (EH-des-sa), which lay east of Antioch, and defeated its ruler. When news of Edessa's downfall reached the pope in Rome, he immediately sent out an appeal for a Second Crusade. Even kings themselves answered the call; the rulers of both France and Germany "took the cross," swearing to raise up another army and march to the defense of the Christian kingdoms of Palestine.

But things went differently this time. The army, and the noblemen that led it, did not seem to have a clear goal. They turned away from Edessa and attacked Damascus in Syria instead, but there they met defeat after only four days and were forced to retreat, embarrassed and humbled, back to their homes in Europe. Edessa remained a Muslim city, and the Muslims, encouraged by the crusaders' failure, turned their eyes toward Jerusalem. All that was required was someone to lead them there.

That someone arose in the person of Saladin (SAL-a-din), one of Islam's greatest warriors. Born into a family of soldiers, he had risen to become the sultan, or king, of Egypt. He had heard all his life the story of Jerusalem's fall to the crusaders, and he was determined to win it back again. By 1187 he had convinced the other Muslim nations to join him in the attempt.

If the crusaders had been patient and wise and awaited Saladin behind Jerusalem's thick walls, perhaps this story would have turned out differently. But convinced of their own courage and success in battle, they rode out to meet the Muslim army in the open country north of the city. There on a dry hilltop far from any reliable source of water, they found themselves surrounded by Saladin's army and were forced to make camp with no hope of food or drink. During the night the Muslims set fire to the dry grass, filling the crusaders' eyes and throats with smoke so that they could hardly move. The next morning when the battle was joined, the crusaders were utterly defeated.

With their army destroyed, the crusaders could not hope to hold Jerusalem. Saladin laid siege to the city, but he preferred to take it with as little bloodshed as possible. He offered *quarter;* that is, he promised the people that if they would surrender, he would allow them to pay a ransom for their lives and leave peacefully. He gave them forty days to come up with the money; soon a steady stream of Christians poured out of the city. Each man paid ten dinars, which was about a year's wages; each woman five and each child only one. But of course there were many in the city who were too poor to pay the ransom, and eventually, as the forty days drew to a close, Saladin allowed most of the poor to escape anyway. Then he declared that any Jews who wished to might return to the city and make it their home once again.

After 88 years as a Crusader kingdom, Jerusalem lay in Muslim hands. But while this news was greeted with joy and celebration in the lands of Islam, it ignited a firestorm of rage and sorrow throughout Europe. Legend says the the pope fell ill and died the day that word of Jerusalem's surrender reached him. When a new pope, Gregory VIII, had been appointed in Rome, he announced at once the formation of a Third Crusade. Kings once more began to sharpen their swords.

One of these was the newly-crowned King of England, Richard I, the great-great-grandson of William the Conqueror. He was a tall, handsome man, and his skill in battle, along with his golden mane of hair, had earned him the nickname "Lionheart." Like his ancestor, William, he was a Norman, and indeed he had spent most of his life in Normandy. He spoke no English; when he knelt at the altar in the great abbey at Westminster in London and received his crown, it was his first visit to England since he had been a little boy. It would be the last, too, for many years. He had no deep love for the land he ruled. "It is always cold and raining," he complained. In any case, England held little interest for Richard; his mind was entirely set on Jerusalem.

The crown had barely settled on his brow before Richard sailed away from his kingdom, having paid his way by first emptying England's treasury and then selling practically everything he owned. He joined forces with the king of France, Philip II, and the Duke of Austria, Leopold V, who both happened to be his cousins. The three kings had expected to be joined by a fourth, Frederick Barbarossa (BAR-bah-ROH-sa), the Holy Roman emperor, but he had drowned while crossing a river and his immense army had turned around and returned home.

Undaunted, Richard and his cousins took aim at the fortress of Acre on the coast of the Mediterranean Sea, the most important port in all of Palestine. It is one of the oldest cities in the world, having been continually occupied by one empire or another for more than 4,000 years. Though it had long been an immensely wealthy crusader kingdom, the banners of Saladin now flew over the fortress walls. Richard swore that he would throw those banners down and then use Acre as a stronghold from which to attack Saladin in Jerusalem.

It wouldn't be an easy assault. Acre's thick walls were lined with hundreds of Muslim warriors, and Richard himself was gravely ill with *scurvy*, which is a sickness that can strike down travelers who haven't eaten enough fresh fruit and vegetables. Weak and lightheaded, Richard nevertheless refused to give up command of the army to either Philip or Leopold. Instead, he was carried to the gates of Acre on a stretcher, and hoisting himself up on one elbow, he spent the entirety of the battle shooting enemy soldiers off the top of the walls with his crossbow.

Saladin's warriors within the city knew that they were outnumbered and quickly agreed to surrender. Saladin's banners were replaced with the flags of the kings, but in this Richard once again refused to give place. When he saw his cousin Leopold's banner raised to an equal height with his own, Richard denounced the Austrian ruler's "arrogance." Richard's men threw Leopold's flag into the fortress' muddy moat, and Leopold, furious, left the crusade at once, taking all his men with him. Soon afterward Philip too abandoned the fight, for he was sick and weary of battle. He returned to France, and Richard alone moved on toward Jerusalem.

Trudging along the coastline, the army was vulnerable to attack. But Richard had learned from the foolishness of others and, so, was careful to march his men only in the cool of the morning and to always pitch his camp where plenty of food and water could be found.

Saladin's forces nipped at his heels, trying to tempt him into battle, but Richard resisted the urge to turn and attack. His army marched steadily toward the goal until finally, tormented beyond endurance by the stinging flights of Muslim arrows, a group of Richard's knights disobeyed his orders and charged Saladin's army. Reacting instantly, Richard flung the rest of his men after them and, most unexpectedly, won a rousing victory.

The Muslims retreated, discouraged and downcast, and now the walls of Jerusalem were in Richard's sight. Surely he would sail upon the wave of triumph through the gates of King David's city!

Meanwhile, as Richard grasped at victory in Palestine, back home in England his kingdom was slipping through his fingers. However, unlike Alfred the Great or Harold Godwinson, Richard was threatened by an enemy who was not an invader from outside his borders; it was his very own brother.

When Richard had departed on crusade, he had left England in the hands of a *chancellor*—a man who would make decisions in the king's name. This did not please Richard's youngest brother, John, who had lingered for many years in the Lionheart's mighty shadow. The king's ship had scarcely disappeared over the horizon before John picked a quarrel with the chancellor, managed to have him exiled from England, and then set himself up as ruler. When Philip of France returned from the crusade, John proposed that they join together in an alliance against Richard.

News of John's schemes reached Richard in his camp outside the walls of Jerusalem. Things had not gone well with his attempts to retake that city. The weather was dreadful, the leaders among his army were quarreling about strategy, and half of his soldiers had departed the battlefield. So in September of 1192, Richard arranged a meeting with Saladin and agreed to make peace. He departed from the Holy Land, and Jerusalem remained under Muslim control.

Richard disguised himself as a simple knight and sailed for England with four loyal attendants. But his ship was wrecked off the coast of Italy. Richard and his men set off on a long and dangerous journey, up the length of Italy and across the lands of the Holy Roman Empire in central Europe. Just before Christmas he reached Austria, the home of his cousin Leopold V, the same Leopold whom Richard had insulted by flinging his banner down into the moat of Acre. Leopold captured him and turned him over to the Holy Roman emperor, Henry VI, who declared Richard his prisoner and locked him up in a castle atop a tall crag, deep in the German countryside.

Richard was mortally offended; first, that anyone would dare to hold him prisoner, and second, that anyone would claim authority over him. "I recognize no superior but God," he declared, refusing to bow before Henry. But despite these bold words, he remained in Henry's power, and Henry insisted that he would not release England's king until England paid him 100,000 pounds of silver in ransom.

For John, back in England, the king's imprisonment was like a belated Christmas gift. He sent a secret message to Henry, offering to send the emperor 50,000 pounds of silver just to keep Richard prisoner.

But there were many in England still loyal to their absent king. Slowly and painfully, the huge sum of money was raised. The treasures of nobles were seized, the golden goblets in churches were confiscated, and new taxes were issued to be paid by every landowner in England. All through that winter, there were clashes and skirmishes between those who longed for Richard's return and those who despised the cost of ransoming the king and supported John instead.

It was during these troubled times that a new legend arose in England—stories about an outlaw living in England's forests, a follower of King Richard who would steal from the corrupt officials and the wealthy landowners who were friends of Prince John and give his ill-gotten gains to the poor and weak. He gathered a crew of "merry men," and together they fought against the injustice of John's attempts to make himself king.

You've heard these stories yourself, I'm sure, and you know the name of this noble outlaw: Robin Hood. Some of the stories even tell of Robin Hood's saving the day by preventing John from stealing the treasure meant to ransom the king.

Of course, just as we saw with the legend of King Arthur, no one can say for certain who Robin Hood really was. But nevertheless, his tales became entwined with the true story of Richard's imprisonment: an outlaw who loved England, championing the king who did not seem to care about England at all.

In any case, whether through the heroics of Robin Hood or the patient labor of Richard's loyal friends, the ransom at last was paid. Richard was set free in February of 1194. The first thing he did was send a message to John: "Look to yourself; the devil is loose."

Was Richard finally returning to England to live and rule there as its rightful king? We will see the answer to that question in just another chapter or two.

Chapter Eighteen

Castles

Fortresses of stone protect the lord and all his people

In the wintertime when the snow gets deep enough, children zip themselves into their warm jackets and boots and pile out into the powdery drifts. Before many minutes have gone by, someone might shout, "Let's have a snowball fight!" The sides are drawn, and everyone scrambles to scoop and shape the snow into the balls that will be the weapons and also into the large walls that will be the snow fort; because everyone knows that the winner of the snowball fight is the team that builds the strongest fortress.

Fortresses have always been important. As you well know, men have been building walls and towers since the earliest days of history. But it was in the Middle Ages that a new kind of fortress began to be built with a tall central stone tower surrounded by a thick wall pierced with watchtowers: a castle. Even now when you think of the Middle Ages, I suspect that one of the first images that pops into your mind is a majestic stone castle on a hill with banners flying from its towers.

In the earliest years of the Middle Ages, when the barbarians were attacking Rome, the Romans abandoned most of their empire in Europe and left behind their walls and forts as well as their smoothly paved roads. Often the people living in those lands reinforced the Roman buildings, sometimes adding a *palisade,* which is a wall made of wooden planks or poles set on end and planted closely together. As life grew more dangerous and uncertain in those early years, with the protection of Rome gone forever and invaders always threatening, people began to build their own larger fortresses. They would find a hill or some other place that was easy to defend and build a wooden tower atop it. Then they would dig a deep ditch all around and surround the whole structure with a tall palisade.

When feudalism became the way of life in Europe, starting in the ninth and tenth centuries, the feudal lords needed even stronger fortresses to protect their lands and wealth. The simple hill and ditch arrangement changed. Now if there was no suitable hill available, the lords would build one; they would command their serfs to construct a massive, flat-topped mound, sometimes as tall as 100 feet, and atop this they would erect a large stone tower, a *keep,* with its own stone wall, which would be the home of the lord and his family. Around the base of this mound, which is called a *motte,* a large open area, a *bailey,* would be enclosed with a second strong wall. The servants and warriors who served the master of the keep made their homes in huts built along this wall. The bailey and its wall in turn were often protected by an enormous ditch filled with water or sharp spikes. Any enemy who sought to conquer this castle would be forced to somehow field the ditch, breach the bailey wall, cross the open space of the bailey, fight through the wall of the keep, and attack the keep itself, all while under fire from the keep's defenders. You can see, I think, why every feudal lord thought it useful to build himself such a well-protected home.

Knights returning from the Crusades, in the eleventh, twelfth, and thirteenth centuries, forced the builders of castles to change their designs yet again, for these warriors came back from their wars with tales of the fearsome siege weapons used by the Byzantines and the Muslims: catapults and trebuchets (tray-

BOO-shays) capable of knocking down thick walls. The castles built in these centuries were more colossal yet, built entirely of stone with walls soaring high into the air. The ditch at the foot of the wall became more formidable with steep sides and deep water—a *moat* to keep enemies further at bay. The only way to cross it was a drawbridge, which could be instantly raised at the first sign of attack. Towers were built at every corner of the outer wall with narrow openings just wide enough for archers to shoot through. The wall's greatest weakness was its doorway, so the gates were often protected with huge, hulking gatehouses and an iron *portcullis,* a heavy grate that could be dropped down with ropes and pulleys to protect the wall's vulnerable wooden doors. If an enemy did manage to break through the doors, the castle was designed to give every advantage to the defenders: spiral staircases that could only be climbed one man at a time; "murder holes" in the ceilings of passageways where boiling oil could be dropped on anyone passing through; and "killing grounds" where attackers could be trapped between an outer and inner wall, with the defenders firing down arrows and heaving heavy stones down on their heads.

As the castle's walls grew ever taller and thicker, the buildings within the wall's embrace became more complex and often more luxurious. The central keep, the lord's home, multiplied from a single tower to a whole collection of buildings and rooms with various purposes.

The largest room in the keep was always the Great Hall, an immense chamber with a high, vaulted ceiling. Here the lord would conduct his business and entertain his guests. There was very little furniture; the hall might contain a few wooden tables and benches, which the servants could arrange for feasts or meetings. During meals the lord and his most important guests sat on a platform, a *dais,* along one end of the Hall. He would recline in a large, elaborately carved chair to emphasize his importance, since everyone else was perched on the backless benches.

Murder hole above the main gate of a castle

Such a large, open room would be damp and chilly, so a great roaring maw of a fireplace spilled out heat and light, and the walls were draped with ornate carpets to block the cold drafts that would creep in through the stone. Carpets were never put on the floor; instead the floor underfoot would be strewn, either loosely or in woven mats, with *rushes,* which were plants harvested from nearby marshes, much valued for their hollow, spongy stems. Over the rushes the servants scattered herbs and flowers, such as lavender and violets, in the hope that these sweet-smelling blossoms would mask some of the miasma of odors that rose up from the rushes. As you might imagine, the rushes collected an astonishing amount of smelly garbage: fragments of food dropped from the feasting tables, splashes of spilled wine and beer, and all sorts of other rather nasty remains. Every so often the rushes would need to be shoveled completely out of the hall and new ones brought in. I suspect that this was not a chore the servants enjoyed!

In the earliest castles the lord and his family would not only dine and entertain in the Great Hall but sleep there as well, in a space at one end that was separated from the rest of the hall with large screens. Soon though, the sleeping quarters for the noble family became more private; separate rooms for bedchambers were added to the keep. They were often on the upper stories of the castle with glass windows for light and a small fireplace for heat in each one. Rich, dark wood paneled the walls on which were hung colorful tapestries or paintings; concealed among these decorations were *squints*, peepholes that allowed the lord of the castle to keep an eye on the goings-on in the Great Hall. An enormous wooden bed-frame enclosed a mattress stuffed with feathers and piled with cotton sheets, quilts, and coverlets made of fur. The bed was furnished with curtains as well, on all four sides, to help keep in the warmth during the cold winter nights.

Many of these bedchambers also contained a tiny niche just wide enough for a bench-like bed where a servant slept, ready to answer at once should his lord or lady call.

Castles in the Middle Ages did not have bathrooms, because the pipes and pumps that make bathrooms possible did not exist in Europe. So instead, a resident of the castle would bathe in his bedchamber in a wooden tub with a canopy and curtains attached. The servants hauled buckets of warmed water up from the kitchen, along with several soft sponges, and sprinkled sweet-smelling herbs in the water. If a person wanted only to wash his face or hands, there were stone basins built into the walls here and there, filled with fresh water each day.

The water, both for bathing and drinking, came from a

cistern—which is a kind of tank that collects rain water, usually kept on the roof—or from a well dug somewhere within the bailey. Some castles were fortunate enough to have a spring of fresh water trickling up from underground, but most had to make do with what the cistern and the wells could provide.

Of course, all of the people living within the castle's walls must be fed, and so every castle had a kitchen. It was a separate room, sometimes a completely separate building, with a large hearth and fireplace for cooking. Meat was stewed in gigantic pots or cooked on rotating spits over the fire. The castle usually had a *buttery*, a room used only for storing wine, and a *pantry*, a place to store and slice bread. Outside the doors of the kitchen, the castle garden bloomed with all of the vegetables, flowers, and herbs that the cooks and servants would use to supply the master's table and to add to the castle's beauty and comfort. Fruit trees were trained to grow with their branches flat against the garden walls, so that they took up less space. The garden sometimes sheltered a fishpond and often a dovecote for the castle's pigeons, who were mostly destined to end up in pies.

Somewhere within almost every castle, there was a chapel. In the Middle Ages people went to church every day, usually in the morning. The castle would have its own place of worship and often its own priest as well. There might also be a *crypt* attached to the chapel, which would contain the caskets and tombs of all the castle's previous lords.

Out along the outer walls, the castle's bustling business ebbed and flowed. Here you would find the stables for the lord's many horses and the workshops and houses for all of the castle's craftsmen and artisans: carpenters, gardeners, metalworkers, blacksmiths. In fact, the castle would often employ hundreds of people, almost like a small town. There would be a mill to grind grain, with a miller and his family, and a little dark chandlery where the candlemaker dipped long wicks into hot wax to make the hundreds of candles that the castle required. Along one wall, close to the well, there would be a laundry with its boiling tubs of sudsy water.

For hundreds of years the castles ruled the countrysides of Europe. But eventually, of course, they lost their importance. Feudalism died away and with it the whole system of lords and knights. The responsibility to protect the land became centered on kings and governments rather than individual noblemen, and so the need for fortified castles fell away. As time went by, most castles were abandoned. They were so huge and so well-built, though, that even centuries could not destroy them, and so they became the romantic ruins that still dot the countrysides of every country in Europe. They stand like silent ghosts now, but if you someday should have the chance to visit one, you might be able to hear, if you listen very closely, the bustling echoes of lords and knights, ladies and gentlemen, servants and craftsmen, all of them living their busy lives within the same castle walls.

Chapter Nineteen

The Great Charter

For the first time, a written document limits the power of a king

King Richard came roaring back to England in 1194, promising vengeance on his faithless brother John. But strangely enough, when John threw himself on his mercy and begged for forgiveness, Richard gave it freely. He clapped his brother on the shoulder, declared that all would be well, and made John the heir to the throne. And then, with that taken care of, he was off again, sailing over to France to wage war on his cousin, Philip II, who had taken advantage of Richard's imprisonment by seizing all of his lands in Normandy.

Five years passed. In 1199 Richard was besieging a tiny, unimportant castle deep in the countryside of France. He was mockingly applauding the defenders on the wall, one of whom was using a frying pan to beat away flying arrows, when a bolt from a crossbow struck him down.

Richard the Lionheart died of his wounds, aged only 42, and his brother John became king in England. But though John had longed for the throne and coveted the crown, kingship did not rest easily on his shoulders.

Of course, for most of the people in England, one king was much the same as another. Since the days of Edward the

Confessor, England's rulers had grown steadily more powerful, governing the land according to their own notions of what might be best and resting securely in the knowledge that the king was above the law. When the reign of one king ended with his death and the Archbishop of Canterbury placed the crown on the head of the next, the lives of the English continued on as they always had. Their days were still filled with labor and toil and the always-present burden of taxes. Noblemen, townspeople, freemen, and serfs—all of them groaned at the knock of the tax collector at their door. They may have understood the king's need for money and yet more money, they may have even agreed with his crusades or his wars, but that didn't make the paying for it any less painful.

King John, much to his people's chagrin, required an unusually large amount of money. After Richard's death Normandy had once again fallen into Philip's hands, and for ten years John struggled to win it back. He taxed the nobles again and again in every way that he could think of. He required a tax to hunt in the forest. He doubled the tax a noble must pay to avoid serving in the army. He introduced the notion of income tax, where every landowner gave up a portion of the money that his estates earned each year. In John's mind all of this was necessary, because he needed ships and armor and arrows and horses and all of the necessities of war. But to the nobles it was unjust and horribly burdensome, and in order to meet John's demands, they in their turn squeezed every last penny they could from the people who lived on their lands. John's name became black indeed among his people, especially when his constant warfare in France bore little fruit and he did not regain the lands he had lost. "Softsword" they called him, muttering darkly. A weak and luxury-loving king.

It wasn't the noblemen alone who hated John; the Church, as well, frowned upon him. In 1205 he had refused to accept the pope's choice for a new Archbishop of Canterbury, who was the most powerful churchman in the land. The pope had responded to John's refusal by placing all of England under a decree called an *interdict,* a locking of the churches. The doors were chained shut, the bells tied and silenced, and for six years every church in England was empty: no weddings, no baptisms, no funerals. You might imagine the distress of the people, who must now marry in chilly, open churchyards or bury their loved ones out in the dark, forbidding woodlands with no priest to pray over them. It was a time of great grief, and the people blamed their king for it.

Finally John relented. He agreed to allow the pope's man to be made Archbishop, and the interdict was lifted. But those years of taxation and distress had left their mark, and John was not a king beloved by his people.

He, in turn, did not seem to love them. He was known to deal out cruel punishments to those who opposed him or even said a critical word. He wielded his great power as king without justice or mercy.

And so in the spring of 1215, his noblemen—his *barons,* they were called—turned against him.

The Archbishop of Canterbury, the very same man so opposed by John, had come to them the year before with an old document. He reminded them that John's grandfather, Henry I, had issued a proclamation on the day of his coronation that promised to free the nobles from over-taxation and unjust commands. It was called the Charter of Liberties; it wasn't a law, really, but it was at least a promise that the king's power would be limited. Naturally, in the hundred years that had passed since then, the kings had conveniently ignored Henry's Charter, but copies of it still existed.

Now the barons saw in it a model that they could use. John had, only a few months before, returned from his wars in France and settled back into his palace in London. The barons, from their meeting place far to the north, sent him a message demanding that he agree to the same limits his grandfather had—limits on taxation, limits on unjust imprisonment, limits on money or property being seized willy-nilly by the king. Confirm the Charter of Liberties, they said, or we will march against you and take your throne.

They began their trek southward toward London, gathering supporters along the way. By May 17th they had reached the city itself, and the city's leaders threw open the gates to welcome them in. The king, barricaded behind his castle walls, could only watch in dismay. He certainly had no intention of surrendering to these rebels, but he also knew that he did not have enough of his own support to defeat them.

So he sent a message asking them to put their demands in writing. He agreed to meet with them in a few days' time on the banks of the Thames River near his castle, in a field called Runnymede. Like its name suggests, this was, quite literally, a soggy meadow.

Imagine the scene that day, if you can. It was early June, and the meadow's pathways were no doubt squelching with mud, but the grass was green and fair and the king's tents would have glowed like brightly-painted carousels, their pennants snapping in the spring breezes. Beneath this shelter, the king was presented with the barons' demands—a simple list that they called the "Articles of the Barons." For the next few days the king and the nobles faced one another in round after round of hard bargaining, neither side willing to give an inch to the other. Scribes were kept busy furiously scribbling as changes were made and then scrapped.

Eventually though, a document took final shape. It was mostly concerned with taxation, as you might imagine; the nobles had had enough of John's taxes and demanded to be made free of them. But this new charter contained other freedoms as well. It guaranteed, first of all, the freedom of the Church in England. It also promised that no man could ever be secretly imprisoned or exiled; everyone accused of a crime was promised a just and civil trial. No one could be denied justice; every person in England was given the right to stand before a judge and plead his innocence. Merchants were promised the right to travel freely from market to market. Towns were given the right to make their own laws.

Most of all, the king no longer lived outside of the law. The Charter decreed that, by giving it his seal, the king was agreeing that he, himself, king though he may be, was subject to the laws of the land.

Of course, Henry I's Charter had made this same promise, but that Charter had been freely issued by the king and just as freely ignored by every king that followed. This one was different; this time the king had been forced to come and compelled to agree. This charter made sure that John would not be able to disregard its promises, because it demanded that he submit himself to the oversight of a Council: twenty-five barons who could meet at any time and overrule the king's decrees. They could even seize the king's houses and lands, if he did something truly horrible, and keep them until he made things right again.

As you might expect, this Council was the final sticking point for John. He was not in the least pleased with such an idea. But in the end, the Council remained a part of the agreement, and on June 19th, 1215, King John attached his seal to the bottom of the Charter. He was no longer an all-powerful king who answered to no one but God. Now he must answer to the law as well.

Thirteen copies were hurriedly made and sent out to every corner of England with the king's seal attached and the signatures of the barons as well. John would not be able to deny the limits on his power. The idea that kings are somehow separate from the law had been defeated forever. A line had been crossed and could never be uncrossed.

The Magna Carta with Seal

Because it was more wide-reaching and powerful than any promise or charter before it, the Charter sealed at Runnymede came to be called the *Magna Carta:* the "Great Charter."

Of course, new ideas do not always sail smoothly out

into the wide open seas of history. The Magna Carta faced its storms soon enough; only three months after it was signed, war erupted once more between King John and the barons when John rejected the Baron's Council. He had hated that idea from the very first, and by November of 1215 he had gathered enough support from the Church and from some of the lesser nobles to turn entirely against it. He mustered an army and attacked the rebel barons directly.

Naturally, a civil war in England was treated as the very best of news by Phillip II, over in France. He saw it as a perfect opportunity to seize power for himself, especially when the rebel barons decided to offer the crown to Phillip's son, Louis, if he would only come over and help them get rid of John. Louis sailed at once at the head of a French army.

English history hung in the balance. The Magna Carta overthrown so quickly? A French prince on the throne?

John led his own army to the south to face Louis and the barons. But disaster after disaster struck him. His baggage train, with all of the king's horses, carriages, and luggage carts, was crossing an *estuary*—a low place where a river meets the sea—when an incoming tide swept them away. All was lost, lost to this day: the king's jewels and gold, even his crown.

Worse, the king himself had grown deathly sick. He tried to struggle onward, but it was too much. He was borne on a litter of willow branches to a nearby town and breathed his last on October 18th, 1216.

But strangely and fortunately, the Magna Carta did not die with him.

John's death put a sudden stop to any French plans for the English throne. The rebel barons at once withdrew their support from Prince Louis, and he was forced to leave England and sail back to France. The noblemen of England, both the rebel barons and those who had remained loyal to John, declared that John's son Henry III would be king. And to ensure the peace and the loyalty of all Englishmen, the Magna Carta was reissued under the young king's name.

And so it continued. Every king for the next 200 years included the Magna Carta as part of his reign until it passed into the standard law-books of England where it has remained ever since.

Some people have said that the Magna Carta is the most important document ever signed. That's a pretty big claim to make for a piece of parchment written hurriedly by scribes in an English meadow eight hundred years ago. But the Magna Carta captured and nailed down a very important idea: that men should be free from tyranny, that no king is above the law, and that every person deserves justice. That same idea has spread from the wet, green field of Runnymede to every end of the earth. Although John "Softsword" was not a good king, the Charter he was forced to sign has been a force for good ever since.

Chapter Twenty

The Mongols

Genghis Khan builds an empire on horseback

When Rome ruled its empire in the years that surrounded the life and death of Christ, much of the world lay at peace. This was the *Pax Romana*, the "Roman Peace," and it existed because of Rome's overwhelming power and wealth. The many peoples that Rome had conquered were not permitted to war with each other; instead they paid their loyalty to Rome, and in return Rome provided them with safety. Merchants could deliver their goods to markets far away; travelers could visit interesting sites with no fear of being set upon by bandits; and letters and scrolls could cross the empire, so literature and art flourished. The conquered peoples had no great love for their Roman overlords, but they nevertheless enjoyed the benefits of the peace that Roman power enforced.

Of course, as we have seen, Rome did not last forever; it fell and the *Pax Romana* shattered. The roads fell into disrepair in many places; bandits once more haunted mountain passes, waiting to attack travelers; and a letter could no longer cross the miles in safety.

And so things remained for hundreds of years until another empire, larger than Rome, arose in the Middle Ages during the 13th and 14th centuries. Unlike Rome, it was not born out of a powerful, gleaming city. Rather, it arose in the windy, empty plains of Asia and swept outward in all directions. It was the creation of one man, with his sons after him. It was an empire built on horseback and in tents and by the edge of the sword. When he was through, he had forged the *Pax Mongolica*, the "Mongol Peace," and the largest empire in history.

As most large stories do, this tale begins small and humbly, with a young boy.

His name was Temujin (tay-MOO-jin). He had been born in 1162 in a comfortable round tent with a peaked roof, a *yurt*. His family were nomads, wanderers, who moved through the land that today we know as Mongolia—a cold, dry, treeless land in the center of Asia, far from any sea, with China to the south and the huge stretch of Russia to the north. The nomads pitched their tents in the *steppes,* which are the broad, flat grasslands that cover most of Mongolia even today. The land was too dry and cold to grow crops, so instead Temujin's people raised animals: herds of sheep, goats, oxen, and especially, horses. The herds roamed freely over the open grass and the people followed after them, pitching their yurts wherever the grazing was best. Temujin's clan was one of many tribes wandering the steppes. They were all called *Mongols,* but they were not in any way a unified nation of people; their loyalty lay only with their own family and with their tribe.

Temujin spent his days on horseback, keeping watch over the herds, racing with his brothers, and fighting mock battles with wooden sticks in place of swords. He had learned to ride almost before he could walk; all Mongol children did, because horses were everything to the Mongol tribes. Their small, sturdy steeds gave the nomads swiftness in battle against their enemies, freedom to travel long distances lightly and easily, and even lifesaving nourishment if it became necessary.

Despite the freedom he found on horseback, Temujin's life was not easy. His family faced a constant risk of raids from other wandering tribes, who were always seeking to steal horses and kidnap women and children as slaves. Under the leadership of Temujin's father, who was the *khan,* or ruler, the men in the tribe must be constantly at watch and ready to leap upon their horses and repel an attack.

Because life was so uncertain, the Mongols expected their children to marry early and start their own families. So one day when he was only nine years old, Temujin rode with his father into the encampment of a different tribe where he would meet the young woman that he would one day take as his bride, a girl named Borte (BORE-tuh). He carried everything he owned in a little roll at the back of his saddle, for the Mongol custom dictated that he must now live with her family and serve them until he was old enough to marry. He clasped his father's arm in a silent farewell, never imagining that this was the last time he would look upon his father's face. For while riding back home, Temujin's father encountered an enemy tribe; he agreed to share a meal with them, but in vengeance for past battles, they poisoned the food they served him.

When he heard of his father's death, Temujin returned at once to his tribe to claim his rightful position as the new khan. But the tribe refused to consider it: he was, after all, still a young boy. Surely someone so inexperienced would only lead them to destruction! Instead, they cast Temujin and his mother and all of his siblings out of the tribe to fend for themselves as best they could.

The next few years were filled with hardship for the little family. They survived with Temujin's mother gathering wild fruits and the boy and his brothers hunting for any game they could find, but their troubles continued. Temujin was captured in a raid and held as a slave by a tribe that had formerly been his father's ally. This was a bitter pill to swallow for the young man, but it also taught him the importance of keeping your allies close: don't let them slip away or someday you might find that they have become your enemies instead.

Temujin waited, watching for a chance to escape and making friends even in the camp of his slave-masters. One night a sympathetic guard allowed him to slip out of the yurt in the darkness. When his captors realized the next morning that he was gone, they searched frantically, but Temujin evaded them by hiding motionless all day under the overhanging lip of a river bank.

His bravery and cleverness did not go unnoticed. He began to gather around himself other young men who recognized in Temujin one who would someday be a powerful leader. When Temujin was sixteen years old, he returned to Borte's family and asked her father's permission to be married to her. He was a young man cast out of his own clan; everyone in Borte's tribe would have understood if her father had rejected him. But instead, Borte's father must have recognized the same strength and ambition in Temujin that his band of young followers did, for he gave him Borte with his blessing and with a rich bridal gift: a long cloak of silky black fur.

Now Temujin had a wife; he also had allies again: Borte's entire tribe. Because his new father-in-law so obviously supported him, other chieftains of other nearby tribes were inclined to look on him with favor as well. Temujin tended these new friendships carefully, always seeking to strengthen his network of allies. He began reaching out, too, toward the tribes that had once supported his own father. He reminded them of the strong leader his father had been and promised that he himself would prove to be equally strong.

But in seeking out his father's old friends, Temujin also roused the ire of his father's old enemies. They remembered well the raids that Temujin's father had ordered even twenty or thirty years in the past. One of these old enemies, a tribe called the Merkits (MAIR-gets), swept into Temujin's camp one day and, purely for revenge, seized Borte and raced away with her.

Temujin was angry and frightened for Borte's life, but even more he was humiliated. This Merkit raid was a direct challenge to Temujin's honor. How would he respond?

He went at once to the most powerful of his father's old friends, Toghrul, a leader in a huge tribe who was called the Prince Khan, the Ongkhan (ONG-khan).

My father looked upon you as a brother, he said. That means that you are as a father to me. Will you help me?

It is easy to imagine what the Ongkhan's answer might have been if Temujin had come to him empty-handed. He would have turned the young man away with barely a thought. But Temujin, though he came humbly, was not empty-handed. The careful nurturing of his alliances had borne fruit, and he had 10,000 Mongol warriors at his back. The Ongkhan considered this, then gave Temujin 10,000 more of his own fighting men.

And so Temujin set out to rescue Borte and also, not insignificantly, to prove himself as a great military leader. At the head of his army, he rode into the Merkit camp in the depths of night, cutting down the enemy warriors as they came stumbling out of their yurts. As he thundered through the camp, he shouted, "Borte! Borte!" But in the darkness and confusion, how would he ever find his wife?

The Mongols' histories, long preserved, tell us what happened:

> *Borte Ujin was among the Merkit who ran in the darkness*
> *and when she heard his voice,*
> *when she recognized Temujin's voice,*
> *Borte leaped from her cart . . . .*
> *and ran to him, finally seizing the reins of his horse.*
> *All about them was moonlight.*
> *As Temujin looked down to see who had stopped him*
> *he recognized Borte Ujin.*
> *In a moment he was down from his horse*

and they were in each other's arms, embracing.

Having found his wife and rescued her, Temujin sent out messengers to his captains and called off the attack. He returned to his own camp, a victor.

While there is no doubt that this adventure was important for Temujin's own happiness, since Borte meant a great deal to him, there is also no denying that his success in this attack greatly elevated him in the eyes of the other tribes of the steppes. This victory over the Merkit probably occurred in the year 1184; up to this point, Temujin was just one of several young, ambitious chieftains among the Mongols. But after his rescue of Borte, Temujin began to grow in power. He had proved himself as a strong leader of men, and now many more warriors followed him, swearing to him their alliance and loyalty. They noticed not only his skill in battle but also his justice and generosity toward his followers. Eventually, sometime in the late 1180s, a number of tribal leaders gathered at the base of the sacred Mount Burkhan and bestowed upon Temujin a new title: Genghis Khan (GHEN-ghis KAHN). Boundless Leader. Lord over all.

Gaining such a masterful title had not been easy, and keeping it was harder still. The Mongols were still a loose collection of tribes, and there were many of those tribal leaders who sought to challenge this new Lord of All. As he began the work of bringing all the tribes under his authority, Genghis Khan also began to transform them as a people.

He chose to delegate authority and reward followers based not on their family ties, as had always been the case among the Mongols, but rather on how well they performed in battle and how clearly they demonstrated their loyalty to him. He also promised to share with all of his followers the spoils of war. Perhaps most importantly, when he had conquered a rival tribe he did not kill and scatter them. Instead he brought them in among his own loyal people; he arranged that orphans be adopted and widows cared for. By doing these things he secured ever-greater loyalty to himself, even among conquered people, and he made himself stronger with each victory.

By the year 1206 Genghis Khan was the only ruler of the steppes; every other tribe had joined him or been defeated by him. But now his restless eye looked outward for the first time to the lands and nations beyond the Mongol plains.

His armies at this point were a sharp and lethal weapon. He had also strengthened the Mongols as a people by creating for them a written code of law. No more kidnapping of women or children, he decreed. No stealing of animals. A lost animal must be returned to its owner. No hunting for more than what you need. No punishment of wrongdoers without a trial. By enforcing these rules, Genghis Khan made the Mongols into one nation; now he was ready to make them into an empire.

First he led his armies into northern China where they were forced to learn a new kind of warfare in order to attack its fortified cities. From there he pushed into Afghanistan and Persia and then into Eastern Europe, panic and fear mounting ahead of him like a cresting wave. Those who surrendered at once were spared, but any city or people who tried to defy him was slaughtered without mercy. He had learned another new weapon, you see: fear. He knew that the word was spreading across the world like a wildfire: beware the Mongol Horde! When you hear the pounding of the horse's hooves, surrender or be killed! The Mongols' swiftness in battle on the backs of their sturdy horses only increased their fearsome reputation. They seemed to come like racing ghosts out of nowhere.

By 1225 Genghis Khan was back in Mongolia, master of an empire that stretched from the east coast of China all the way to the Caspian Sea, from Siberia in northern Russia to Arabia in the far south. It was the largest land empire that history had ever seen. Genghis Khan was a greater conqueror than Julius Caesar or Alexander the Great, and across all of those conquered lands he spread the *Pax Mongolica*. He created an efficient mail system using horseback riders. He made all of the roads safe from bandits, to encourage merchants to travel and trade. He declared that all peoples in his empire were free to practice any religion they chose and that teachers and doctors were free from paying taxes.

Soon though, he was back at war when one of his conquered territories rose up in rebellion. And so it was that in 1227, at the age of sixty-five, Genghis Khan fell from his horse during a battle and died there on the ground. Years before, he had decreed that at his death he wished to be buried without ceremony. His followers did as he commanded, and to this day no one knows the location of his grave.

Genghis Khan was one of history's greatest warriors, and as is so often the case with such men, he is remembered very differently by those he conquered and those who rode beside him. To most of the world, his was a name wrapped in fear and dread: the coming of the cruel and terrible Mongol Horde! But to his people, he was their greatest leader, the source of their laws and their pride, and their truest hero.

Chapter Twenty-One

The Travels of Marco Polo

*A merchant from Venice explores
the far reaches of the East*

In the Middle Ages there was no nation of Italy. Instead, in what had been the heart of the Roman empire, a patchwork of small kingdoms vied for power and wealth, each centered on a single city. The greatest of these was Venice, tucked into the curve at the very top of Italy's boot.

Venice was a city like no other. It was built on hundreds of small islands in the center of a vast, shallow lagoon, and instead of streets and alleyways, it was pierced and threaded with canals. Its people used boats and barges rather than carts to make their way from house to market. And Venice in those days was very interested in markets, because it was a city made fabulously wealthy by trade. Its merchants sent their ships to every corner of the Mediterranean Sea and even further, to the islands of Indonesia with their sweet spices and to the faraway shores of India. They brought back all the exotic goods of Asia: spices, silk, gemstones, fragrant wood, and incense. These luxuries were then sold to the countries of Europe for very pretty prices indeed, and the city of Venice grew ever more rich, its harbor crowded with ships from every nation. It was the center of an empire of merchants, and people everywhere called it *La Serenissima,*

The Most Serene. Few cities in Europe were more wealthy or powerful.

So it was that in 1269 in the great city of Venice, there lived a young man of fifteen years who, that year, met his father for the very first time.

This was not because the father, a merchant named Niccolo Polo (NEE-koh-loh POH-loh), had abandoned his son. Fifteen years before, Niccolo had kissed his wife farewell and set out with his brother, Maffeo Polo (MAH-fay-oh), on a trading voyage. The two men often traveled together, venturing far to the east to trade the goods of Venice in faraway lands. This occupation had made them both wealthy, but it came at the cost of much time spent away from home.

A month after their departure, Niccolo's wife gave birth to a fine, healthy son. She named him Marco and all was well.

But when the boy was only five years old, his mother died. His father and uncle were still away, far to the east in Constantinople, and so Marco went to live with an aunt and uncle who promised to care for him until, someday, his father would return. He went to school and learned reading, writing, arithmetic, and geography, as well as the subjects that Venetians thought most important of all: how to inspect the cargo on a merchant ship, how to tell the difference between one foreign coin and another, and how to judge the worth of a bale of silk.

But one day Marco found two strange men sitting at the table in his uncle's house. His father had returned after fifteen years to finally meet his son. He came bearing marvelous tales of the places he and Maffeo had been; they had journeyed far, far beyond Constantinople into the realm that the people of Europe called "Cathay" (CATH-ay), which we today know as China. They had brought back a fortune in gemstones and silk, but in amongst this cargo were two very curious items: a letter written on soft, strange paper and a long, thin tablet made of pure gold. These two items had been placed in Niccolo's hands by the magnificent Kublai Khan (KOO-blay KAHN) himself, the Mongol emperor of China.

Kublai Khan was the grandson of Genghis Khan, whom you have already met. In the years since Genghis Khan's death, his sons and grandsons had expanded his empire even farther. It stretched from the Pacific Ocean to the Black Sea, one fifth of the total land on Earth. As ruler of such an enormous kingdom, Kublai Khan was always eager to hear news of the lands beyond his borders; he had welcomed Niccolo and Maffeo into his court and spent much time in conversation with them. When they decided to return to Venice, the Khan made them promise to return, and he gave them the two treasures. The letter was written to the Pope, the leader of the Church in Rome, asking for one hundred Christian scholars to come to China and teach the court about Christianity. The golden tablet was called a *paizah* (PIE-zuh): it was like a passport, guaranteeing whoever was holding it safe passage through all the Khan's lands.

Niccolo and Maffeo intended to go back to China at once, this time taking Marco with them. But they were disappointed to learn that the Pope had recently died; there was no one to whom the Khan's letter could be given. For two years the Polos waited in Venice for a new Pope to be chosen, but as the process dragged on and on, they decided at last to set out for China anyway without the Christian scholars the Khan had requested. They were afraid that he would be angry if their return was too long delayed, and they would lose the trading opportunities that China could give them.

So in 1271 Niccolo, Maffeo, and Marco departed from Venice at the head of a long caravan loaded with goods. They had only gone a short way, however, when a message reached them: a new Pope had finally been elected, and he wanted to honor the Khan's desire to learn about Christianity. They detoured south to the old crusader fortress of Acre on the shores of the Mediterranean. They presented the Pope's orders to the

simplycharlottemason.com 169

monks there; in the end, only two were willing to brave the long, uncertain journey. With the two monks in tow, the Polos' caravan made its way north and east into Asia Minor.

Marco, though only a very young man, proved to be an eager and observant traveler. He noticed everything: the landscapes, the customs and past-times of the people, the products sold in markets. He stared in awe as the caravan made its way along the foot of Mr. Ararat and wrote in his journal about the ice-capped peak "on which Noah's ark is said to have rested."

The caravan crossed into Persia, aiming south now toward the coast of the Persian Gulf. Niccolo had no wish to walk all the way to China; he wanted to hire ships to take them around the horn of India and through the Indian Ocean. But when they finally reached the seaport of Hormuz (HOR-muhz) and gazed upon the ships that lay at harbor there, they were filled with disappointment.

"The ships are very bad," Marco wrote.

So they turned their backs to the sea; they would walk to China after all. They would have to take their chances on the Silk Road.

When you think of a road, perhaps you think of the smooth pavement running in front of your house or a busy highway filled with cars. But the Silk Road was a beaten dirt pathway that stretched for 4,000 miles across the length of Asia, from the eastern coast of China all the way west to the Mediterranean Sea. It passed through green valleys and over soaring mountains, through deserts so dry that water had to be carried on camelback by the merchants, soldiers, monks, and wanderers that traveled along the Road's twisting length. Its sole purpose was trade, a way for the silken cloth and tea of China to go west and the goods of Europe and Africa—ivory, wool, silver, cotton—to go east. The Silk Road had existed since ancient times; silk from China has even been found in the buried longships of Vikings and the tombs of ancient Egypt. Under the reign of Kublai

Khan, travel and trade on the Road reached its peak because merchants were honored in the Mongol empire and protected by patrols of Mongol warriors.

Despite the soldiers' presence, the Silk Road was not without danger. Bandits and wild animals lurked in the desolate stretches where towns were few and far between; sudden storms could rise up in the high mountain passes, smothering a caravan in snow and icy winds; and the eastern portion of the Road passed through a corner of the Gobi Desert, a place of trackless, blowing sand that whispered hauntingly to itself, so that people insisted it was filled with evil spirits.

The three Polos squared their shoulders, prepared to go forward into these dangers. But the two monks who were traveling with them were not; they refused to follow the Road into China and returned to the west.

Undaunted, the Polo caravan set out from Hormuz. The difficulties they encountered were many. In eastern Persia they were set upon by bandits and lost many of their servants and much of their caravan. In Badakhshan (bah-DAK-shun), which is today in the country of Afghanistan, one of their party—it may have been Marco himself—fell very ill and they were forced to linger there for almost a year. After leaving there, the Road led them over the high Pamir Mountains in central Asia, a place that the people living nearby called the "Roof of the World." For fifty-two days they struggled forward, seeing not a single other person. Then after making their way through the plains of western China, they faced the Gobi desert with its terrifying, whispering sands. They were afraid; Marco described one of their fears:

"There are some who, in crossing this desert, have seen a host of men coming towards them, and, suspecting they were robbers, have taken flight; so, having left the beaten track and not knowing how to return to it again, they have gone hopelessly astray."

Most scholars today think that Marco is here describing a *mirage,* which is a ghostly illusion caused by the light dancing and reflecting off the waves of heat that rise from the desert sand. You may have seen a mirage yourself while riding in a car in the summer with your family. Have you ever looked ahead, down a long flat road, and seen in the distance a shimmering sheet of water stretching across the highway? As the car draws closer, it disappears, because, of course, it wasn't really there. It was an illusion created by the heat and the light.

The mirages may have been fleeting, but the fear of losing the pathway was very real indeed. Marco wrote that travelers took many precautions to stay on course. "Before they go to sleep they set up a sign pointing in the direction in which they have to travel. And round the necks of all their beasts they fasten little bells, so that by listening to the sound they may prevent them from straying off the path."

Despite these dangers, both real and imagined, the Polos safely crossed the desert. Now they found themselves in the region of Cathay, the heartland of Kublai Khan's vast kingdom. To their surprise, messengers sent from the Khan were there to greet them. With this escort they made their way toward Shangdu (SHANG-doo), the Khan's summer capital, and arrived there in 1275. The entire journey from Venice had taken them three and a half years.

They had seen many marvelous sights on their travels but surely none more amazing than Shangdu itself. One hundred thousand people lived there surrounded by walls eighteen feet high. In the city's center, protected by a second wall, rose an artificial mountain built of rock and earth, atop which stood the Khan's palace "all gilded and wonderfully painted," Marco wrote later, "so well and cunningly that it is a delight to see."

There was also within the city a huge walled park, its hills and streams filled with animals of every kind, where the Khan would go to hunt with his falcons and tame hunting-cheetahs.

And in the center of this park stood a golden palace with a roof held high by pillars carved in the shape of roaring dragons. It was built of light wood and anchored to the ground with silken ropes, so it could be moved from place to place within the park whenever the Khan desired.

Such a sight was Shangdu! So amazing that hundreds of years later, inspired by Marco's descriptions, one of England's great poets, Samuel Taylor Coleridge, would write one of his most famous poems:

In Xanadu did Kubla Khan
A stately pleasure dome decree
Where Alph, the sacred river ran
Through caverns measureless to man
Down to a sunless sea.

Kublai Khan was pleased to see Niccolo and Maffeo once again. When he inquired about this young man who had come with them, Niccolo introduced Marco to the king. The Khan made Marco welcome; from that moment, Marco entered the king's service and did not leave it for more than twenty years.

The Khan discovered quickly that Marco was a young man with a talent for observation and reporting, as well as languages: he had learned both the Persian and Mongol languages during the three years of their journey. So the king sent him out to the far reaches of the Mongol empire to observe his subjects and report back on their welfare. Everywhere he went, Marco watched and learned and noticed, and he remembered. And all the while he was reporting to the Khan, he was also observing the Mongols themselves.

He admired them. He wrote about their use of paper money rather than heavy metal coins. He noticed how they burned strange black rocks—coal—to keep their homes warm. He tried their foods and wrote about them, including the long, thin strands of boiled dough that we call noodles and Marco knew as pasta. He enjoyed traveling on their smooth, paved roads.

As Marco traveled hither and yon for the Khan, Niccolo and Maffeo remained in Cathay carrying out their usual trading ventures and growing ever more wealthy. At last though, after twenty years, the two older Polos were yearning for home, and they asked the Khan for permission to return to Venice. The king refused; he wanted them to stay and even offered them double the value of all the wealth they had acquired if they would agree to never leave.

But then, unexpectedly, his mind was changed. He received a message from the king of Persia: his wife had died, and he wished to take a Mongol princess as a new bride. The princess, a young lady named Kokachin (CO-cah-CHEEN), was frightened to embark on such a long journey. Her advisors had heard of Marco's wide travel on behalf of the Khan, and so they requested Marco's company as an escort. Reluctantly the Khan agreed, and in 1291 a fleet of ships—with the Princess, all of her servants, and the Polos aboard—set out across the South China Sea toward the Indian Ocean and home.

It was a dreadful journey, filled with delay and bad weather; but thirty months later the ships limped their way into the port at Hormuz, the same city from which the Polos had begun their journey on the Silk Road so many years before. They bid farewell to the Princess, though Marco tells us that she wept at the thought of leaving them, and made their way to Constantinople, from which it was but a short sea journey to reach, at last, in the year 1295, the arched bridges and watery canals of Venice.

Home.

It was said in later days that they pounded on the gate of the family estate, only to be turned rudely away by the family members who were living there. So many years of travel had left them ragged and worn, and no one recognized them. But then, the legend says, they ripped open the seams of their travel-stained cloaks and a fortune in gemstones—rubies, emeralds, diamonds—cascaded out upon the floor and suddenly their family recognized them after all.

That was the end of Marco's journeys, for they received word that Kublai Khan had died, and the loss of his favor, Marco wrote, "entirely put an end to all prospect of our revisiting those regions."

I suppose, like every traveler, Marco entertained his friends and family with the stories of his experiences. After all, he had seen far more of Asia than any European before him. But those tales would have died with Marco himself had it not been for one more remarkable adventure.

The city of Venice went to war with the city of Genoa over trade routes and control of the Mediterranean. As a loyal Venetian, Marco was given command of a warship; but it was captured and everyone aboard thrown into a Genoese prison. There Marco sat, bored and uncomfortable, for more than a year.

Now it happened that his cellmate was a writer, a man named Rustichello (ROOS-tee-KEL-low). Since there was little to do each day but talk, he encouraged Marco to share memories of his travels. As Marco talked, Rustichello wrote, and between the two of them they created a book, which Marco called *A Description of the World*. It became enormously popular, and eventually it was copied into almost every European language.

After a year in prison, the Polo family finally ransomed Marco, and he returned to his quiet life. He died on January 9, 1324, still the best-known traveler the world had ever seen. Rustichello said of him, "There was never a man, be he Christian or Saracen or Tartar or heathen, who ever traveled over so much of the world as did that noble and illustrious citizen of Venice, Marco Polo."

Chapter Twenty-Two

Salt, Books, and Gold

*In Africa, all roads lead to
the fabled city of Timbuktu*

In our Castle of the Middle Ages, we can imagine that there is an enormous chamber locked away and hidden from the vaulted rooms where the people of France and England and the Holy Roman Empire and the rest of Europe are gathered. They have heard rumors about this secret place and they know that it exists, but few have ever ventured out to find it, afraid perhaps to wander too far from the familiar pathways at the castle's heart. But if they were to pass through the chamber's door, they would find treasures in every corner: ivory elephant tusks, snowy white bricks of rock-hard salt, stacked logs of black ebony wood, and most of all, the gleam of gold. These treasures and more were the wealth and strength of Africa.

Of course, if you spin your globe or take out a map of the world, you can well understand why the people of Europe would have little knowledge of the great continent to the south. Between the green valley of the Nile and the coastline of Morocco, over which the Rock of Gibraltar sits like a watchtower, the northern reaches of Africa are taken up with the mighty Sahara Desert. Crossing such a dry and forbidding land was a dangerous, perhaps fatal, journey. And so, though the land beyond the

Sahara was green with thick jungles and blue with rushing rivers and immense lakes, no one knew of it. The many people who lived in the central and southern parts of Africa lived their lives and fought their wars and told their stories, and the world to the north beyond the uncrossable Sahara knew nothing about them.

At one edge of the Sahara, though, there was a place that did make itself known; it reached out past the desert sands and beckoned the world with salt, books, and gold, all offered for sale in the markets of the city of Timbuktu.

Timbuktu lies on the banks of the Niger River, on the southern edge of the great desert. If you study a map of Africa you can see the Niger tracing an enormous curve above the bulging coastline of northwestern Africa through the modern-day countries of Guinea, Mali, Niger, and Nigeria; Timbuktu lies at the topmost arch of the river's curving course. The desert stretches away like a limitless carpet, but the riverbanks are green with life, and so Timbuktu perches on a narrow limb between water and sand, ready to welcome travelers from either direction.

Throughout the Middle Ages, Timbuktu was a crossroads, a gathering place for all of the wealth of Africa. From the south came traders laden with bars of pure gold taken from mines in western Africa whose locations were kept secret for hundreds of years, giving rise to rumors throughout Europe that somewhere in Africa there ran a river flowing with gold instead of water. From the north the desert nomads would bring caravans of camels loaded with rock salt cut into bricks and slabs; salt was exceedingly valuable in the Middle Ages because it could be used to preserve food. In the markets of Timbuktu they would be traded, salt for gold and gold for salt, with both sides paying a portion of each sale as a tax to the governors of the city. Though its people neither mined gold nor cut salt, Timbuktu grew very rich through the buying and selling of both.

Just to the west of Timbuktu lay the empire of Ghana. Through the early years of the Middle Ages, Ghana had grown into a powerful kingdom whose rulers also charged a tax upon the caravans of gold and salt that traveled through, bound for Timbuktu. Ghana was rich in gold mines, as well, and the kings decreed that any gold nuggets dug out of the earth belonged to the palace; the miners could keep the tiny grains of gold dust as their wages. The kings of Ghana covered themselves in gold; when the king sat in his court to judge his people, he sheltered beneath a golden tent and surrounded himself with guards carrying golden swords. His officials wrapped themselves in gold-threaded cloaks and braided gold into their hair. Even the king's slim, elegant dogs, who sat by his side whenever he held court, wore collars of solid gold.

By the twelfth century Ghana had become a Muslim country, filled with traders and scholars who followed Islam. But its rulers had grown weak, and during the 1100s Ghana was overrun and conquered by a neighboring people, the Sosso (SO-so). They were not Muslim at all and their leader viewed Islam as a terrible threat because it came from outside of Africa and did not follow African ways. Fearing for their lives, the Muslim scholars of Ghana fled to the nearest place that would seem to offer friendly sanctuary: Timbuktu.

And so it was that the city of gold and salt also became the city of books. Scholars from all the lands of Islam traveled there, for the city became famous for its bustling book market and its libraries, all of them stacked with thousands of books. Books were brought into the city from across the Muslim world to be copied and then stored in the libraries. And as the libraries swelled in size, so also did the number of scholars, who came not only to study the books but to write even more.

In Ghana, meanwhile, the kingship of the Sosso rulers had been short-lived. They had been swallowed up by the empire of Mali, whose fierce prince, Sundiata (SOON-dee-AH-ta), was nicknamed The Lion King. The rulers of Mali were called "mansa," a word that means "master"; by 1312 Mali was ruled by Sundiata's grand-nephew, Musa (MOO-sah), who would be remembered as Mali's greatest king and who would in time turn his attention to Timbuktu.

Mansa Musa was a devoted follower of Islam, and his greatest wish in life was to make a pilgrimage to the city of Mecca, the holiest place in the Muslim world. In 1324 he set out toward Arabia with an enormous caravan of thousands upon thousands of servants and attendants, as well as all his friends and relatives. Some observers wrote that his train included sixty thousand people! Among them were twelve thousand slaves, each carrying bars of shining, unmarked gold, and eighty camels bearing bags of gold dust. Everywhere he went, Mansa Musa gave away gold. In Egypt, he left so much gold behind that it lost much of its value; no one wanted any more because everyone had some. News of his fabulous wealth spread far beyond the Sahara. A map drawn in Spain in 1535 shows Musa seated on a golden throne with a golden scepter in one hand and, in the other, a large gold nugget. Many of those who heard the stories of Musa's journey to Mecca came to believe that in Africa, gold could be plucked up from the ground like a handful of pebbles.

On his trip back home to Mali, Musa stopped at Timbuktu and declared his intention of adding it to his empire. There does not seem to have been any disagreement with this plan, for very shortly thereafter, history tells us that Musa began the construction of a palace for himself in Timbuktu and a large *mosque*, which is a place for Muslims to worship. Then he brought to the city a famous architect from Spain to build a *university*, a place where scholars and students from all over the world could live and study. The architect fashioned the school entirely out of mud bricks, with wooden posts poking out of the smooth walls like the quills on a porcupine. In this way, once every year, workmen could clamber up the walls to repair the damage caused by rain and wind. When the building was finished, Musa paid him for his work with 400 pounds of gold.

University at Timbuktu

By the end of Musa's reign, the University of Timbuktu had already grown into a marvel. Its library held more than 500,000 books and scrolls; there were living quarters for 25,000 scholars. Timbuktu was the center of Muslim learning. The people who lived there said of their city, "Gold comes from the south, salt from the north, and silver from the country of the white men, but the treasures of wisdom are only to be found in Timbuktu."

At the height of their power, the kings of Mali held more than four hundred cities and towns and ruled almost twenty million people. But the wealth they gained from the trading of gold and salt was a mighty temptation to other kingdoms. Eventually, in the 1460s, Mali was conquered and absorbed into a new empire: the Songhai (song-HI). Its leader, Sonni Ali (SOO-nee ah-LEE), though a Muslim, did not respect the scholars and the libraries of Timbuktu. He burned much of the city and killed the scholars or drove them away. Those who fled took many of the city's precious books and scrolls with them; thousands more were saved from destruction, hidden away in the thick walls of houses or in secret, walled-up chambers. Under the Songhai, Timbuktu became once again known mostly as a crossroads, for the trading in gold and salt was as busy and prosperous as ever, and now it was joined by traders in copper, ivory, kola nuts, and sadly, in slaves. The gold of Africa began to appear in the coins and jewelry of Europe as merchants out of Venice and Genoa made themselves part of the long chain that had its ultimate end in Timbuktu.

In 1510 a Spanish scholar named Leo Africanus (AH-fri-CAH-nus) visited Timbuktu, drawn by its fame and the rumors of its wealth. A few years later, when he was summoned to Rome and asked by the pope to write a book about Africa, he described the fabled city. He wrote about the ruler with his "plates and scepters of gold," and the citizens who were "very rich." Their coins were unmarked discs of pure gold, he said. He talked about their comfortable lives, with plenty of cattle, milk, and butter, even though the city had no gardens or orchards.

Leo Africanus' book, which he called *Description of Africa*, became well-known throughout Europe in much the same way that Marco Polo's had, setting fire to the imaginations of those who read it. Africa, the land of gold! For the explorers who were already seeking ways to sail south along the coast of Africa, some of whom we'll meet in a chapter ahead, the book confirmed what they already suspected: Africa was a treasure chest just waiting to be opened.

As for Timbuktu itself, the fame it enjoyed slowly changed. Where once it had been a synonym for gold and wealth, slowly, as the years went by, it became something else: a symbol of a place so far away, so mysterious, that it could never be reached. Or if someone were to stumble upon it, a place from which he might never return. Timbuktu came to mean the great unknown, the farthest place a person could possibly go. It seemed like a legend. Even now, in our modern world, there are many people who don't believe that Timbuktu is a real city.

But you know better. Timbuktu lives on; nowadays it is a small, sleepy place. The people carefully repair the mud brick walls of the University each year, just as they have done for hundreds of years, and eye the desert fearfully as it creeps ever closer. Though the city is diminished and its fame forgotten, they still remember that Timbuktu was once the greatest crossroads of wealth and learning in the world, a gathering place for scholars and merchants, a treasure house of salt, books, and gold.

Chapter Twenty-Three

A Fresh Breeze

Giotto di Bondone transforms the art of painting

The city of Florence lies in the center of Italy's boot. The River Arno winds its way past the magnificent, red-domed cathedral at the city's heart; the pale stone buildings and crooked streets spread out to fill a low, wide valley; and it is all surrounded by gently rounded hills where, around the year 1277 or so, a citizen of Florence went out for a stroll.

This Florentine was named Giovanni Cimabue (JEE-oh-VAN-nee CHEE-mah-BOO-eh). He was renowned as a painter and a maker of *mosaics*, which are large pictures created by pressing thousands of tiny tiles into damp cement. He often traveled far from Florence to decorate the walls and ceilings of churches all over Italy, for since the days of Emperor Constantine, when Christianity was made the official religion of Rome, and all through the Middle Ages, most art was created by and for the Church. Cimabue always had plenty of work. The Italian historian Giorgio Vasari (JOR-joh vah-SAH-ree), who lived in the 1600s and wrote a long book called *Lives of the Artists,* explains that "he painted in churches both in Florence and Pisa, and made the name of Cimabue famous everywhere."

When Cimabue walked up into the hills above the city that day, he could not have guessed that he would come home

simplycharlottemason.com   185

again with something unexpected: a student. For as he made his way along the path, he came upon a bored young shepherd, a ten-year-old boy named Giotto di Bondone (JOT-toh dee bon-DOH-neh), who was amusing himself by sketching pictures of his sheep upon a flat stone. Vasari describes for us what happened:

> *One day Cimabue, going on business from Florence to Vespignano, found Giotto, while his sheep were feeding, drawing a sheep from nature upon a smooth and solid rock with a pointed stone, having never learnt from any one but nature. Cimabue, marvelling at him, stopped and asked him if he would go and be with him. And the boy answered that if his father were content he would gladly go. Then Cimabue asked Bondone for him, and he gave him up to him, and was content that he should take him to Florence.*

Cimabue asked Giotto's father if he would allow the boy to become his *apprentice*. This was a common practice in the Middle Ages; a skilled craftsman, perhaps a blacksmith or a weaver, would invite a promising boy to come and live with his family and work in his shop. The craftsman would then teach the boy all that he knew, and in return the young man would serve his master doing chores and keeping the shop clean. After a period of time, usually seven years or so, when the master thought that his student had learned all that he could, the apprentice would set up a shop of his own. This system worked very well, because the apprentice learned a useful trade and the master received the help he needed to run his shop.

It might seem a bit strange to think of painters and sculptors as shop-owners, as if they were no different from tanners or shoemakers, but during the Middle Ages, painting was not considered a special gift or talent. Painters, sculptors, mosaic-makers, architects—they were all seen as craftsmen who were hired to do their specific jobs and who could pass on their same skills to others. A well-known painter would run a large workshop and employ any number of apprentices, all of them learning to paint just like him.

The art of the Middle Ages was, you see, very *stylized*. This means that most artwork looked similar, and the work of any one painter would be very much like any other. In the centuries after Rome's fall, the world had lost, or turned away from, the artistic triumphs of the ancients, their *realism*. The statues that are left us from ancient Greece and Rome look as if they were actual humans, frozen in stone or marble. But the art of the Middle Ages was not realistic at all. The paintings, while very beautiful, show us people with slim, *elongated*—stretched out—bodies, and stern, expressionless faces that stare straight-forwardly out toward the viewer. They look flat, like cut-out paper-dolls individually pasted to the wall. The people are arranged according to their rank, with important people painted tall and imposing and less important people meek and tiny at their feet. The paintings have no backgrounds—usually the area behind the figures is a solid sheet of gleaming gold leaf or vivid blue paint—and the gowns and robes in the paintings hang in stiff, flat folds, as if they were carved from wood, with no hint of the actual body that might lie beneath them. The paintings are not concerned with telling a story; all the important happenings of any event are often shown all at once, with the main actors appearing multiple times in the same scene.

Cimabue was a master of this kind of painting, and it was to his workshop, to learn this skill, that Giotto came in the year 1280. It must have quickly become apparent that those life-like sheep were no accident. Vasari shares the tale that once, while still just a boy in Cimabue's worksop, Giotto drew a gleaming black fly on the nose of a face in one of his master's paintings. Later that day, when Cimabue returned to work on the painting, he tried several times to brush the insect away.

News of the astonishing skill of Cimabue's apprentice

found its way all the way to Rome. The pope, curious if the rumors were true, sent one of his courtiers to find out. As he made his way to Florence, the courtier visited other painters and collected a painting or drawing from each to give to his master. So of course, when he came to Cimabue's workshop, the courtier rather imperiously demanded of Giotto a "little drawing." Giotto was a polite young man, but he also possessed a mischievous sense of humor. He dipped a pen into red ink, and with a whisk of his wrist, formed a large, perfect circle.

"Here is the drawing," he said, offering it to the courtier with a flourish.

The courtier was certain that he was being insulted. "Am I to have nothing more than this?" he sniffed.

"This is enough and too much," Giotto replied. "Take it and include it with the others, and see if it will be understood."

The courtier returned to Rome and presented his collection of drawings to the pope, who, upon seeing the perfect circle drawn in one quick sweeping line, declared that surely Giotto would surpass all the painters of his time.

And indeed, Vasari says that Giotto soon "equalled his master." But more importantly, the historian also tells us that the young painter "freed himself . . . and brought back to life the true art of painting." By the time he left Cimabue's workshop, around 1290, Giotto was creating paintings that were unlike any the world had seen for a thousand years.

The people in Giotto's pictures are not flat and stylized. They look solid and natural with rounded arms and curved cheeks. Their clothes flow softly over the curves and angles of their bodies. They stand in detailed landscapes with rocks and trees and skies. Most of all, Giotto's pictures tell stories. The faces are filled with real feelings—hope, sorrow, puzzlement, fear—and the people reach out and touch each other or make gestures with their hands like real men and women do. Some of them are turned so that we see only their backs or the sides of their faces. They peer at each other rather than out at the viewer, and Giotto invites us, as viewers, to become part of the painting, too, by arranging the scenes so that it feels as though we are standing right there, a spectator and participant in the painting's great events.

Like all artists of the Middle Ages, Giotto painted scenes from the Bible for churches or monasteries. In 1304 he traveled to Padua, a town northeast of Florence, to decorate a chapel built by a wealthy nobleman on the site of an ancient Roman arena. He stayed there for several years, covering the walls of the Arena Chapel with thirty-seven scenes from the Bible, each telling a dramatic story from the life of Jesus. One shows the betrayal of Christ, as Judas reaches forward to bestow his traitor's kiss. In Giotto's painting we can see the deep sorrow and compassion on Jesus' face, even as the Roman soldiers press forward to seize Him. In another, Giotto shows us the terrible sadness of Mary as Jesus' body is taken down from the cross; the angels in heaven are looking down, their faces crumbled as they weep bitterly.

With his paintbrush Giotto showed people their own faces, because in his figures they saw the same joy, grief, excitement, and rage that are part of any person's life. Even though his paintings depicted famous characters from Bible stories, they didn't seem like distant, stony saints. They seemed like neighbors and friends.

Giotto's paintings were *frescos*. This means that they were painted directly onto a newly-plastered wall while the plaster was still wet. The colors of the paint would sink into the damp plaster, so that when it dried, the painting would actually be part of the wall. Fresco painting was a difficult task; the artist needed to work quickly on large sections of the wall, and once the painting was done, it could not be altered. If the artist made the slightest mistake, the plaster on that entire section would have to be removed. Although this painting technique had been used since ancient times, it was the Italians who gave it the name

The Arrest of Christ by Giotto

"fresco" from a word that means "fresh."

    Giotto's paintings were fresh in ways beyond just the plaster on which they were painted. They were so different, so new, that other painters traveled from all around Italy in order to study them. Others began to use Giotto's ideas in their own work: telling a single story in their paintings, making the people look solid and real, and arranging them in natural-looking groups. In the century after Giotto's death, Italy became a paradise of painters, with men like Michelangelo and Leonardo da Vinci expanding and extending Giotto's realism.

    Giotto died in 1337. He was buried in the cathedral of Florence, Vasari tells us, under a slab of white marble. Hundreds of years later, in the 1970s, some bones were uncovered beneath the cathedral's floor; when they were studied, it was determined that they had belonged to a man who was very short, less than five feet tall, whose neck bones showed that he had spent much of his life staring upward. The bones were filled with arsenic and lead, which were used, in the Middle Ages, in artist's paints. After the examination the bones were reburied with great ceremony, for most people believed that they were Giotto's remains.

If they were, it reminds us that a person may be short of stature and yet still cast a very long shadow. Giotto's marvelous paintings opened a window through which a fresh breeze began to blow. The lost realism of the art of Greece and Rome experienced a rebirth—a *renaissance*—as artists followed Giotto's lead and turned away from stale, stiff, staring figures. Over the next two hundred years, that renaissance breeze would escape the artist's workshop and grow in power until it became a hurricane. It would sweep away the old ways of seeing the world and stir up new ways of thinking and believing. In Giotto's lovely paintings, we can see the wind changing—the beginning of the end of the Middle Ages.

Chapter Twenty-Four

Freedom Fighter

In Switzerland, William Tell strikes a blow against tyranny

Every year on the first day of August the people of Switzerland gather to celebrate their nation's independence with parades of paper lanterns, fireworks, and bonfires on hilltops. Some of them come to the shores of Lake Lucerne, to Rutli (ROOT-lee) Meadow, a small swath of grass, glowing green amongst the shadows of tall oak trees. There, sitting on the soft grass or standing in small groups, they watch as several men dressed in medieval hats and cloaks act out the swearing of an oath. As the Swiss flag snaps briskly in the breezes that blow off the lake, they bow their heads in gratitude to the few men who, seven hundred years ago, made a promise to each other, a promise that created Switzerland and set her people free.

Those men were there because of a farmer and herdsman named William Tell. He did not set out to be a hero or to found a nation, but in the legend that grew up around him, that is exactly what he did.

Seven hundred years ago, in the last years of the thirteenth century, there was no such place as Switzerland. The mountains and valleys that today make up that nation were part of the Holy Roman Empire. Mostly, however, they ruled themselves, for they were so remote and the land was so rugged that, for most of the early years of the Middle Ages, the empire and its rulers spared them very little thought.

Their land lay within a great range of mountains—the Alps. These peaks were a giant wall, cutting the Holy Roman Empire off from Italy and France, with only a few low passes as gateways. But by the middle of the 13th century, the clever men who lived in those high valleys had found a way to build a bridge over one of the most impassable gorges, and from there to build a road directly through the peaks and down into Italy. It created a broad, open doorway from northern Europe to the markets of Venice and Genoa and Milan, and suddenly it was easy and convenient for merchants and travelers to make the journey, as long as they were willing to pay the men of the mountains for food and shelter.

This bridge had been built by the men of Uri (OOR-ee), which was one of the mountain *cantons*. A canton is like a state, though the word meant "edge" or "corner." Each mountain valley, tucked away in the corners of the empire, was really a country of its own with its own laws and rulers. As more and more travelers made their way across Uri's bridge, it grew ever more wealthy. The emperor took notice and gave to Uri, as well as to its neighboring cantons Schwyz (SCHWEETS) and Unterwalden (OON-ter-VAHL-den), a special status called "Immediacy." This meant that these cantons were free from interference from any local lord and would answer to the emperor alone.

In 1273, however, a new emperor came to the throne—Rudolph I, Count of Hapsburg. The Holy Roman Empire had, since the days of Charlemagne, been an uneasy conglomeration of German estates and Italian cities. Though it ruled over most of central Europe, its strength depended entirely on the ambition of whoever was currently occupying its throne and how much money he was willing to pay to stay there. Large parts of the empire often acted as if the empire did not actually exist, going their own way. The emperor himself, you might remember, was elected by the various princes and dukes and earls over which he was then expected to rule. Having gained their votes, Rudolph I was determined that his family, the Hapsburgs, would keep the throne for a very long time.

Hapsburg Castle, the home of Rudolph I, lay deep in the Alps close to Uri and the other mountain cantons. Hungry for the gold to be gained from taxing the steady stream of bridge-crossers, Rudolph took from the cantons their "immediacy"—their independence, really—and declared that they would be governed by his own officials.

And so it was. The cantons chafed under the unjust Hapsburg rule, but what could be done?

One morning, then, the farmer William Tell, with his little son at his side and his crossbow on his back, came strolling into the market square of Altdorf, which was Uri's only town of any size. There he stopped in surprise, for a tall pole had been erected in the center of the square, guarded by frowning soldiers, and atop it perched a fancy hat clearly marked with the Hapsburg coat-of-arms. As the townspeople hurried by, they each paused in front of the pole to bow their heads, the men carefully removing their own hats as a sign of respect.

William Tell caught a passing boy by the elbow.

"What's this all about?" he asked.

The boy looked down at his toes. "It's the bailiff's command. We must bow before the hat, to show that we submit to the emperor."

The bailiff of Altdorf was a man named Gessler (GUESS-ler), who had been sent by Rudolph to govern Uri and collect tax money. William Tell looked up at the hat on the pole and then, with an arm curved tightly about his son's shoulders, he stepped forward. What happened next has passed into legend and story, a story celebrated in Switzerland every August.

For William Tell walked past the pole and did not remove

his hat. He was seized at once by the guards and dragged before the bailiff to answer for this insolence. Gessler declared that both this man and his little son must die for showing such disrespect, but then he spotted the crossbow slung across William Tell's back and an evil plan occurred to him.

"You deserve your death," he said. "But I have heard that you are an excellent bowman, William Tell, so I will allow you to earn back your life and the life of your son."

He ordered the guards to take both man and boy back out into the square. There, in a loud voice, he announced that William Tell must demonstrate his skill with the bow by shooting an apple off the head of his own son. If he succeeded, they would both go free. But if he failed, and killed his son, he himself would also die.

We can only imagine the agonized glance that must have passed from father to son as the boy was marched 120 paces across the square and a single red apple was balanced atop his head. With his lips pressed into a grim line, William Tell slid two crossbow bolts out of his arrow case; he slipped one into the pocket of his coat and notched the other into the bow. Then in the deep silence that filled the square, as the people looked on in dismay and fear, he took a single breath, aimed his crossbow, and shot. With a thunk, the arrow split the apple in two, and the little boy stepped away, unhurt, to run back across the square into his father's arms.

"You have saved your son's life and your own," Gessler said. "But why did you hide a second arrow in your coat?"

"Because," answered William Tell, "if the first arrow had struck my son, I would have used the second to kill you."

Gessler was enraged by this answer, as you might well imagine. He could not order a second execution upon William Tell, since he had already promised to spare him, but he decreed that the farmer had best say farewell to his son, for he would never see him again. He would be locked in the dungeon of the

Castle Kussnacht (KOOS-nakt), on the opposite shore of Lake Lucerne, and there, the bailiff said, William Tell would never again see either sun nor moon.

The guards bound William's arms and propelled him down to the lakeshore with the angry Gessler in their wake. They boarded Gessler's own small boat and began to row across the lake, but when they were far out upon the water, a storm broke over their heads. The boat shuddered and bucked in the waves, and the guards could make no progress toward the shore no matter how hard they pulled at the oars.

"We must release him," they shouted at Gessler, pointing at William Tell, with his strong hands and broad shoulders. "We'll never survive without another man at the oars."

Frightened, Gessler agreed. The bonds were cut from William Tell, and he stepped into the helm and rowed with all his strength. Then, just as they reached the rocky slabs of the shore, he leaped from the boat, whipped around, whip-quick, and kicked the boat, with the guards and Gessler still aboard, back out into the heaving waves.

Now William began to run, through the dark forests and over rocky ledges, toward the Castle Kussnacht, for he guessed that the bailiff and his men, if they survived, would come to the castle in search of reinforcements. And that they did, beaching their half-sunken boat and racing up a narrow road toward the castle gates. But from behind a fallen tree, William Tell aimed his crossbow, armed with the second arrow that he'd hidden in his coat, and fired one shot. If flew, straight and true, and killed the evil bailiff there on the castle road.

William Tell was not the only man who had been wronged by the bailiff's cruelty. There were other stories of Hapsburg tyranny, of unjust punishments and foolish judgments. And so, not long after William Tell's escape on the lake and his shooting of the unjust bailiff, three men of the mountains met in Rutli Meadow—one man each representing Uri, Schwyz, and

Unterwalden—and together they swore an oath: "To assist each other with aid and every counsel and every favor, with person and goods, with might and main, against one and all, who may inflict on them any violence, molestation or injury, or may plot evil against their persons or goods." Even today in Switzerland every schoolchild knows this oath by heart.

They were small things, just a promise made between a few men, just one arrow from William Tell's crossbow, but even tiny pebbles can start an avalanche. When Rudolph died that same year, the three cantons—Uri, Schwyz, and Unterwalden—determined to uphold the Rutli oath and fight to secure their freedom from the Hapsburgs. Together they signed the Federal Charter of 1291, the oldest declaration of independence in the world. This was the foundation of Switzerland, a name which was taken from the little canton of Schwyz. The Hapsburgs sent mighty armies to squash them, but each time they were beaten back by the stalwart men of the mountains. As their rebellion against the Hapsburgs grew, more cantons joined with them. By 1386 the Swiss cantons had defeated the Hapsburgs completely and secured their independence, which has lasted for more than 700 years.

Now so far removed in time, no one knows how much of the story of William Tell is history and how much is legend. But it is certain that something happened in the waning years of the thirteenth century in the deep valleys and high peaks of Uri and Schwyz. There a small group of people decided that they would govern themselves and not submit to the authority of a tyrant, however great that tyrant's power might be.

Every August the Swiss people remind themselves of this truth. They remember William Tell, who refused to remove his hat to please an evil ruler's whim, and who inspired the men of Rutli to stand up before the tyrant and swear their courageous oath.

Chapter Twenty-Five

The Black Prince, the Black Death, and the White Knight of Orleans

England and France fight the Hundred Years War

Sometime around the year 1340, shortly after he became king, Edward III of England declared that his Lord Chancellor, chiefest of his advisors, must from that day onward conduct all of his council meetings while seated on an overstuffed sack of sheep's wool.

This may perhaps have seemed as odd to the Lord Chancellor as it does to you and me, but the king had good reason for making such a decree. Wool, after all, was very important to England; the hills and fields were white with flocks of sheep, and every year after the shearing, bales and bales of English wool were loaded aboard ships for a brief journey across the sea to the county of Flanders, there to be spun into thick, strong cloth in the Flemish mills.

Flanders is north of France—it lies in Belgium now, in modern times. Cloth from Flanders was highly prized and traded throughout all of Europe and even into Asia and the Muslim lands. But to manufacture their cloth, the millers and weavers of Flanders needed that English wool, and they paid well for it. And so, for a while, all was well and the wool merchants and sheep farmers of England made a fine living, and the king's treasury filled with gold from the taxes paid off each bale of wool.

But, unfortunately for England, the counts of Flanders were vassals of the kings of France. If you will think back to what we've learned about the feudal system, you'll remember that this meant Flanders owed loyalty and allegiance to France, however much they might love the English and their woolly sheep. As Flanders grew richer, the king of France began to press for more control over the county, even though it had long governed itself. He wanted some of those tax dollars for himself.

Edward III, as king of England, could not allow that. The wool trade with Flanders kept his treasury well topped with gold. When the Flemish mill-owners and weavers declared that they would go to war against France rather than submit to French control, Edward agreed to support them.

Edward's quarrel with the king of France went far deeper, though, than merely a scuffle over wool and cloth. Since the days of William the Conqueror, who had left behind his enormous estates in the south of France when he had sailed the channel for England, the English kings had claimed vast portions of the French countryside as their own fiefs. This meant, of course, in theory, that they must swear homage to the king of France as his vassals, but as you can well imagine, no English king was eager to do so.

The French, too, viewed the situation with a sour and bitter eye and through the years had done their best to cut and shave away at the English holdings in France, reclaiming a castle here or a village there, and occasionally, as Phillip II had done, seizing entire fiefs outright. To the kings of France, it seemed as if the English kings were reaching across the channel with grasping hands, and they would have been most content to see the English lose their grip on every claim they made to French land. There was constant bickering along the border between the English-held fiefs in the south and the rest of France. And now, with Flanders rising up in arms in the north, the king of France was caught between an army of angry Flemish millers and the threat of English invasion.

To make matters worse, from a French point of view, their king, Charles IV, had died without an heir. His sister, Isabelle, had married King Edward II of England the year before, and their son was Edward III. This meant, of course, that the closest relative of the French king sat upon the throne of England and was the obvious choice to inherit the throne of France as well.

But the French could not abide the thought of Edward as their king. When Charles IV died, a group of French lawyers dug up an old, old law—the Salic law—which decreed that a woman could not inherit the throne. If Isabelle could not reign in France, neither could her son. And turning their backs on Edward, they gave the crown to a man named Philip of Valois (VAL-wah), who had been Charles IV's cousin.

Edward could have let it stand and focused his attention on England alone. After all, France was the strongest country in Europe, with many more knights ready for battle and a much larger treasury than England boasted. But Edward's England supported him in his desire to go to war; he was young—only eighteen years old—and strong, his own knights were battle-tested, and his cause seemed just. He was, after all, truly the heir to the French throne. He sent a letter to King Philip in France: "We are heir to the realm and crown of France by a much closer degree of kingship than yourself. . . . Wherefore we give you notice that we shall claim and conquer our heritage in France." He added tersely, "We consider you our enemy and adversary."

So in 1340 a war began between England and France, a war that would, in fits and starts, last for more than a hundred years.

At first the French aimed to control the English Channel. After all, if Edward were going to aid the Flemish millers, he would need to send ships across the water. An enormous fleet of French ships was assembled at a port town called Sluys

(SLUHZ), anchored side by side like cars caught in a traffic jam on an enormous freeway. But before they could sail out to battle, English sailors attacked, setting fire to the French ships and battling sword to sword and hand to hand across the closely-packed decks, like soldiers on a wooden battlefield. When the Battle of Sluys was over, the French fleet was destroyed and England was entirely safe from French invasion. English ships ruled the channel for the remainder of the war.

In 1345 Edward arrived in France at the head of his army, with his son at his side. His men were not in fighting shape; many of them had fallen ill on the crossing. Rather than risk an open battle, he led his soldiers across the countryside, pillaging as they went, always moving northward toward Flanders but evading the huge French army for as long as he could. Finally, just south of the port town of Calais (CAL-ay), Edward could avoid facing Philip no longer, and he prepared his men for battle.

The prospect did not look hopeful for the English. They were outnumbered almost three to one, and they were sick and weary from marching. Philip rode toward them with row upon row of the finest knights in France arrayed in shining armor. But the English, despite their ragtag appearance, had come to France bearing a weapon that would give them an awesome advantage in battle: the longbow. These bows were carved from the supple yew trees that filled the English forests. Each one was as tall as a man and could fire an arrow across an entire battlefield to strike a target with tremendous force.

Edward positioned his men along a hilltop and waited, throughout the day, as the French army marched ever closer. When Philip finally caught sight of his adversary late in the afternoon, he recklessly gave the command to attack at once, not realizing, or perhaps too angry to care, that the English stood with their backs to the setting sun and the brilliant, blinding light was shining directly into the French soldiers' eyes. The long ride up the hill slowed and wearied the knights' horses. And then the command was given and the English archers fired.

Out of the blistering glare came a storm of arrows. The French fell into a horrified confusion of wounded men. The archers continued to fire, over and over; the English pressed forward, down the hill, and the French were forced back, little by little. As dusk fell, Philip called for a retreat.

Edward, meanwhile, had scaled a nearby windmill in order to view the battle's progress. He saw, down amongst the still-desperate fighting, his son, sword flashing. "Let the boy win his spurs," he said, when an officer asked if they should go to the prince's aid. When the battle had ended, with most of Philip's grand and glorious knights fallen on the field, Edward presented his son with a black sword as a reward, and he was called the Black Prince from that moment forward.

With this great victory in hand, Edward was poised to claim all of France. He had secured the town of Calais, which gave him a port for his ships, and the French were discouraged by the loss of so many of their noble knights. But instead, both England and France were shortly to face an enemy far more merciless than each other. In 1347 the Black Death came to Europe.

This terrible, sweeping sickness had begun ten years earlier far to the east in the land of China. Slowly, like a spreading pool of spilt ink, it made its way westward, killing as it came. In Constantinople half of the city perished. In Florence the streets stood empty. Eight hundred people died every day in Paris, and when the sickness crossed the English Channel, nearly half of England's people were swept away by its cold hand.

In all, millions of people were killed.

No one knew what it was or where it came from, only that it was a deadly sickness that struck suddenly and mercilessly. Now we have learned that it is caused by a certain kind of infection carried by fleas that rode upon the backs of rats, who in turn were to be found in the ships that sailed throughout the medieval world. Shipping and trade brought great wealth to the

Middle Ages, but it also brought death. It seemed to the people living then that the end of the world had come.

Finally, by 1350 the wave of deadly sickness began to recede. The survivors faced a changed world with empty villages and deserted cities. There were so few workers in the fields and towns that ordinary goods, such as milk or bread, became three or four times more expensive than they had been before.

Surely such catastrophe would bring an end to Edward and Philip's warring! And indeed, in 1350 Philip died, claimed by the same Black Death that had killed so many of his subjects. His son, John II, was quickly crowned, and he and Edward signed a truce. But by 1356 Edward had rejected it and sent his son, the Black Prince, to once again plunder the French countryside. He hoped to force the French, so weakened by years of war and sickness, to once and for all recognize his claim to the throne.

John II marched out to meet the Black Prince at a place called Poitiers. The French were once again confident of victory, with their well-mounted knights and superior numbers. But the English longbows proved just as deadly this time as they had in the past, and King John of France was taken captive. The Black Prince greeted him with respect, but nonetheless, bundled him into a ship and sent him as a prisoner back to England.

This was most unwelcome news for the French! Edward told them that he would be pleased to release their king if they paid an enormous ransom of three million crowns. Though he was given a comfortable tower and treated with honor, John was still a captive in London when he died in 1364.

Meanwhile in France, the Black Prince had grown sick, so he returned to England. He died in June of 1376 much to the sorrow and dismay of his father, who was himself growing old and frail. When Edward, too, went to his grave the next year, he was succeeded as king by his little grandson Richard II, the oldest son of the Black Prince, who was only a boy of ten.

A brief peace descended then, with a child on the throne

in England and Philip's teenaged son Charles ruling in France.

By 1413 Richard II had lost his throne; he had angered his nobles and all of his people with foolish decisions and heavy taxes, and the king in England was Henry V, a great, great grandson of Edward III. As soon as the crown had settled on his brow, he raised an army and returned to France, determined to at last achieve what all of his forefathers had not and sit as king in Paris. Henry was a war leader of astonishing skill and courage. At the battle of Agincourt (AH-jin-coort), near Paris, he defeated the French despite being outnumbered four to one, with his men charging forward through a field knee-deep with mud. He forced the French to surrender and signed a treaty which declared that he would marry the French king's daughter, Princess Catherine. Their children would sit upon the thrones of both England and France; Catherine's brother Charles, who had been the crown prince, would never be king. England was triumphant.

And yet, perhaps not.

The people of France had no desire to accept this English conqueror as their king. When Henry V died suddenly in 1422, after just ten years of rule, many of them rallied behind the young Charles, hoping to drive the English out of France and crown him king. But Henry had left behind an infant son, Henry VI, who was declared king of England and France despite being only nine months old.

The baby king's regent, the Duke of Bedford, took up the battle against Charles. He marched to the city of Orleans (aw-lay-ahwn) and besieged it; if it fell, the duke would have a clear path to pursue Charles and the battered French army all the way through the south of France and perhaps force him to flee the country altogether.

And then, suddenly, the duke and the besiegers of Orleans came under attack. To the Englishmen's astonishment, the army assaulting them was led, not by Charles or any of his mighty knights, but by a small figure dressed in gleaming white armor, a seventeen-year-old girl. Her courage and her very presence seemed to inspire the French soldiers. They fought with an enthusiasm and strength that had previously been lost, and in a few short battles, they drove the English away from Orleans.

Her name was Jeanne d'Arc. The English called her Joan of Arc; the French, the Maid of Orleans. She had come to Charles and told him that, in a dream, God had assured her that he would be king of France. He, in turn, had allowed her to lead his men into battle.

Lead them she did. Throughout the summer of 1429 the armies of France followed young Joan, seeming to draw strength from her example and her fervent belief that France would be rescued from the English. And in battle after battle the French prevailed, turning back the tide of English success that Henry V had unleashed.

Finally though, in September of that year, the English managed to capture her. Due to her great effect upon the French, the Duke of Bedford and the other English noblemen knew that they must be rid of her forever. For two years they kept her a prisoner, unsure of how to accomplish that goal. Eventually, they accused her of being a witch and put her on trial for sorcery. They gave her no lawyer and the verdict was assured. On May 30, 1431, she was led away from the English courtroom to her death.

The English leaders hoped that by killing Joan, they would also kill the renewed heart that had filled the French army. But they were wrong. The people of France and all of her noblemen united completely behind Charles and defeated the English, thoroughly and finally, at the Battle of Bordeaux (bore-DOH) in 1453. The kings of England would make no more claims upon the throne of France.

Though history has come to call this conflict the Hundred Years War, it actually lasted for 116. It left both England and

France with empty treasuries, many, many deaths, and much ill will toward each other. It also destroyed much of the flower of chivalry that had bloomed in both nations, with the deaths of so many knights. But it created heroes, as well, in the mighty prowess in war of Henry V and the delicate white Maid of Orleans, who died believing that France should be free.

And in England, to this very day, the Speaker of the House of Lords, the leader of the British Parliament, still conducts his business while seated on a sack of wool.

Chapter Twenty-Six

Conquerors of the Green Sea

*Prince Henry of Portugal unlocks
the Age of Exploration*

One August morning in 1415, Prince Henry of Portugal set out with his father and brothers to hunt pirates.

Portugal is a small nation snugged up next to Spain on the western edge of its peninsula, like a mask on an enormous face peering out over the Atlantic Ocean. In those early years of the 1400s, Portugal had only existed as a separate nation for little more than a century. For five hundred years, since the conquests of Tariq-ibn-zayid in 711, the land of Portugal had been part of the Muslim caliphate of Al-Andalus. Then in 1249, with the help of crusaders marching toward Jerusalem, the Christians of Portugal had driven the Muslims out of their country and established their own independent kingdom. Prince Henry was the third child of Portugal's king, John the Good.

With its long coastline facing the Atlantic's wild waters, Portugal had been, throughout much of its short history, easy prey for the dreaded Barbary Pirates. Sailing out from their home base in North Africa, these lawless men would attack villages all along the coast, emptying them and carrying all of the people off into slavery in Africa and Arabia. King John and his sons were determined to put a stop to these horrible raids, if they could, by capturing one of the pirate's main ports, the north African town of Ceuta (SAY-oot-ah), which lay just across the Strait of Gibraltar from the great cliff-face itself.

The attack was an overwhelming success. Caught by surprise, the pirates were swiftly overcome, and by nightfall the town belonged to the Portuguese. For a while at least, the pirates had been defeated and King John could rest easier, knowing that he had successfully defended his people from evil.

For Henry the battle of Ceuta brought more than just honor and glory, although he fought valiantly despite a deep wound in his thigh. In the days that followed, as his father and brothers dealt with securing their conquest of the town, Henry found himself increasingly fascinated by the marvelous treasures to be found in its markets: bags of rich spices, sleekly-woven rugs of silk and wool, sparkling plates of gold. Henry had never visited Africa before, for as we have seen, Africa was entirely unknown to most Europeans. But here suddenly, as Henry feasted his eyes on the wealth of Ceuta, a hunger awakened in him. He saw that Africa was full of knowledge to be sought and riches to be gained, and he wanted Portugal to have a part in it.

King John, perhaps noticing his son's awakened interest, put Prince Henry in charge of Portugal's trade and exploration. After giving some thought to the mysteries confronting him, Henry began to collect maps and travel journals. He ordered that any sailor who passed through his city must come to his palace and share the story of his journey. He sent out investigators to the other kingdoms of Europe with instructions to discover and record their knowledge of navigation on the open sea. And he built a home for himself on the southern tip of Portugal, close to the sea, where he could stand on the edge of his homeland and feel the warm winds of Africa upon his face.

In the years that followed, Prince Henry began to explore the western coast of Africa. He did not go himself, for he was devoted to the service of his father and did not feel free to sail off into the unknown. Instead, he became a sponsor; he paid for the ships and the crews, and he told them where to go and what to look for.

Like many others in Europe, he had heard the tales of Mansa Musa and his heaps of gold, and he knew that somewhere in West Africa were enormous gold mines. He had learned, too, of Muslim maps that showed a river of pure gold, a Rio do Oro, flowing through the heart of Africa. Sailors' stories had also come to him of beautiful, green islands somewhere off Africa's coast; he wanted to find them. He knew, as well, that Africa's people were pagan, and he felt strongly his duty as a Christian to bring to them the Word of God. And finally, in the midst of all these practical plans, he very much desired to find the kingdom of Prester John.

Do you know the myth of the lost island of Atlantis that sank into the ocean and disappeared over the course of one night and one day? Or perhaps you have heard of the mystical land of Shangri-La, a beautiful valley in the Himalaya Mountains where, the story goes, people live for hundreds of years and never grow old. In many ways, the legend of Prester John was like these stories—a fantastical tale of a magical kingdom.

Prester John was a king, the stories said, a descendent of one of the Three Magi who had come to visit the infant Christ. Carrying a scepter carved from a single emerald, he ruled over a land full of riches far to the east, and his kingdom was home to marvelous creatures and brave Christian knights. Some of the stories whispered that in Prester John's lands lay the Garden of Eden or a Fountain of Youth that would give eternal life to any who drank of it.

Hand-copied manuscripts describing his marvelous kingdom spread everywhere in Europe during the Middle Ages, and for most people, the story seemed to be nothing less than the truth. The pope in Rome had sent out letters addressed to Prester John in 1177. Crusaders desperate to retake Jerusalem prayed for the day when Prester John and his army of knights would march over the eastern horizon and crush the Muslims. Marco Polo mused that perhaps the kingdom of Prester John might be found in Ethiopia, in eastern Africa.

Prince Henry was intrigued by the idea that he might find Prester John's lands if only he pressed far enough along the coast of Africa. How much of Africa did the Muslims actually control? Could he sail clear around the bottom of Africa and reach Asia by sea? If so, perhaps he could find John's lost, gold-bedecked kingdom and join forces with him! Along with the lure of gold and the mystery of Prester John, the thought of finding a way to sail to Asia fired his ambition to push ever farther south.

In doing this, he was asking great bravery of his sailors. The coast of Africa, after all, was utterly unknown. The Muslim traders and merchants who lived in North Africa had little interest in venturing to the west; they already possessed the well-traveled caravan routes across the Sahara and had no need to find any other way. They called the Atlantic the "Green Sea of Darkness" and the "Sea of Obscurity."

The Europeans had their own reasons for avoiding any travel to the south. The few expeditions that had sailed down that way had never returned. If they dared to discuss it at all, most sailors agreed that a great wind, along with a strong ocean current, would prevent anyone who sailed too far to the south from turning around and voyaging back home. And there were also stories of dense, mysterious fogs that might swallow a ship to its doom or sheets of flame pouring down from the sky that caused the sea to boil. It was whispered that even the air itself was poisonous.

Filled with the fear of these unknown dangers, no European had ever sailed beyond Cape Bojador (BOH-ja-dor), the "bulging cape" which lies on the west coast of Africa where the land begins its great curve out into the Atlantic. If you take a moment to study Africa on your globe, you can find Cape

Bojador just to the southeast of the Canary Islands. If Henry wanted to fulfill all of his dreams of Africa, he must somehow get his ships beyond this one fateful spot.

First, then, they needed ships that could sail against the wind, so they could travel both north and south. For twenty years the ship builders of Portugal labored at Henry's command to come up with a vessel that could manage this feat. Eventually, they developed a new type of ship, which was called a *caravel*. It was light and fast and easy to steer, and most importantly, it had slim sails shaped like triangles, which allowed the ship to sail backward into the wind as well as forward with it. In a caravel, a sailor no longer needed to fear the wind—he could sail any way he pleased!

Henry offered a large reward to anyone who would sail beyond Cape Bojador and return, and one of his captains, Gil Eannes (JILL EE-ah-nays), took up the challenge. His first attempt failed when an unexpected wind threw him far off course. After he had limped his ship home, he suggested to Prince Henry that the journey was simply far too dangerous. But Henry dismissed his lack of courage with a sharp rebuke. "There is no peril so great," he said, "that the hope of reward will not be greater." Then he sent Captain Eannes out once again.

The cautious captain managed to pass the "bulging cape" this time. Timidly, he landed on a desert beach just beyond and dug up a small, succulent cactus that was growing there. He packed it carefully in a barrel and shipped it off to Portugal as proof that he had actually broken the barrier of Cape Bojador. And even better news! The seas did not boil, the air did not poison his crew, and his ship was not swallowed in a deadly mist. The Green Sea of Darkness was not so dark, after all. Despite all of the frightening stories, the coast of Africa was explorable.

But if he had hoped that this would be sufficient and he would be allowed to retire in glory and honor, he was mistaken. The next year, in 1435, Prince Henry dispatched him off again

A Portuguese Caravel

on yet another excursion with instructions to go as far as he could. This time they sailed more than one hundred miles past the cape until they came to a river filled with small red fish. Pleased with themselves, they returned to make their report to their prince.

Certain now that he was on the right track, Henry sent out more ships the next year, telling his captains to "look for the River of Gold, bring back some of the people so that I can talk to them, seek for the kingdom of Prester John, and, most of all, find a way around the bottom of Africa!"

Slowly, slowly, the captains attempted to do as they were commanded. They sailed ever farther south along Africa's coast. Although they did not find the River of Gold and there was no sign of Prester John, they found seals and camels. They found strange birds and shoals of fish. And eventually, they found African people.

In 1441 one of Prince Henry's ships returned from Africa with several captives, including an African man named Adahu, who could speak Arabic. When he learned that several of Henry's officials could also speak this language, he made an offer to them. If they would allow him to return home, he would repay them with ten more Africans. The Portuguese agreed and took Adahu back to the river mouth where they had captured him. Just as he promised, he returned a week later with a column of men and women chained together. They were slaves.

The Portuguese had known about slavery, of course. They knew of the slave markets in Timbuktu and across Arabia; they hated the Barbary pirates who kidnapped coastal villagers and sold them into slavery. Slavery was nothing new; sadly, it has been a part of human history for as long as there has been history. And yet, despite this knowledge, the Portuguese willingly entered into the terrible business themselves. They took the ten slaves and returned with them to Portugal. And then they began to come back, again and again, for more. They began to buy and sell these fellow men to work in the fields and farms of Portugal and, eventually, its colonies.

Henry's aim in exploring Africa was certainly not to capture slaves. But he truly believed that in bringing them to Portugal, he was doing them a great service, because they could be introduced to Christianity and hear the Gospel of Christ. The terrible injustice of slavery, which would mark the Old World and the New for the next four hundred years, did not seem to occur to him.

Meanwhile, he continued to send out his ships. By 1460, the year that he died, his men had reached the coastline of the present-day nation of Sierra Leone. He had added two thousand miles to the maps of Africa. Twenty-eight years later, in 1488, a Portuguese captain named Vasco de Gama sailed safely around the bottom of Africa and reached India by sea, just as Prince Henry had planned.

Though he did not sail the seas himself, Henry opened the door to what we now call the Age of Exploration. It was Henry and his caravels that showed the course to Columbus and Vespucci and Magellan and John Cabot. He was the one who pointed the way; history remembers him as Prince Henry the Navigator. When he died and was buried in a tomb next to his father, these words were carved in tribute on his grave: "He possessed a hunger to perform great deeds."

Chapter Twenty-Seven

An Explosion of Words

*Johannes Gutenberg makes the wisdom of God
and man available to everyone*

Sometime during the 1450s, in his workshop in Mainz (MINES), Germany, Johannes Gutenberg set off an explosion.

Of course, at the time no one, certainly not even he himself, realized the impact of what he had done. Gutenberg was an unknown craftsman, and the project he had been working on for many years, the project that lit the fuse of the explosion, was something that he would have preferred to keep to himself. He had not set out to change the world; in fact, what he really wanted to do was make a lot of money. And he had decided that the way to make money was to find a better way to make books.

Books were very valuable in the Middle Ages, because it took so much time and trouble to produce one. Before Gutenberg came along, every book in Europe had been painstakingly copied by hand in scriptoriums, such as the one we have already seen in Lindisfarne, or in candle-lit workshops. Each word on every page was drawn with a hand-sharpened pen dipped in watery ink; the pages themselves were also handmade, either from paper or thin sheets of leather, and then the whole book was carefully sewn together between two thick covers of leather-covered wood. It might take a year or more to make just one book, and each of those books was worth a fortune. There were men in the Middle Ages who boasted of their "great libraries," which consisted of perhaps one short shelf. In the monasteries and castles, books were often kept chained down so thieves would not be tempted to make away with them.

Johannes Gutenberg wanted to try something different. He wanted to *print* the books instead of copy them.

Have you ever tried printing? Perhaps you've carved a simple shape—a heart or a star—into the end of a raw potato or out of a piece of sponge. Then you dipped your shape into ink or paint and stamped it onto a piece of paper. You could cover an entire sheet with hearts or stars and they would all look exactly the same, because they all came from the same source, your carved stamp.

In the same way a page of a book could be printed if someone took the time to carefully carve all the sentences into a block of wood and then coat it with ink and stamp it onto sheets of paper. This kind of printing, which is called *block printing*, had been used since ancient times in China, as Marco Polo discovered. But it would take a very, very long time indeed to carve out all the blocks of wood needed to make all the pages for even one book. You can see why block printing, which worked fine for Chinese money, never caught on as a way to make books.

But Gutenberg did not want to print from blocks. Instead, he had thought long and hard about what it might take to print pages quickly and easily, and he had come up with an answer: he invented *movable type.*

Here is what he did.

First he realized that if a person were to create individual letters rather than entire blocks, he would be able to reuse them, time and time again, to form different words. So in his workshop he created *molds,* one for each letter, by carving a letter out of the tip of a slim metal peg and then hammering that peg into a small block of soft copper. The peg's tip made an impression of the letter in the copper—a mold—and into that mold he poured melted, liquid metal. When the metal cooled and hardened, he could pop it out of the mold and he would have a small, crisp-edged metal letter, ready to be coated with ink and stamped onto paper.

Gutenberg made thousands of these letters, which are called sorts, and sorted them into a rack of small boxes, so that he had a little bin of *A*'s and one of *B*'s and so on—all of the alphabet and all of the punctuation marks and also a few decorative swirls and curlicues.

Metal movable type arranged in a column

Now he had all the individual letters, but he needed a way to organize them into words and sentences. So he created a sort of frame out of metal or wood, a frame in the size of the finished book. Inside this frame he spelled the words and stacked up the sentences, line by line, until he had formed with his metal letters an exact replica of the page in the book.

Next it was time for ink. But he could not use the inks that scribes had been using for centuries. The inks of the hand-copied books in the Middle Ages were made from charcoal or soot or iron dust mixed with water. This was a fine black ink, but it would not work for Gutenberg's letters because it was too watery to cling to the metal. So in addition to inventing the frame for the letters, he also needed to invent a new kind of ink. He finally devised a deep black, sticky, oily ink that was thick enough to cling to the metal and yet flexible enough to smoothly print the letters onto the paper. We do not know exactly how long it took him to concoct the perfect ink, but I suspect he spent many long days trying batch after batch until he got it right. Even today, all these hundreds of years later, the deep, crisp black of Gutenberg's letters is deeply admired by printers.

So with page and ink ready, Gutenberg needed one thing more: he required a way to press the paper smoothly and evenly down onto the prepared frame, so each of the letters would bite into the paper and leave a nicely-printed mark. To do this, he took another ancient device—a wine press—and adapted it to suit his purposes. A wine press is a heavy plate with a large screw attached to the top. When the screw is turned, the plate presses down on the grapes and squeezes out the juice. Gutenberg saw that he could use that same mechanical idea for printing his pages.

As clever as all of this thinking was, Gutenberg wasn't the first to have these ideas. Smiths in both China and Korea had come up with the idea of movable type many years earlier and had even printed a book or two. But both the Chinese and Korean languages are written with thousands of different symbols, which makes it laborsome and difficult to make enough molds. The European languages, though, such as English or French or Latin, use mainly the twenty-six letters of the alphabet. The simplicity of the alphabet is what made printing truly workable.

And so, on that day in the early 1450s, Gutenberg and his crew of printers set to work. For the last five years they had been preparing, creating the metal letters, collecting enough paper, and building the press itself. They had tested their work by printing a copy of a German poem for practice. Now though, they were going to create something rich and astounding: 180 printed copies of the Holy Bible in Latin.

After each page of movable type had been laid out in the frame, it was coated with the sticky ink and then carefully placed on a small, wheeled table. A fresh piece of clean paper was laid atop the inked letters, and the table was rolled beneath the press. The screw was tightened to lower the heavy plate, which pressed the paper down firmly and smoothly onto the letters. When the screw was loosened and the plate lifted, a workman drew the freshly-printed page off of the letter-frame and hung it on a nearby line to dry. Then the letters were re-inked, a new piece of paper laid down, and the process began again. One hundred-eighty times for each page of the Bible; 1,286 pages in all.

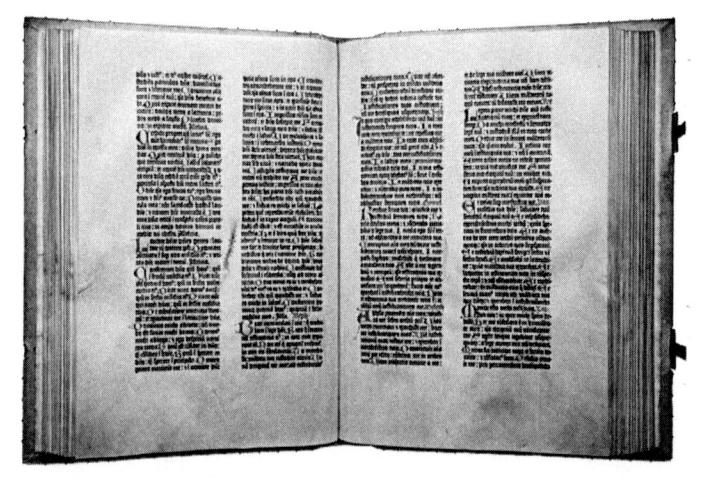

The Gutenberg Bible

It took Johannes Gutenberg only three years to print all of his Bibles. Three years! When it might have taken twenty years for a single monk to copy just one. For Gutenberg, though, three years was too long, despite the astonishing speed of production.

He badly needed to finish the job, because he had borrowed a lot of money to buy and make all the equipment in his print shop and the time had come to pay it back. Each one of his Bibles would sell for 30 *florins,* which was almost three years' wages. Even though only a rich man could afford to buy it, every one of the 180 copies sold as soon as it was printed.

Gutenberg hoped to keep the process a secret, in his hands alone. But he wasn't able to repay his debts, and he lost his print shop, his press, and half of his beautiful Bibles. Soon print shops appeared in other cities in Germany, and then throughout Europe. Where once books had been scarce and precious, now within just a few years, they were common. By the year 1500 more than two hundred cities in Europe had presses, which had printed more than twenty million books. And the more books were printed, the less they cost. During the 1500s a book fair became a yearly event in most cities; almost everyone could afford to buy at least one or two. And in the great castles and monasteries, libraries expanded from one or two shelves to fill entire rooms.

As a consequence of all of this, more and more people learned how to read. Once, reading had been a rather unusual skill reserved for monks and wealthy noblemen. A common smith or farmer would have had no reason to learn his letters, since the only books available were priceless, hand-copied manuscripts chained to the shelf at the church. This meant, too, that most Europeans had little knowledge of the Bible or of philosophy or of the law or of the world beyond Europe, because they could not read it for themselves and were forced to depend solely on what they were told by the Church and by their rulers.

But now, suddenly, knowledge was available to all. Gutenberg's press caused an explosion of words: people were writing books, people were buying books, and people were reading. Suddenly a man in France could read the thoughts of an English philosopher; a German Christian could read the Bible for himself for the first time; an Italian merchant could read about the silk markets in China. The fuse that Gutenberg lit in his workshop would lead to the earth-shaking explosions of the Renaissance, the Reformation, and the Scientific Revolution, which we will learn about in the chapters to come—three earth-shaking ideas in and of themselves, and all fueled by the explosion that Gutenberg ignited.

As for Gutenberg himself, the press did not bring him the wealth he had hoped. After losing his press, he worked in other men's print shops, using the machines that he had invented at no profit to himself. During his lifetime he received no fame or praise for the astounding work that he had done. And yet, in the year 2000, Johannes Gutenberg's invention of the printing press was named the most important event in the last one thousand years. After Gutenberg's Bible, the world would never, ever be the same.

And as you sit there in your warm, comfortable chair or curl up in your bed to read your favorite novel or even reading this book, aren't you glad?

Chapter Twenty-Eight

The Conquest of Constantinople
One empire meets its end at the hands of another

Constantinople was the capital of the Byzantine Empire for more than a thousand years, carrying the banner of "Rome" through the Middle Ages even though Rome itself had fallen centuries before. Enemies had besieged it many times since the long-ago days of Justinian the Great, but the city had stood firm. I suspect you may remember why: perched on a tall peninsula jutting out into the Bosphorus Strait, Constantinople was surrounded on three sides by deep water, and on the fourth it was protected by an enormous, triple-layered wall. The wall bristled with towers from which the city's defenders could fire down arrows and balls of burning tar upon the heads of any attackers. On the city's east edge ran a deep harbor, the Golden Horn, and here, between the city and the opposite shore, the emperors had strung a massive chain just below the surface of the water, past which no enemy ship could sail. Even if it were somehow able to get past, the city's walls were protected by an enormous moat, sixty feet wide.

Formidable though these defenses were, Constantinople was still a magnificent prize, too tempting to resist. The Muslims, especially, had thrown themselves against the city again and again; when Charles Martel had closed the door to

Europe at the Battle of Tours, the armies of Islam had looked to Constantinople. If it were theirs, it would become a secure base from which they could sweep north into Europe and Asia with no worry of attack from the rear. And of course, the city was the New Rome, and rumor abounded that it was stuffed with silver and gold, a wealth that the Muslims would have been happy to take for their own. But their wars against the city had always failed. Its wall remained, whole and unbroken.

The Muslims were not the only people who coveted Constantinople. During the ninth and tenth centuries the city found itself under fire from a very different direction: the north.

These new attackers were the descendants of Viking warriors who had left their homes in Scandinavia to explore eastward. They wandered into the farthest reaches of Europe and, liking what they saw, decided to stay. They had conquered the people living there, the Slavs, and set up their own kingdom. The conquered Slavs called them "Rus" (ROOS), after the name of their leader, Rurik (ROO-reek). A Muslim traveler who visited their lands in 922 described them:

> *I have seen the Rus. . . I have never seen more perfect physical specimens, tall as date palms, blond and ruddy; they wear neither tunics nor caftans, but the men wear a garment which covers one side of the body and leaves a hand free. Each man has an axe, a sword, and a knife, and keeps each by him at all times.*

Like their Viking ancestors, the Rus were canny traders and fearless travelers. It wasn't long at all until they had found their way south, sailing their nimble longships across the Black Sea to Constantinople, which they called "the Great City." There they sold honey, furs, and leather to the city's merchants in return for Byzantine silks, spices, and gems. The Byzantines were pleased to welcome the Rus to their markets, but perhaps the sight of those axes, swords, and knives should have given them pause.

For just before sunset one summer evening in 860, a fleet of longships loaded with warriors appeared most unexpectedly in the Bosphorus Strait and immediately attacked the small towns and villages surrounding the city. They were open and unprotected; the emperor and most of the Byzantine army were off fighting Muslims, and the Rus appeared out of nowhere just like, as one onlooker described them, "a swarm of wasps."

History is a bit unclear as to what happened next. The Byzantine stories say that when the emperor came hurrying home to defend his people, he dipped a holy relic into the waters of the Bosphorus, causing a wild storm to blow. The Rus ships were scattered hither and yon, and by the time they had recovered, the Byzantine army had returned. Defeated, the Rus retreated back across the Black Sea.

But as Alfred the Great could have warned them, and the Byzantines were soon to learn, when Vikings retreat they are merely gathering strength for the next battle.

Over the next two centuries the Rus attacked Constantinople six more times, but despite their considerable enthusiasm and skill as warriors, each time they failed. After that first skirmish, the Byzantines were on their guard. They kept the chain strung across the harbor, they manned the towers, and most of all, they manufactured Greek Fire.

This was their secret weapon, so secret that we still don't know what exactly it was. The histories of those battles describe it; some kind of oil or sticky pitch was loaded into tubes and then sprayed over the enemy "like a fiery whirlwind." Its victims said that it looked like "liquid fire," and it filled the air with smoke and thunder. Greek Fire burned continuously, even across the surface of the sea, and it produced a wall of flame that forced enemy ships to either retreat or be consumed.

Greek Fire was such a terrifying weapon that, at last, the Rus gave up, which is a most unusual outcome in a war with Vikings! As a sign of peace and good will, a Rus prince, Vladimir

I (VLAD-ee-MEER) of Kiev, sent six thousand of his choicest warriors to Constantinople. The Byzantine emperor, who at that time was a man named Basil II, was mightily pleased to receive them, since he had come to suspect the loyalty of his own army. He called the Rus warriors the Varangian (vah-RAN-jee-in) Guard and made them his personal bodyguards.

As time went on, the Varangians kept that post, and once their fierceness in battle became known, they formed a large part of the Byzantine army as well.

For their part, the Rus continued to flourish, so much so that their lands became known as Russia, the kingdom of the Rus, a name which that country keeps to this day.

Constantinople, however, did not flourish. The city had fought off the Rus and the Muslims, but even Greek Fire could not protect it from the Black Death, which stalked through the streets like a lion, killing more than half of the city's people between the years of 1346 and 1349. As the centuries crept by, the city gradually lost its empire; by 1453 the only thing that remained of Byzantium was the city itself. And so it was, that at its weakest hour Constantinople was faced with its strongest foe, the Ottoman Turks.

They seem to have been, at first, just a scattered tribe of nomads, wandering through Asia, scouting for pasture land for their flocks. But in fear of the Mongols who had, as you know, made all of Asia their own, they moved to the west. Eventually, they settled down along the edges of the old Seljuk empire in Asia Minor and acquired a *sultan*—a king—a man called Osman, who gave his name to the people as a whole. They also acquired a religion, for they absorbed the teachings of Muhammad and became Muslims.

As Byzantium's star dimmed, the Ottoman fire blazed more brightly. Slowly throughout the fourteenth century, Ottoman armies captured larger and larger chunks of the lands that had belonged to Constantinople until all of Turkey was theirs. Then they conquered the land of Thrace, which was the country that lies just to the west of the city itself. Thrace had been the last province left of the Byzantine Empire, the last land that was still loyal to Constantinople. Now it fell and the city stood alone, its wall still strong but surrounded on every side by the Ottoman Turks. And they were determined to succeed where none had before; they set out to breach the wall and conquer the city.

The young Byzantine emperor, Constantine XI, called for aid. He sent out messages to London and Paris and Rome, begging the kings of Europe for help. But the centuries of crusades had taken a terrible toll, and the kings of the west had little stomach to once again march to war against a Muslim foe. No help came. And so, because he knew that the city must attack the enemy rather than merely wait in terror behind its walls, Constantine hired an expert to build him some cannons.

By this time in history the invention of the cannon had changed warfare. You have surely seen pictures of these powerful weapons: long, hollow tubes into which a heavy iron ball is loaded along with an explosive charge to send it flying toward the enemy. Constantine's expert, a man whose name was Orban, had built many of them for the princes and dukes back in his home in the Holy Roman Empire. He agreed to do the same for the Byzantines, but only if they paid him an enormous salary. When Constantine refused, unable to come up with that much portable gold, Orban presented himself to the Ottomans instead, promising that he would make them a weapon that could crumble "the walls of Babylon itself."

The Ottoman leader, Sultan Mehmet II (MEH-met), was perfectly willing to give Orban as much gold as he could carry. For the next three months, Orban labored to forge the largest cannon that anyone had ever seen, the "Basilica," which measured 30 feet long and fired a cannon ball that weighed half a ton. It was so heavy that it had to be pulled by a team of sixty oxen, and it grew so hot when it was fired that it could only be used seven times a day.

Meanwhile the Turks laid siege to the city. Food became scarce and the wells ran dry. The people grew desperate, but they refused to surrender even when Mehmet offered to let them go if they would leave all of their possessions behind. Perhaps they did not believe that their city could ever actually fall.

After six weeks of siege, Orban's monstrous cannon had done its work. A section of the city's ancient wall finally began to crumble. Though Constantine threw aside his purple emperor's cloak and personally led his men into the battle, they were not enough to overcome the Ottoman soldiers pouring through the breach in the wall. The dam had been broken and the flood was unstoppable. Constantine was killed as he fought in the streets.

Some people were certain, though, that the emperor did not really die that day. For hundreds of years afterward many believed that Constantine escaped his enemies and hid himself away within the city's wall. There he waits still, the story says, and someday when the city lies once again in Christian hands, he will emerge as its rightful king, like Arthur arising out of the mists of Avalon.

The few who survived the city's fall may have comforted themselves with such a tale, but it was a cold comfort. Most of the citizens were killed; a visitor from Venice, who was there in the city and later wrote about it, said sadly, "All through the day the Turks made a great slaughter of the Christians." The Turkish soldiers emptied houses and shops and then set them on fire, destroying large portions of the city. After three days of this, when the Sultan entered the city, he ordered the looting stopped. The stories tell us that he exclaimed with tears in his eyes, "What a city we have given over to plunder and destruction!"

But tears or no, Mehmet was victorious. He set up his throne in the Hagia Sophia, the beautiful church that Justinian had built, and ordered his men to transform it into a Muslim mosque. And he renamed the city: no longer would it bear the name of Constantine, the Christian emperor of Rome. It would be called instead Istanbul, which means in the Turkish language "where Islam abounds."

The city's defenders had fought with great courage, but Constantinople was gone. Istanbul stood in its place, as it still does today. The Ottoman Empire would last for hundreds of years, until it was at last blown away itself in the whirlwind that was World War II. Empires rise and fall; this is one of the unchanging lessons of history.

The conquest of Constantinople was met with shock and lament in every corner of Europe. It was the end, after almost 1500 years, of the last windswept remnants of the Roman Empire.

Chapter Twenty-Nine

Rebirth

The Renaissance fans the winds of change

When last we visited the city of Florence, we were contemplating the bones of Giotto, the short-statured man who cast such a long and wonderful shadow over the art of painting. But even though Giotto had lived and worked there, for much of the Middle Ages when people thought of Florence, they thought not of art but of money.

In the 1400s Florence was a city of banks. Its golden coins, which were called *florins,* were used to pay for all sorts of endeavors. It took thirty florins, you might remember, to buy a Gutenberg Bible. When the kings of England and France fought the Hundred Years War, they used florins to pay their soldiers and build their ships. When the Church in Rome sought to construct ever more magnificent cathedrals, the bankers in Florence smoothed the way. When merchants and kings and mill owners needed loans, they made their arrangements in Florence. The city was one of the wealthiest places on earth.

At the calm eye of this hurricane of riches lay the Medici (MAY-dee-chee) family. During the first half of the fourteenth century, Cosimo de'Medici (CO-see-MO) owned the largest bank in Florence, and in fact in all of Europe, and with his wealth he gained control of the city's government. Even though

Florence was a democracy and Cosimo was not a king, his florins gave him a very powerful voice. When he spoke, the city listened. And because Cosimo loved art and architecture and poured an unceasing cascade of money into paintings and sculptures and palaces and gardens, other Florentines did the same. The city became a haven for artists.

In 1469 the reins of the family's power were held by Cosimo's 20-year-old grandson, Lorenzo. Like his grandfather, Lorenzo was indisputably the ruler of Florence though he never actually held any elected office. He worked hard to maintain peace with Florence's neighbors and encourage trade with the Holy Roman Empire to the north and the Ottoman Empire to the east. But mostly he focused on art. Although he wrote poems and tried his hand at painting, he did not consider himself an artist. Instead, he was a *patron*.

A patron is a person who gives money and aid to an artist. Through most of the Middle Ages the Church was the patron, by far the most prolific employer of painters, but the Medici family changed that. Lorenzo, especially, supported many artists. He paid generously for paintings and sculptures. He provided living quarters and workshops; the great painter Michelangelo, for example, lived with the Medici family for five years. Lorenzo might introduce a favored artist to his wealthy friends, who paid handsomely to hire the renowned artists of Florence—men like Leonardo da Vinci and Sandro Botticelli (BO-tih-CHELL-ee)—to paint a portrait or decorate a chapel on the family estate. Lorenzo also used his power and wealth to secure important commissions with the Church for his Florentine artists, such as painting the Sistine (SIS-teen) Chapel in Rome.

In making it easier for artists to live—for who can paint a masterpiece if he is worrying about buying bread?—Lorenzo was fanning the breeze that began a century earlier with the astonishing paintings of Giotto. Giotto showed the painters of Italy how to make their work come alive, a rebirth of the beauties of the ancient world's lifelike statues. Lorenzo gave the artists a safe and prosperous place to work, and as a result Florence became a fountain of new and beautiful art.

In Florence artists began to experiment for the first time with different kinds of paints. By mixing powdered colors with oil, they could create a paint that would dry incredibly slowly, so that, unlike a quick-drying fresco, an oil painting could be worked and adjusted and changed over the course of many weeks. They also began to experiment with light and shadow—Leonardo da Vinci called this *chiaroscuro* (KEE-ar-ohs-COO-roh), which comes from the Italian words for "light" and "dark." The paintings became ever more realistic; they looked *three-dimensional* rather than flat, as if the painting were a stage filled with light and air and you could step right inside of it.

The rebirth of art was joined, like two horses in harness, to a rebirth of ideas. During the same years that Giotto was re-creating the realistic art of Greece and Rome, another Italian was re-discovering their books. His name was Francesco Petrarca (fran-CHESS-ko pe-TRAR-kah), though nowadays we know him as Petrarch. Though he had been born in Italy, in the countryside outside of Florence, he had spent his youth in France dutifully studying law and religion as his father required. Those studies involved a deep knowledge of Latin, since both the law and the Church conducted their business in that language, and Petrarch soon found himself much more interested in the Latin itself than in the Church doctrine or records of old lawsuits. He was developing, as he remarked later, "an unquenchable thirst for literature."

As soon as he was able, he returned to Italy and entered the service of the Church; he became an *envoy* for the pope, which is a sort of diplomat. It was the perfect occupation from Petrarch's point of view, because it allowed him to travel all over Italy; to France, Spain, and Constantinople; and all across the Holy Roman Empire. Everywhere he went, he searched for ancient

Latin manuscripts, immeasurably pleased when he found one, no matter how tattered. Eventually he collected books of poetry and science, medicine and astronomy, and even some letters penned by the famous Roman writer Cicero (SIS-er-oh), which he rescued from a pile of scrap paper.

As he studied them, he grew astonished at the thoughts that they contained. He admired the minds of the ancient writers, their curiosity about the world, the cleverness of their observations, and their stirring, dramatic poetry. He began to believe that darkness and ignorance had shadowed Europe since the fall of Rome because these writings and thinkers had been forgotten. He wrote to a friend:

> *Each famous author of antiquity whom I recover places a new offence and another cause of dishonor to the charge of earlier generations, who, not satisfied with their own disgraceful barrenness, permitted the fruit of other minds, and the writings that their ancestors had produced by toil and application, to perish through insufferable neglect. Although they had nothing of their own to hand down to those who were to come after, they robbed posterity of its ancestral heritage.*

But despite these gloomy words, Petrarch was convinced that all was not lost. Men were still men, after all; if they had, in the days of the ancients, reached such heights of mind and heart, surely they could do so again. This belief—that humans are capable of greatness, and that each man should aspire to greatness and should study the greatness in other men—is called *humanism*. The ancient Greeks had said that "man is the measure of all things." Many historians call Petrarch the "father of humanism," because he introduced that idea back into the world. He was the midwife at its rebirth—the starting point, those same historians say, of the period in history that we call the Renaissance.

What does it mean to say that man is the measure of things? For the scholars and thinkers of the Renaissance, it meant looking back to the great thinkers of the past and learning from them. It meant that people should see themselves as individuals, who should strive to learn and grow. It meant that men should immerse themselves in the world around them, rather than retreat from it into a monastery. It meant that people should try to discover for themselves the answers to life's questions, rather than depending on their rulers or on the Church.

The Renaissance rebirth was greatly hastened, strangely enough, by the death of Constantinople; for that old city had been home to many churches which had carefully preserved, for centuries, an enormous stockpile of scrolls written in ancient Greek. The city's scholars had fled the Turks, carrying the scrolls with them, and so brought into Europe a treasure trove: Greek copies of the Bible, books about astronomy and navigation, the writings of early Church fathers, textbooks for mathematics and architecture. Eager scholars set to work copying them, translating them into Latin or English or French, and sending them to the closest print shop. Petrarch had needed to travel the world to find his ancient texts; now, thanks to the Ottoman Turks and Gutenberg's press, they could be purchased at a bookseller's stall in any city market.

The Renaissance blossomed in Florence, with Giotto's art and Lorenzo de'Medici's patronage and Petrarch's tattered scrolls, and then spread to all of Europe. As it transformed the way people thought about themselves, it also changed their daily lives. Without the feudal pyramid to keep everyone frozen in place, there were many more craftsmen and merchants, artists and shopkeepers. They were a *middle class,* neither noblemen nor peasants. They lived in the cities rather than on farms out in the countryside, and they had money of their own, perhaps not much, but enough to make their lives a bit more comfortable: to buy nicer clothing, better food, a few books. They sent their children to schools, where the teachers taught them to read and write, to study Latin and poetry, grammar and music, arithmetic and astronomy.

Most of all, they were no longer citizens of the Middle Ages. The Renaissance beckoned them forward into the modern world.

Chapter Thirty

Reformation

*With his pen and his hammer,
Martin Luther seeks to change the Church*

One autumn evening in 1517, in the town of Wittenberg in Germany, the thick wooden door of All Saints' Church suddenly rang with the steady blows of a hammer. A man dressed in monk's robes stood on the steps outside, his face grim and determined as he drove a nail through a sheaf of papers. They were covered with a long, numbered list, written in Latin and printed in thick black ink: 95 *theses*—statements that he believed to be true. By posting them on the church door, he was challenging scholars and churchmen to read his list and refute his statements if they could. His name was Martin Luther. He meant to begin an argument, but what he started instead was a revolution: the Reformation of the Church.

Our Castle of the Middle Ages had many rooms but only one Church. Christianity had ruled Europe for more than a thousand years, led by the pope in Rome, and the Church was an essential part of every person's life. Be he a king or a beggar, a shopkeeper or a knight at arms, the Church held the keys to salvation in the next life and well-being in this one. No one could baptize his child, marry his wife, or bury his dead without the Church's blessing.

simplycharlottemason.com

But as we have seen, the Renaissance was opening doors in people's minds. They were reading books and moving to the cities to open shops; they were sending their young men to universities and making more comfortable lives for themselves. They could move and change and grow. And as people grew in wealth and opportunity and education, they turned their eyes more and more to the pursuit of those very things.

The Church was no different.

Just like the people around them, the Church's clergy gradually increased the comfort and safety of their lives. Many of them began to love the trappings of wealth: fine fabrics for their clothes, expensive furnishings for their houses, delicious food and drink on their tables. The Church itself, too, was ever in need of money, at first to support crusades and missionary efforts but also, as time went by, to build larger and more beautiful cathedrals. The Church had always received gifts from its people; now that wasn't enough. Some new way must be found to increase the coins in the Church's offering boxes.

At first Church officials decided to make money by selling *missals*. These were the prayers and chants used in church services, printed in conveniently-sized little books so worshipers could follow along and read the service for themselves. But when this idea first took root, many people were still not able to read, and few of the missals were sold.

So the churchmen sought something more lucrative, something that would appeal to everyone and bring in a constant flow of gold. Someone within the Church came up with a startling idea: what people really wanted was deliverance from sin; could the Church perhaps sell it to them?

The Church had always provided paths for forgiveness in the form of penance, such as Pope Urban offered to the first crusaders, or as *indulgences*. An indulgence was granted to a sinner as a reprieve from the punishment his sins demanded, but indulgences had always had to be earned by serving the needy or making a pilgrimage. During the Renaissance, the Church decided to sell them. Any sinner who could afford the price could purchase forgiveness for his offenses whenever he liked.

At first the Church used the increased income for good causes: hospitals were built, orphans were cared for, missionaries were sent out. But as often happens when great sums of money come into the hands of powerful people, the flow of gold was soon diverted to many other less holy purposes. On every level, from lowly monks to the highest officials in Rome, churchmen began to take advantage of the Church's new wealth by enriching themselves. In the beginning, writes one historian, the leaders of the Church "had withdrawn from the world and its temptations. Now they became indistinguishable from the nobility."

Many men entered the Church only to further their own ambitions, to live in luxury and indulge their own pleasures. Such a one was Giovanni de'Medici, second son of Lorenzo de'Medici, whom you have already met. He was elected Pope Leo X in Rome in the year 1513. Upon receiving word of his election, he is rumored to have said, "Since God has given us the papacy, let us enjoy it."

For Leo X, enjoyment came in the form of laughter, entertainment, and art. He filled his court with Renaissance humanists and valued wit and cleverness more highly than goodness. His palace thronged with dancers, actors, jesters, and musicians, and he funneled a constant stream of gold into the purses of painters and sculptors, for, like his father, he was a passionate patron of art. In just eight years, he drained the Roman Church's treasury dry.

A few years into his reign as pope, Leo decided to undertake a new and grand project. He would rebuild the Church of St. Peter, where Charlemagne himself had been crowned, and make it a truly magnificent cathedral. This was perhaps a worthy goal, but there was no money to pay for it. Undaunted, Leo turned to a source of income that had never failed.

On March 15, in 1517, Leo issued a proclamation. Anyone who donated money to his cathedral would be granted an indulgence. Help me build St. Peter's, he said, and "I will absolve you from all thy sins, transgressions, and excesses, howsoever enormous they may be."

Churchmen were dispatched throughout Europe to proclaim Leo's offer. Among them was a monk named Johann Tetzel (YO-han TET-sel), who made his way to Germany, selling the indulgence everywhere he went. In his enthusiasm, he began to hint to his customers that anyone who purchased this indulgence would be free not only of past sins but of any future transgressions as well.

When he reached the town of Wittenberg, he found many eager buyers. But a few were not certain; how could they buy forgiveness for sins they hadn't yet committed? They decided to ask the opinion of a local monk, one they knew well and trusted: Martin Luther.

Luther lived and worked at the University of Wittenberg. He was a teacher of theology, which means the study of the nature of God. In the course of teaching such an important subject, Luther had spent many hours reading and studying the Bible, seeking to know God better. And as he studied, he came to believe that God's forgiveness could not be bought or sold. God gave forgiveness freely when a person came to Him in faith. Faith alone was the key to salvation, not good works or penance or obedience to the Church. Luther was appalled by Tetzel and his indulgences.

So he began to write—ninety-five reasons why the Church was wrong, why indulgences were evil, why people were being led astray from the truth of God. He knew that All Saint's Church was expecting a large crowd of people that autumn, coming to view a display of holy relics, and he wanted them to be greeted at the door by his list of arguments. He gave copies of the list to several of his friends, as well, hoping that they would join him in discussing this problem. One of them decided that the discussion should go further still, and he gave the list to a printer. From there it passed from hand to hand, and within a few months, Luther's *Ninety-Five Theses* had spread to every country in Europe.

Luther was not alone in questioning the Church. His voice was quickly joined by others who were equally concerned. None of them sought to destroy the Church or to flee away from it; most of them were churchmen themselves, who had given their lives in service to God. They wanted to *reform* the Church, to take it by the hand and lead it away from its preoccupation with wealth and luxury and back to the way it had been in the beginning. They wanted to remove the barriers that the Church had put between God and man by requiring penance and ritual and good deeds, and preach instead a different doctrine: that salvation could be had by faith alone. They wanted people to be able to go to God themselves without resorting to the Church's priests.

News of Luther's writings soon reached the ears of Pope Leo. In 1518 he summoned Luther to appear before some of his officials in a meeting called a *diet,* which is rather like a trial. For three days Luther stood before a panel of Church judges, defending his words as the truth that he had gained from studying the Bible. The churchmen cautioned him that he was in danger of *heresy,* which was the crime of contradicting the Church's established doctrine. But despite their warnings, Luther refused to change his opinions.

In 1519 the pope declared that Luther's writings were "scandalous and offensive to pious ears." He issued a decree that Luther must *recant,* or deny, the things that he had been teaching. Luther again refused and in January of 1520 Pope Leo excommunicated him: he declared that Luther was no longer a part of the Church. He also declared that Luther's *Ninety-Five Theses* was banned; any Christian caught reading it was committing a sin by this decree. Luther remained convinced of the truth he had learned. That same year he was called before another diet, this one conducted by the Holy Roman emperor himself. Luther was brought into the courtroom and shown his writings laid out along a table. "Are these your books?" he was asked. "Do you stand by what they say?" Knowing that he would be declared an outlaw, Luther faced his judges and said, defiantly, "Here I stand. God help me. I can do no other."

Luther was standing in protest of the Church; he and the others who shared his beliefs came to be called Protestants, and many flocked to join them. They became a church of their own. From this point forward the church—the people who were followers of Christianity—would be split in two. Some would continue to follow the Church in Rome, and they are called Roman Catholics. Some would turn instead to the Protestant Church, which has divided up over the centuries into a number of different groups: Lutherans, Baptists, Methodists, Episcopalians, Presbyterians.

The Reformation, then, did not succeed in reforming the Roman Church; instead it formed a different church altogether. Little did Martin Luther know, when he nailed his ninety-five theses to the door of the church in Wittenberg, that the strokes of his hammer would shake the Church apart and build something entirely new.

Chapter Thirty-One

Revolution

Nicholas Copernicus invents a new universe

For most of the people who lived in our Castle of the Middle Ages, the sky arching over their heads was a mystery. They watched the sun climb over the rim of the world in the morning and sail across the sky to disappear in colorful fire at dusk. The moon soared overhead as well, changing its shape each night as it flew, and the stars wheeled across the sky in a constantly shifting picture-show. All of this dancing, weaving motion while the earth under their feet stayed rock solid and still.

The astronomers, learned men who studied the sky, believed that the earth lay fixed at the center of the universe and around it spun a giant, transparent sphere—a hollow glass ball embedded with the glowing points of light that were the stars. Within it, nested together like a set of Russian dolls, were other spheres, one for each of the planets and the sun and, closest to Earth, the moon. They were all made of a delicate crystal called *aether* (EE-ther), and some men believed that the spheres created a beautiful, humming music as they spun, all of them at different speeds, around the unmoving earth at their center.

The astronomers of the Middle Ages had not come up with these ideas on their own. Indeed, this vision of the earth and the sun, which is called the *geocentric model* of the universe, had been devised by the great thinkers of ancient Greece, who sought to explain the movement of the stars and planets, moon and sun, that they observed in the sky overhead. The spinning, clockwork spheres, complicated and elegant, provided an answer that seemed to make perfect sense. This idea, the work of several centuries of Greek astronomy, was written down by a philosopher and scientist named Ptolemy (TALL-uh-mee) in a book called the *Almagest*. Ptolemy's book was one of the first rediscovered by the scholars of the Renaissance, who were entranced with its ideas. It explained the heavens! Ptolemy's book was accepted as the only possible truth.

But on the rooftop of a house in Italy, a young student named Nicholas Copernicus (cuh-PER-ni-kiss) gazed up at the stars and saw, not the arching roof of a great sphere embedded with sparkling light, but many individual stars, each moving on its own. He began to wonder if perhaps, after all, the Greeks were wrong. He began to think about revolution.

By the time he arrived in Italy, in 1496, to study at the university in the city of Bologna, Nicholas Copernicus had already been a student for many years. He had been born into a well-to-do family in Poland, and when his father had died and Nicholas was only ten years old, his uncle had arranged for the boy to go to school. First he had attended the Cathedral School in a nearby town, and then, when he turned eighteen, he had spent four years at the University of Krakow in Poland's capital city. His uncle wished him to study law and philosophy, and Nicholas agreeably did so, but the books that he purchased during those years, which are now kept carefully preserved, show that his interests had begun to swerve into an entirely different direction. Along with a few books of law, Nicholas collected book after book about mathematics and astronomy, and his handwritten notes from those years show that he read them all.

Nicholas traveled to Italy at the direction of his uncle, who instructed him to spend three years studying the laws of the Christian Church. Then, his uncle hoped, Nicholas would be able to become a *canon*, a kind of church official, back home in Poland. The canons received a good salary from the Church; this would be an excellent way for Nicholas to make a living.

Nicholas obediently signed the register in the University of Bologna, listing himself as a student of law, but just as before, he revealed his true interests almost at once. He attended many lectures, but they were given by mathematicians rather than professors of law. Very soon he met Bologna's most famous astronomer, a man named Domenico Maria Novara da Ferrara (doh-MEN-i-CO ma-REE-ah no-VAR-uh da fer-RAH-ruh), and before long he was living at Novara's house and working as his assistant. Night after night the teacher and student would climb to the rooftop to watch the stars overhead and observe the motion of the moon. It was here, on Novara's rooftop, that Nicholas' doubts began to grow. He was no longer certain that Ptolemy was right.

For three years in Bologna, Nicholas read everything he could find. He learned ancient Greek and read the thoughts of the ancient philosophers, discovering different ideas about the way the universe was organized and arranged. One thinker in particular, named Aristarchos of Samos (AH-ri-STAR-kus of SAH-mos), had suggested two thousand years before that it was the sun, and not the earth, that sat at the center of things.

Could this be true? Was it possible that the earth, which seemed so solid and still, might actually be moving? Throughout all the rest of his years in Italy, this idea simmered in Nicholas' mind.

There were others who questioned the truth of Ptolemy's geocentric model, particularly in Muslim lands, where Ptolemy's book had been translated into Arabic in ancient times and had never been lost. In 1020, for example, a Muslim astronomer named Abu Said al-Sijzi (AH-boo SAH-eed al-SEE-ja) suggested that the earth rotates and that "the motion we see is due to the earth's movement, and not to that of the sky." A few others, in their observatories in the deserts of Arabia and Persia, wrote books that questioned the accepted truth that the earth must be the center of the universe.

Perhaps in his wide-ranging study, Nicholas read some of these. In any case, when he returned to Poland at the age of 30, ready at last to take up his job as a church canon, he had already concluded that Ptolemy and the Greeks were indeed mistaken and the truth must be found.

For the next 40 years, until his death in 1543, Nicholas lived quietly in Poland, fulfilling his duties to the Church and to his uncle. But while his life was quiet and predictable, he continued to study the sky, and his thoughts were whirling into giddy, new circles. By 1514 he felt ready at last to share a new view of the universe.

In a little hand-written book, barely forty pages long, he set forth the ideas that had been swirling through his thoughts for so long. They went like this:

The earth is not the center of the universe.

The sun is the center of the universe.

The stars are actually individual suns of their own, and they are very far away.

The stars and the sun seem to move because the earth is rotating.

The earth, and all the other planets, revolve around the sun.

This revolution, once per year, is the cause of the four seasons.

Nicholas' little book did not contain the complex mathematics that were needed to prove these ideas. He saw these forty pages as just a sort of sketch, a mere outline of the work that was to come. He showed it to a few of his most trusted friends, fearing all the while that he would be mocked or perhaps even severely criticized. But his friends must have encouraged him, because he set about turning those forty pages into his greatest work, a book of revolution.

By this time Nicholas had moved to a different house on the outskirts of the city, where the sky was darker at night and thus better for watching the stars. A small tower jutted up from the roof, and there Nicholas collected his observations. He had only his eyes, of course, since the telescope would not be invented until twenty years after his death, and the sort of simple measuring instruments that Ptolemy himself had used 1500 years before. From his tower he made detailed notes of the movements of Mars and Saturn, Venus and Mercury, and the position of the stars when compared to the sun. He measured the moon as it wandered through its phases; he created charts and diagrams and spent long hours working the complex mathematics that described the motion he saw.

By 1532 he had finished writing his book, *The Revolutions of the Celestial Spheres*. It explained as thoroughly as possible Nicholas' certainty that the earth orbits the sun. But though the work was done and the book written, he did not publish it. He was afraid that he would be punished for suggesting such new and startling ideas, especially by the Church. After all, the Church clearly taught that God had created the heavens and the earth, and surely God would have put the earth, as His highest work, at the very center of His creation. Nicholas feared that the Church would look harshly upon him for suggesting otherwise.

So rather than sending it off to the printing press, he showed it instead to a few more of his friends. Seven years went by as word slowly leaked out that Nicholas Copernicus believed the earth was moving. But despite his fears, he received no punishments or condemnation. Instead, whispers reached him that people, even learned men within the Church, wanted to hear more.

Meanwhile, in 1539, a German mathematician named Georg Rheticus (JAY-org REH-ti-kus) came to study Nicholas' ideas. He believed very strongly that those ideas were correct. He urged Nicholas to go ahead and publish his book and, finally, in 1543 Nicholas relented. By this time he was very sick, and perhaps he finally agreed to send his book out into the wider world because he knew he would soon pass beyond the reach of any critics.

Rheticus supervised the printing. The final pages were completed in May of 1543 and brought to Nicholas as he lay, weak and dying, in his bed. Legend tells us that as he drew his final breaths, he looked upon the printed pages of his book, smiled, and died in peace.

The Revolutions of the Celestial Spheres was not an immediate success. Everyone had believed for so long that the earth was the center of the universe, and many people were not able to understand the careful mathematics that Nicholas used to prove that the earth was actually moving. The Church, as Nicholas feared, disapproved of the book, afraid that it would lead people away from the truth of God as the Creator. In 1616, in fact, his book was banned, just like Martin Luther's *Ninety-Five Theses;* the pope proclaimed that no true Christian could read it.

But slowly, despite the ban, Nicholas' ideas began to gain ground, because other astronomers could see for themselves that it explained, in ways that Ptolemy's book did not, the motion of the moon and planets in the sky and the seasons on the earth. Other men built on Nicholas' work, using his mathematics and his ideas to sharpen their understanding of the earth and sky. And so, in telling the world that the world was moving—that the earth made a revolution of the sun—Nicholas started a revolution of his own.

Today, looking back at history, we call it the Scientific Revolution. Because Nicholas had the courage and the curiosity to question an idea that had remained stuck in place for more than 1500 years, other thinkers began to question as well. After all, if Ptolemy had been wrong about astronomy, perhaps some of the other old ideas were wrong! Scholars began to delve more deeply into mathematics and chemistry, into the study of human bodies and all other living things, into the forces that caused water to flow and volcanoes to erupt. Beginning with Nicholas' book in 1543, thinkers and philosophers became scientists, and history swept forward out of the Middle Ages into a new world. The Modern Age had begun.

Chapter Thirty-Two

One Thousand Years of History

*At the end of a long journey together,
we bid farewell to the Castle*

When we first saw the Castle in 476 A.D., it was new and rough, just taking shape amid the dust and chaos of Rome's long fall. Some of its chambers were already in place: the Byzantine emperors were strengthening Constantinople's mighty wall and the Saxons were stirring on the cold northern plains of Germany, looking across the sea to Britain's unprotected shores.

But in those first years of the Middle Ages, many of the Castle's trappings still lay far in the future. The monks had yet to dip pen into ink and begin the labor of copying the Word of God, and the Franks had not crossed the Rhine, and over in Arabia Mohammad had not been visited by dreams. The Castle was a single tower, perhaps, surrounded by a bailey wall.

By 800 A.D. the Castle had grown. Now its walls were thick, and the keep at its center housed the lord and his family. Its chambers were filled with Vikings' longships and Frankish battle-axes and, in a corner far away from all the rest, the brilliant green feathers of a quetzal bird. The Great Hall rang with the shouts of battle and the clash of swords as Charles Martel battled the armies of Islam and Charlemagne gripped the pommel of Joyeuse and settled the emperor's crown more firmly on his brow.

simplycharlottemason.com

In 1200 the walls of the Castle's many chambers were hung with the portraits of kings: Alfred the Great, William of Normandy, Richard Lionheart, and Genghis Khan. Powerful warriors stalked the halls, knights and samurai, while Saladin looked toward Jerusalem and Robin Hood lingered in the shadow of an English oak, restlessly waiting for his king to come home.

The Castle of 1400 had begun to change. Giotto's paintings graced the walls, and Petrarch's tattered manuscripts lay open for all to read. Marco Polo returned from his journeys bearing news of a wider world. The gleam of gold beckoned from Mali and Timbuktu, and in Sweden the oath of freedom had been sworn. The kings of France and England marched toward a war of a hundred years. In Portugal Prince Henry was still a little child, but he was already hungry to perform great deeds.

And then in 1453, our Castle was shaken to its core by the enormous cannon of the Ottoman Turks. Every soul in the Castle cowered in shock and fear as they heard the news: Constantinople was no more.

But a fresh breeze was blowing through the Castle's many rooms. New doors and windows were flung open as the halls echoed with the thud of the printing press and the determined strokes of Luther's hammer. High above, Copernicus sat on the roof and watched the planets gently circle the sun.

What a marvelous place it has been to visit! We've walked together through a thousand years of history; we've watched empires rise and fall. We've seen kings both noble and dreadful, and craftsmen and artists who changed the world. We turned our eyes from the tragedy of sickness and war, to rejoice in the triumphs of freedom and forgiveness.

Though we are leaving it now and saying farewell, remember that you can always return. The Castle stands ready to welcome you back and invites you to linger anew in the splendors of its many rooms.

Endnotes

Chapter 1: The Long Fall

St. Jerome's lament upon the fall of Rome is taken from William James. *The Decline and Fall of the Roman Empire*. Westport, Conn: Greenwood, 2004. p. 144.

The description of Attila the Hun is taken from the historian Jordanes, cited by William Stearns Davis, ed., *Readings in Ancient History: Illustrative Extracts from the Sources,* 2 Vols. Boston: Allyn and Bacon, 1912–1913. p. 322.

Chapter 2: Justinian the Great

The description of the Hippodrome comes from *Robert of Clari: The Conquest of Constantinople,* translated by Edgar Holmes McNeal. Columbia University Press, 1964. p. 109.

The stirring words of Theodora's are attributed to her by the historian Procopius: Procopius, *History of the Wars,* I, xxiv, translated by H.B. Dewing, New York: Macmillan, 1914, pp. 219–230, slightly abridged and reprinted in Leon Barnard and Theodore B. Hodges, *Readings in European History.* New York: Macmillan, 1958. pp. 52–55.

Theophanes describes the Nika Riots in his *Chronicle*: Theophanes, Cyril A. Mango, Roger Scott, and Geoffrey Greatrex. *The Chronicle of Theophanes Confessor: Byzantine and Near Eastern History,* A.D. 284–813. Oxford: Clarendon, 1997. p. 280.

Chapter 3: King Arthur and the Saxons

The quotations from Hengist and the *Historia Brittonum* are taken from J. A. Giles, ed. (1847) *Nennius: Historia Brittonum. The History of the Britons (Historia Brittonum).* Robbins Library Digital Projects at http://d.lib.rochester.edu/.

The quotation regarding the Battle of Badon is taken from the Annals of Wales, *the Annales Cambriae,* which can be found at the Medieval Sourcebook hosted by Fordham University at http://legacy.fordham.edu/Halsall/sbook.asp.

Chapter 4: The Monastery

All quotations taken from Benedict and Timothy Fry. *The Rule of St. Benedict in English.* New York: Vintage Books, 1998.

Chapter 5: The Earliest Explorers

The quotations from Eric the Red are taken from a digital copy of *Voyages to Vinland,* a translation of the Icelandic sagas by Einar Haugen, New York: Alfred A. Knopf, 1942. It can be found at https://archive.org/details/voyagestovinland013593mbp.

Chapter 6: Making a Nation

The quotation is from Gregory of Tours, a primary source for Clovis' life. Gregory of Tours. *The History of the Franks.* Harmondsworth: Penguin, 1974. p. 143.

Chapter 8: Charles the Hammer

The words from Tariq-ibn-Zayid's sermon to his troops are recorded by Suzanne McIntire and William E. Burns. *Speeches in World History.* New York: Facts on File, 2009. p. 85. Some traditions also tell us that, before giving this speech, Tariq ordered that the ships upon which they had arrived be burnt, so that his soldiers would have no hope of retreat.

Chapter 9: Charlemagne

Quotations from Einhard are taken from his *The Life of Charlemagne,* translated by Samuel Epes Turner in 1880. Einhard wrote his *Life* shortly after Charlemagne's death. The entire text can be accessed at Fordham University's superb Medieval Sourcebook: http://legacy.fordham.edu/Halsall/sbook.asp.

The sword Joyeuse is described in "The Song of Roland," an epic medieval poem composed in France in the eleventh century. The English translation: Dorothy L. Sayers, *The Song of Roland.* Harmondsworth, Eng.: Penguin, 1957. p. 147.

Chapter 10: The Rushing North Wind

The lines of poetry describing the cruel "North Wind" were

written by the Irish monk and teacher Sedulius, as quoted by P. H. Sawyer, *The Oxford Illustrated History of the Vikings*. Oxford: Oxford University Press, 1997. p. 95.

The quotation from Alcuin is taken from Killeen, Richard. *A Brief History of Ireland*. Philadelphia, PA: Running, 2012. p. 30.

The little Viking poem comes from the *Havamal*, the "Sayings of Odin," a collection of verses and wise bits of advice from the Viking Age. This particular verse is #75. An online translation of the *Havamal* can be found here: http://pitt.edu/~dash/havamal.html.

Chapter 11: The Meeting at Egbert's Stone

The description of the battle is taken from a biography of Alfred written during his lifetime by Bishop Asser, translated by Alfred Smyth: Asser, John, Alfred P. Smyth, and Byrhtferth. *The Medieval Life of King Alfred the Great: A Translation and Commentary on the Text* Attributed to Asser. Houndmills, Basingstoke, Hampshire: Palgrave, 2002. pp. 26–27.

The quotation from Charles Dickens may be found in his charming book *A Child's History of England*. New York: Harper & Bros., 1854. p. 16. Available to read in its entirety at http://gutenberg.org.

Chapter 13: The Battle of Hastings

The details regarding William's preparation for invasion come from an account by a poet named Robert Wace, who lived in the 12th century. He claimed that these eyewitness accounts had been passed down in his family, and he wrote about them in the *Roman de Rou*, a digital copy of which can be found at http://archive.org.

William of Poitiers, friend and chaplain to William the Conqueror, wrote an account of the battle, called the *Gesta Guillelmi*, which reports William's stirring words to his men. This quotation from that account was taken from the University of Chicago's excellent history website:

http://penelope.uchicago.edu/~grout/encyclopaedia_romana/britannia/anglo-saxon/hastings/william.html.

The quotation describing Harold's "hewing to pieces the Normans" comes from "The Song of the Battle of Hastings," written (possibly) by a French bishop in the eleventh century. Quotation taken from "Harold and the Arrow" at http://www.dot-domesday.me.uk/arrow.htm.

Chapter 15: The Way of the Warrior

Mototada's letter taken from "The Last Statement of Torii Mototada," found here: https://tgace.wordpress.com/2008/11/03/the-last-statement-of-torii-mototada/.

Statements regarding the Code of Bushido are taken from Inazō Nitobe, *Bushido: The Soul of Japan.* Tokyo: Kodansha International, 2002. p. 37.

Chapter 16: The Cross Upon the Shield

Pope Urban II's promise of absolution is quoted by Jonathan Phillips in his article "The Crusades: A Complete History" in *History Today,* Volume 65, Issue 5, May 2015.

Chapter 17: Lionheart and Robin Hood

Richard's boast that he bows to no one but God can be found in many accounts of the king's life. It is one of his more famous utterances.

Richard's warning to John is quoted by Dan Jones. *The Plantagenets: The Warrior Kings and Queens Who Made England.* New York: Penguin, 2014. p. 121.

Chapter 20: The Mongols

The verses describing Borte's rescue are taken from the "Secret History of the Mongols," quoted by Frederick W. Mote, *Imperial China, 900-1800.* Cambridge, MA: Harvard University Press, 1999. p. 418.

Chapter 21: The Travels of Marco Polo

All quotations from Marco Polo taken from his book: Marco

Polo, A. C. Moule, and Paul Pelliot. *The Description of the World.* New York: AMS, 1976. Since the invention of the printing press, Marco's book has never been out of print.

Chapter 22: Salt, Books, and Gold

The saying that wisdom can only be found in Timbuktu comes from an old West African proverb, which is cited by *Timbuktu Heritage* at http://timbuktuheritage.org.

Chapter 23: A Fresh Breeze

All quotations from Vasari are translated by Adrienne DeAngelis and are taken from her online version of *Lives of the Artists,* found here: http://members.efn.org/~acd/vite/VasariLives.html.

Chapter 24: Freedom Fighter

The version of the Rutli oath translated in this chapter was taken from this interesting little book by Diccon Bewes: *Swisscellany: Facts & Figures about Switzerland.* Basel: Bergli, 2012. p. 68.

Chapter 25: The Black Prince, the Black Death, and the White Knight of Orleans

Edward's letter to Philip of France is quoted by Susan Wise Bauer. *The History of the Renaissance World: From the Rediscovery of Aristotle to the Conquest of Constantinople.* New York: W.W. Norton, 2013. p. 499.

Chapter 28: The Conquest of Constantinople

The Arab traveler was Ahmad Ibn Fadlan, famous for his accounts of his many journeys. His description of the Rus is quoted by Gwyn Jones: *A History of the Vikings.* London: Oxford University Press, 1968. p. 164.

The "swarm of wasps" comment comes from the Patriarch of Constantinople, Photius I. Some sources quote him as saying a "swarm of bees."

The doctor's eyewitness statement is quoted by Ruth Feldman, in *The Fall of Constantinople.* Minneapolis, MN: Twenty-First Century, 2008. p. 100.

Chapter 29: Rebirth

The quotation from Petrarch is one of his more famous sayings and can be found in numerous sources. I took it from the short biography of Petrarch in the New World Encyclopedia: http://www.newworldencyclopedia.org/entry/Petrarch.

Chapter 30: Reformation

The quote regarding the clergy being indistinguishable from the nobility is taken from William Manchester. *A World Lit Only by Fire: The Medieval Mind and the Renaissance: Portrait of an Age.* Boston: Little, Brown, 1992. p. 41.

Chapter 31: Revolution

The Islamic astronomer Abu Sa'id Sijzi is discussed here: Seyyed Hossein Nasr. *An Introduction to Islamic Cosmological Doctrines.* New York: SUNY Press. p. 135. I accessed this book through Google Books: https://books.google.com/books?isbn=0791415155.

Bibliography

Baker, G. P. *Justinian: The Last Roman Emperor.* New York, NY: Cooper Square, 2002. Print.

Barber, Richard W. *Myths and Legends of the British Isles.* Rochester, NY: Boydell, 1999. Print.

Benedict, , and Timothy Fry. *The Rule of St. Benedict in English.* New York: Vintage Books, 1998. Print.

Brengle, Richard L. *Arthur, King of Britain: History, Chronicle, Romance, & Criticism, with Texts in Modern English, from Gildas to Malory.* New York: Appleton-Century-Crofts, 1964. Print.

Brownworth, Lars. *The Sea Wolves: A History of the Vikings.* U.K.: Crux, 2014. Print.

Creasy, Edward Shepherd. *The Fifteen Decisive Battles of the World: From Marathon to Waterloo.* New York: Dorset, 1987. Print.

Currie, Stephen. *Miracles, Saints, and Superstition: The Medieval Mind.* Detroit, MI: Lucent Books, 2007. Print.

Danziger, Danny, and John Gillingham. *1215: The Year of Magna Carta.* New York: Simon & Schuster, 2004. Print.

Davis, William Stearns, ed., *Readings in Ancient History: Illustrative Extracts from the Sources, 2 Vols.* Boston: Allyn and Bacon, 1912–1913. Print.

Dickens, Charles. *A Child's History of England.* New York: Harper & Bros., 1854. Print.

Ermatinger, James William. *The Decline and Fall of the Roman Empire.* Westport, CT: Greenwood, 2004. Print.

Esposito, John L. *The Oxford History of Islam.* New York, NY: Oxford University Press, 1999. Print.

Feldman, Ruth. *The Fall of Constantinople.* Minneapolis, MN: Twenty-First Century, 2008. Print.

Gregory of Tours. *The History of the Franks.* Harmondsworth: Penguin, 1974. Print.

Howard, Nicole. *The Book: The Life Story of a Technology.* Westport, CT: Greenwood, 2005. Print.

Howarth, David Armine. *1066: The Year of the Conquest.* New York: Viking, 1978. Print.

Hughes, Ian. *Belisarius: The Last Roman General.* Yardley, PA: Westholme, 2009. Print.

Ingram, James, translator. *The Anglo-Saxon Chronicle.* London: Everyman Press, 1912. Print.

James, Edward. *The Franks.* Oxford, UK: B. Blackwell, 1988. Print.

James, Edward. *The Origins of France: From Clovis to the Capetians, 500-1000.* New York: St. Martin's, 1982. Print.

Jarrow, Gail. *A Medieval Castle.* Detroit: KidHaven, 2005. Print.

Johnson, Paul. *The Renaissance: A Short History.* New York: Modern Library, 2000. Print.

Jones, Dan. *The Plantagenets: The Warrior Kings and Queens Who Made England.* New York: Penguin, 2014. Print.

Jones, Gwyn. *A History of the Vikings.* London: Oxford University Press, 1968. Print.

Killeen, Richard. *A Brief History of Ireland.* Philadelphia, PA: Running, 2012. Print.

Kirby, D. P. *The Earliest English Kings.* London: Routledge, 2000. Print.

Kure, Mitsuo. *Samurai: An Illustrated History.* Boston: Tuttle Pub., 2002. Print.

Manchester, William. *A World Lit Only by Fire: The Medieval Mind and the Renaissance: Portrait of an Age.* Boston: Little, Brown, 1992. Print.

Mansfield, Peter. *A History of the Middle East.* London: Penguin, 2010. Print.

McIntire, Suzanne, and William E. Burns. *Speeches in World History.* New York: Facts on File, 2009. Print.

Nardo, Don. *The Medieval Castle.* San Diego, CA: Lucent, 1998. Print.

Nicolle, David, and Graham Turner. *Poitiers AD 732: Charles Martel Turns the Islamic Tide.* Oxford: Osprey, 2008. Print.

Nitobe, Inazō. *Bushido: The Soul of Japan.* Tokyo: Kodansha International, 2002. Print.

Oliver, Roland, and Anthony Atmore. *Medieval Africa, 1250–1800.* Cambridge: Cambridge University Press, 2001. Print.

Phillips, Jonathan. "The Crusades: A Complete History." *History Today.* May 2015. Web.

Pollard, Justin. *Alfred the Great: The Man Who Made England.* UK: John Murray Pubs, 2007. Print.

Polo, Marco, A. C. Moule, and Paul Pelliot. *The Description of the World.* New York: AMS, 1976. Print.

Rosewell, Roger. *The Medieval Monastery.* Oxford: Shire Pub, 2012. Print.

Sawyer, P. H. *The Oxford Illustrated History of the Vikings.* Oxford: Oxford University Press, 1997. Print.

Sayers, Dorothy L. *The Song of Roland.* Harmondsworth, Eng.: Penguin, 1957. Print.

Severin, Timothy. *The Brendan Voyage.* New York: Modern Library, 2000. Print.

Seward, Desmond. *A Brief History of the Hundred Years War: The English in France, 1337–1453.* London: Robinson, 2003. Print.

Shuter, Jane. *Life in a Medieval Castle.* Chicago: Heinemann Library, 2005. Print.

Smyth, Alfred P. *The Medieval Life of King Alfred the Great: A Translation and Commentary on the Text* Attributed to Asser. Basingstoke, Hampshire: Paulgrave Houndmills, 2002. Print.

Stefoff, Rebecca. *Marco Polo and the Medieval Explorers.* New York: Chelsea House, 1992. Print.

Strathloch, Robert. *Marco Polo.* Chicago: Heinemann Library, 2002. Print.

Theophanes, Cyril A. Mango, Roger Scott, and Geoffrey Greatrex. *The Chronicle of Theophanes Confessor: Byzantine and Near Eastern History,* A.D. *284–813.* Oxford: Clarendon, 1997. Print.

Thorpe, Lewis G. M., Einhard, and Notker. *Two Lives of Charlemagne.* Harmondsworth: Penguin, 1969. Print.

Vasari, Giorgio. *Lives of the Artists.* trans. Adrienne DeAngelis. "Lives of the Artists," http://members.efn.org/~acd/vite/VasariLives.html. Web.

Weatherford, J. McIver. *Genghis Khan and the Making of the Modern World.* New York: Crown, 2004. Print.

Wilson, Peter H. *Heart of Europe: A History of the Holy Roman Empire.* Oxford: Belknap, 2016. Print.

Photo Credits

Chapter 4: The Monastery
    Lindisfarne Priory Ruins
    Photo Credit: Nilfanion

Chapter 5: The Earliest Explorers
    St. Brendan's Currach model
    Photo Credit: Michealol

Chapter 9: Charlemagne
    The Iron Crown of Lombardy
    Photo Credit: James Steakley

Chapter 10: The Rushing North Wind
    The Gokstad Ship
    Photo Credit: Anders Beer Wilse

Chapter 12: Cornstalks and Quetzal Feathers
    Goal Hoop on a Mayan Ball Court
    Photo Credit: Brian Snelson

Chapter 13: The Battle of Hastings
    Bayeaux Tapestry scene
    Photo Credit: Myrabella

Chapter 15: The Way of the Warrior
    Bonsai tree
    Photo Credit: Ragesoss

Chapter 16: The Cross Upon the Shield
    Hereford Map
    Photo Credit: UNESCO

    Krak de Chevaliers illustration
    From *Guillaume Rey: Étude sur les monuments de l'architecture militaire des croisés en Syrie et dans l'île de Chypre* (1871).

Chapter 18: Castles
    Murder Hole
    Photo Credit: Jonathan Oldenbuck

Chapter 19: The Great Charter
    Magna Carta with Seal
    Photo Credit: J.delanoy

Chapter 22: Salt, Books, and Gold
    University at Timbuktu
    Photo Credit: UNESCO

Chapter 23: A Fresh Breeze
    The Arrest of Christ by Giotto

Chapter 26: Conquerors of the Green Sea
    Portuguese Caravel
    Photo Credit: PHGCOM

Chapter 27: An Explosion of Words
    Metal movable type
    Photo Credit: Willi Heidelbach

    The Gutenberg Bible
    Photo Credit: Library of Congress

For Further Reading

Children's Books

The Middle Ages

Beckett, Wendy, and Jean De France Berry. *The Duke and the Peasant: Life in the Middle Ages: The Calendar Pictures in the Duc De Berry's Très Riches Heures.* New York: Prestel, 1997.

Biesty, Stephen. *Stephen Biesty's Cross-Sections Castle.* New York, NY 10016: Dorling Kindersley, 2013.

Burch, Joann Johansen. *Fine Print: A Story about Johann Gutenberg.* Minneapolis: Carolrhoda, 1991.

Cels, Marc. *Life in a Medieval Monastery.* New York: Crabtree Pub., 2005.

Cels, Marc. *Life on a Medieval Manor.* New York: Crabtree Pub., 2005.

Coggins, Jack. *The Illustrated Book of Knights.* Mineola, New York: Dover Publications, 2006.

Eastwood, Kay. *Medieval Society.* New York: Crabtree, 2004.

Macaulay, David. *Castle.* New York: HMH for Young Readers, 2013.

O'Brien, Patrick. *The Making of a Knight: How Sir James Earned His Armor.* Watertown, MA: Charlesbridge, 1998.

Rumford, James. *From the Good Mountain: How Gutenberg Changed the World.* New York: Roaring Brook, 2012.

Templeman, Henry. *Knights: Secrets of Medieval Warriors.* UK: Carlton Kids, 2015.

The Fall of Rome

Hodges, Margaret, and Barry Moser. *St. Jerome and the Lion.* New York: Orchard, 1991.

Kroll, Steven, and Robert Byrd. *Barbarians!* New York: Dutton Children's, 2009.

Mellor, Ronald, and Marni McGee. *The Ancient Roman World.* Oxford: Oxford University Press, 2004.

The Byzantine Empire

Feldman, Ruth. *The Fall of Constantinople.* Minneapolis, MN: Twenty-First Century, 2008.

Phillips, Robin. *Who in the World Was the Acrobatic Empress?: The Story of Theodora.* Charles City, VA: Peace Hill, 2006.

VanVoorst, Jenny Fretland. *The Byzantine Empire.* North Mankato, MN: Compass Point, 2013.

The History of England

Brocklehurst, Ruth, G. Gaudenzi, and Jane Chisholm. *Roman Britain.* London: Usborne, 2006.

Daugherty, James. *The Magna Charta.* San Luis Obispo: Beautiful Feet, 1998.

Green, Roger Lancelyn. *The Adventures of Robin Hood.* London: Puffin, 2010.

Green, Roger Lancelyn. *King Arthur and His Knights of the Round Table.* London, England: Puffin, 2008.

MacDonald, Fiona. *Anglo-Saxon and Viking Britain.* London: Franklin Watts, 2003.

Tanaka, Shelley. *In the Time of Knights: The Real-life History of History's Greatest Knight.* New York: Hyperion, 2000.

Tappan, Eva March. *In the Days of Alfred the Great.* Boston: Lee and Shepard, 1900.

Explorers

Andronik, Catherine M. *Copernicus: Founder of Modern Astronomy.* Berkeley Heights, NJ: Enslow, 2002.

Freedman, Russell. *Who Was First?: Discovering the Americas.* New York: Clarion, 2007.

Fritz, Jean, and Enrico Arno. *Brendan the Navigator: A History Mystery about the Discovery of America.* New York: Coward, McCann & Geoghegan, 1979.

Sansevere-Dreher, Diane, and Ed Renfro. *Explorers Who Got Lost.* New York: TOR, 1992.

Schiller, Barbara, and Hal Frenck. *Eric the Red and Leif the Lucky.* Mahwah, NJ: Troll Associates, 1979.

The History of France

Maurice, Boutet De Monvel Louis. *The Story of Joan of Arc.* Mineola, NY: Dover, 2010.

Rice, Earle. *The Life and Times of Clovis, King of the Franks.* Hockessin, DE: Mitchell Lane, 2010.

The Middle East and Africa

Burns, Khephra, Leo Dillon, and Diane Dillon. *Mansa Musa: The Lion of Mali.* San Diego: Harcourt Brace, 2001.

Henty, G. A. *The Boy Knight: A Tale of the Crusades.* Mineola, NY: Dover Publications, 2006. (historical fiction)

Kelman, Janet Harvey. *Stories from the Crusades.* Chapel Hill, NC: Yesterday's Classics, 2005. (Originally written in 1907, this is the Crusades told from a Christian point of view.)

McKissack, Pat, and Fredrick McKissack. *The Royal Kingdoms of Ghana, Mali, and Songhay: Life in Medieval Africa.* New York: H. Holt, 1994.

Stanley, Diane. *Saladin: Noble Prince of Islam.* New York: HarperCollins, 2002. (This short biography looks at the Crusades from a Muslim point of view.)

Wilkinson, Philip, and Caroline Stone. *Islam.* New York: Dorling Kindersley, 2005.

Holy Roman Empire

Buff, Mary, and Conrad Buff. *The Apple and the Arrow.* Boston: Houghton Mifflin, 1951.

Early, Margaret. *William Tell.* New York: Harry N. Abrams, 1991.

MacDonald, Fiona. *The World in the Time of Charlemagne.* Philadelphia: Chelsea House, 2001.

Maier, Paul L. *Martin Luther: A Man Who Changed the World.* St. Louis, MO: Concordia Pub. House, 2004.

Willard, Barbara, and Emil Weiss. *Son of Charlemagne.* Warsaw, ND: Bethlehem, 1998. (historical fiction)

The Vikings

D'Aulaire, Ingri, and Edgar Parin D'Aulaire. *D'Aulaires' Book of Norse Myths.* New York: New York Review of, 2005.

Thompson, Ben. *Guts & Glory: The Vikings.* New York: Little, Brown, 2014. (some discussion of violence)

The Americas

Coulter, Laurie. *Secrets in Stone: All about Maya Hieroglyphs.* Boston, MA: Little, Brown, 2001.

Lourie, Peter. *The Mystery of the Maya: Uncovering the Lost City of Palenque.* Honesdale, PA: Boyds Mills, 2001.

Asia

Demi. *Genghis Khan.* Tarrytown, NY: Marshall Cavendish Children, 2009.

Krull, Kathleen. *Kubla Khan: The Emperor of Everything.* New York: Viking, 2010.

MacDonald, Fiona. *A Samurai Castle: Spectacular Visual Guides.* UK: Book House, 2015.

Major, John S., and Stephen Fieser. *The Silk Route: 7,000 Miles of History.* New York: HarperCollins, 1995.

McCarty, Nick. *Marco Polo: The Boy Who Traveled the Medieval World.* Washington, D.C.: National Geographic, 2006.

Park, Louise, and Timothy Love. *The Japanese Samurai.* New York: Marshall Cavendish Benchmark, 2010.

Turner, Pamela S. *Samurai Rising: The Epic Life of Minamoto Yoshitsune.* Watertown, MA: Charlesbridge, 2016. (This book, while engaging and exciting, does not shy away from depicting the violence of a samurai's life.)

For Interested Adults

Asbridge, Thomas S. *The Greatest Knight: The Remarkable Life of William Marshal, the Power behind Five English Thrones.* New York: Ecco, 2015.

Bauer, Susan Wise. *The History of the Medieval World: From the Conversion of Constantine to the First Crusade.* New York: W.W. Norton, 2010.

Bauer, Susan Wise. *The History of the Renaissance World: From the Rediscovery of Aristotle to the Conquest of Constantinople.* New

York: W.W. Norton, 2013.

Brownworth, Lars. *The Sea Wolves: A History of the Vikings.* UK: Crux, 2014.

Carlsen, William. *Jungle of Stone: The True Story of Two Men, Their Extraordinary Journey, and the Discovery of the Lost Civilization of the Maya.* New York: William Morrow, 2016.

Heather, P. J. *The Fall of the Roman Empire.* London: Macmillan, 2005.

Kure, Mitsuo. *Samurai: An Illustrated History.* Boston: Tuttle Pub., 2002.

Morris, Marc. *A Great and Terrible King: Edward I and the Forging of Britain.* New York: Pegasus, 2015.

Morris, Marc. *The Norman Conquest: The Battle of Hastings and the Fall of Anglo-Saxon England.* New York: Pegasus, 2014.

Pollard, Justin. *Alfred the Great: The Man Who Made England.* UK: John Murray Pubs, 2007.

Tuchman, Barbara W. *A Distant Mirror: The Calamitous 14th Century.* New York: Knopf, 1978.

Wilson, Peter H. *Heart of Europe: A History of the Holy Roman Empire.* Oxford: Belknap, 2016.

The Roman Empire in the 4th Century

Europe in the Time of Odoacer

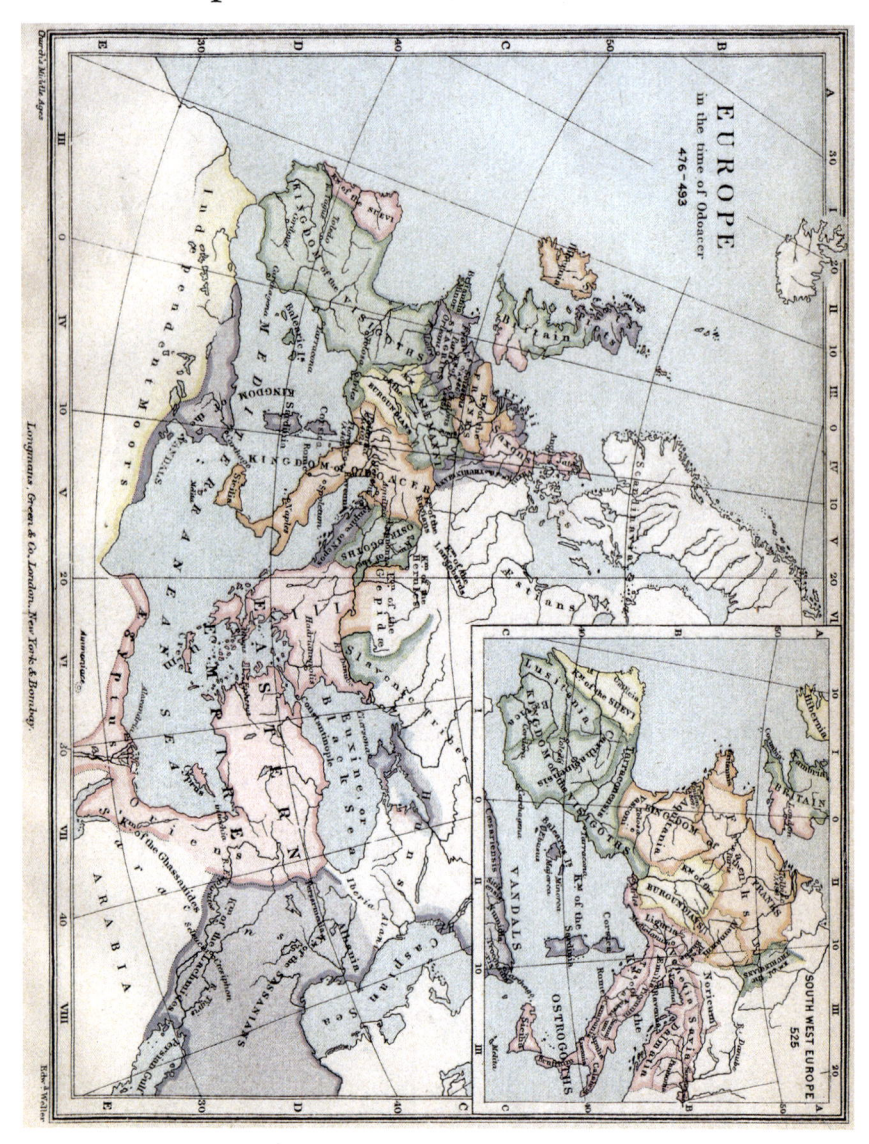

Roman Britain

England after the English Conquest

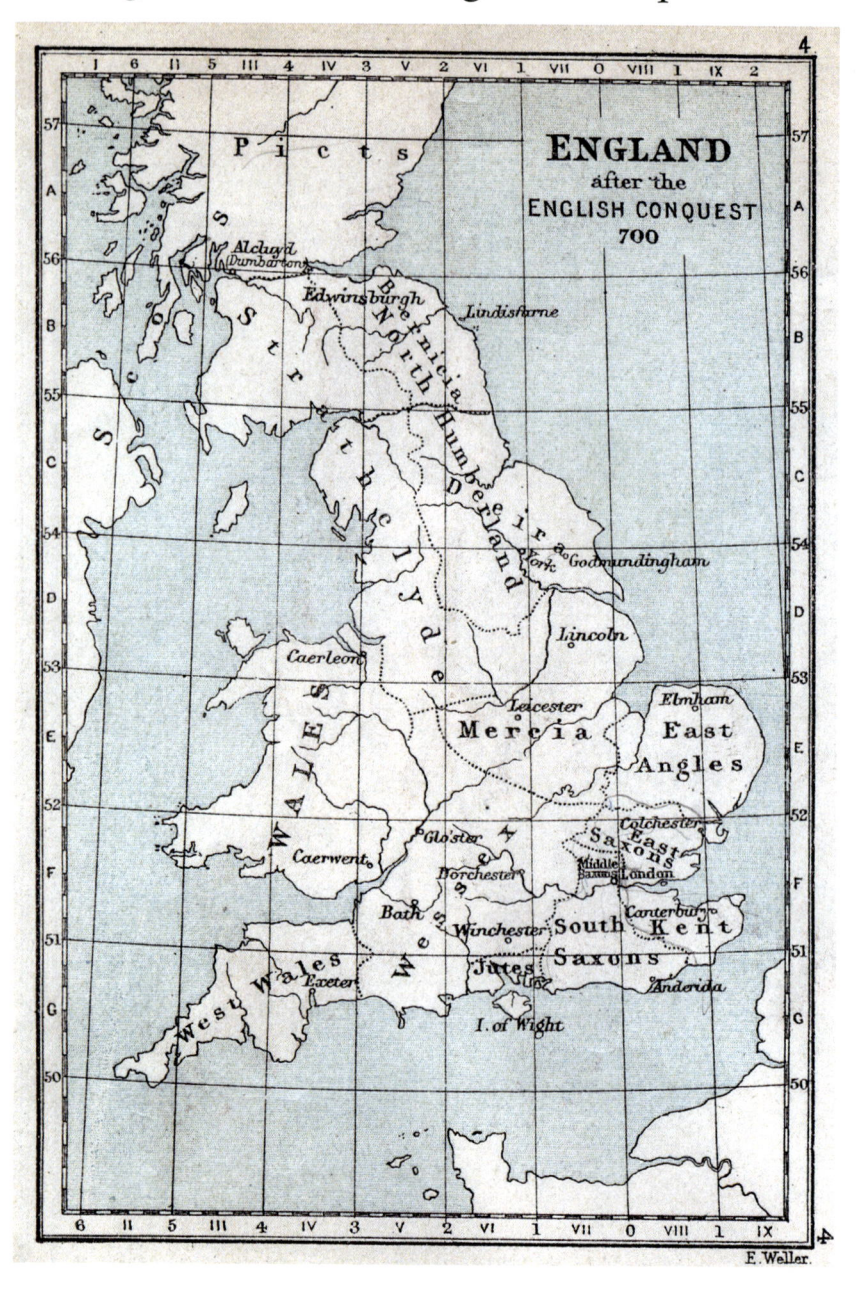

England after the Peace of Wedmore

Europe at the Death of Charles the Great

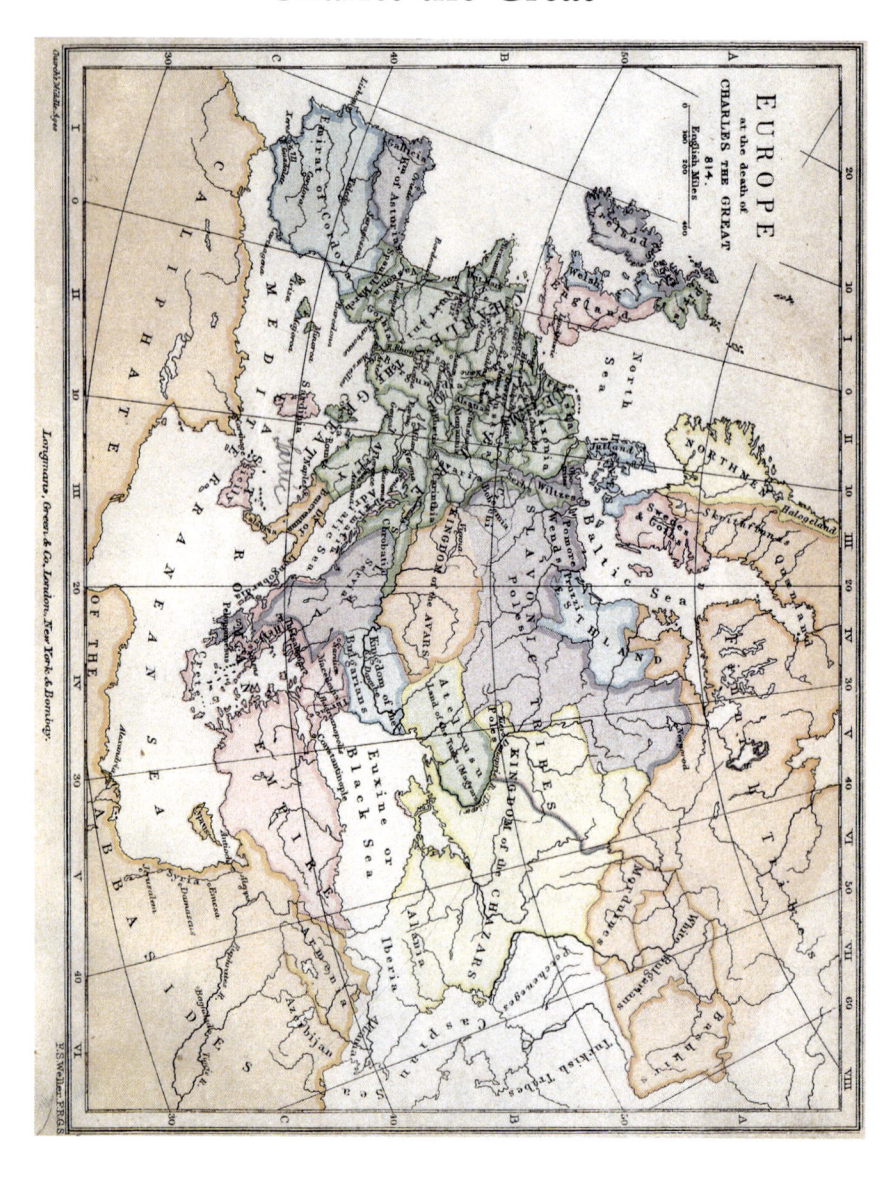

Europe in 912

England in 1065

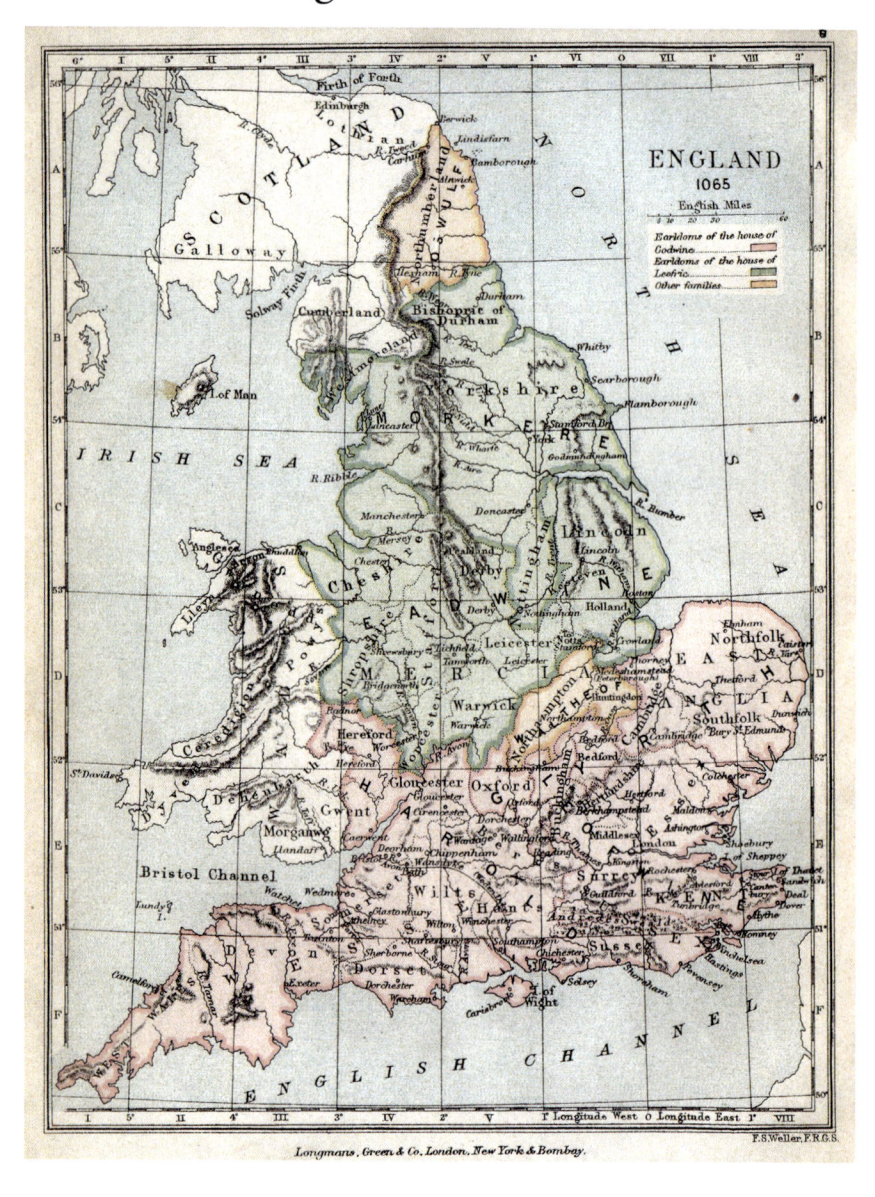

Era of the Crusades

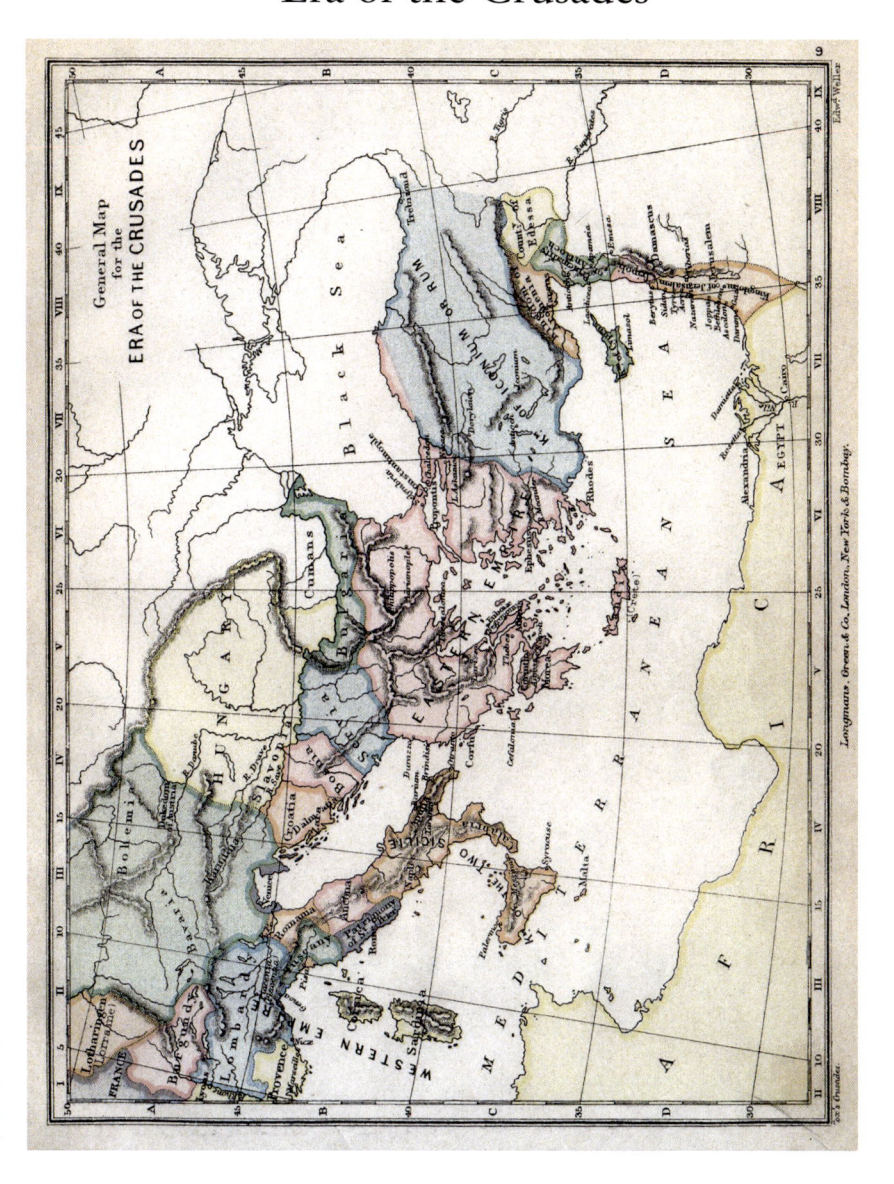

Europe in the 14th Century

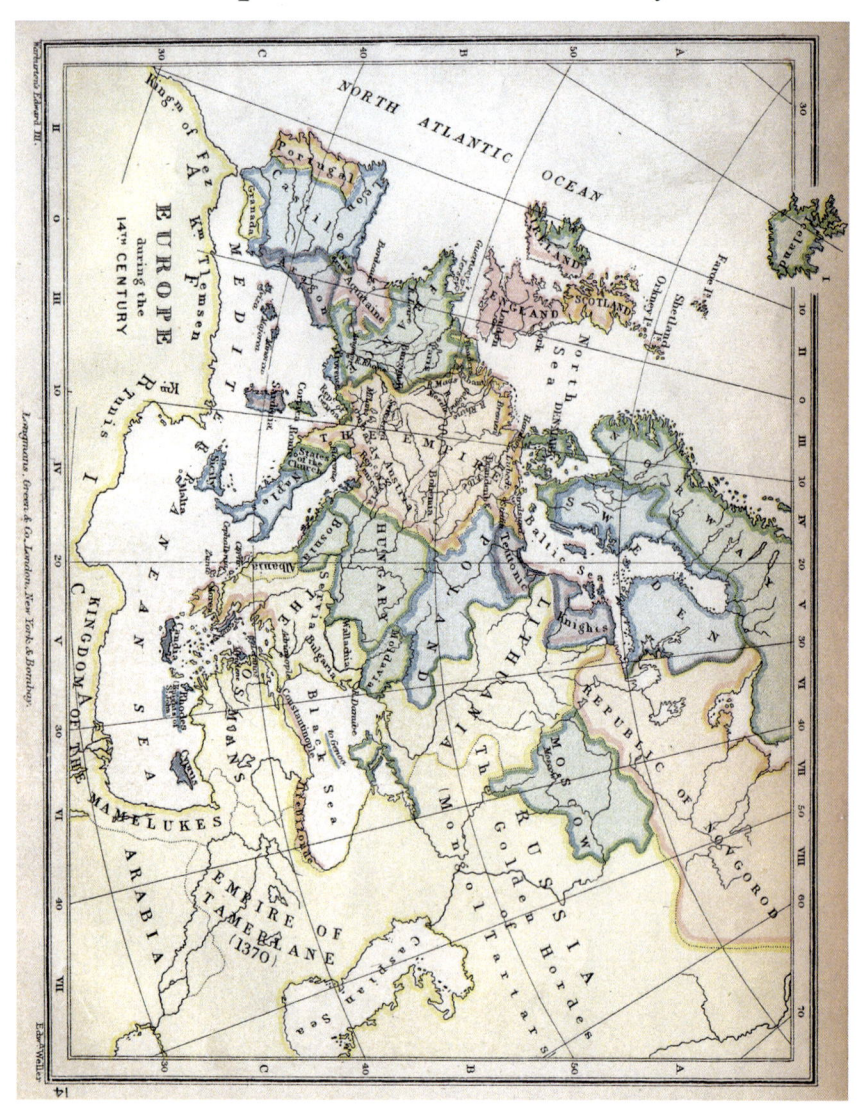

Europe in the 15th Century

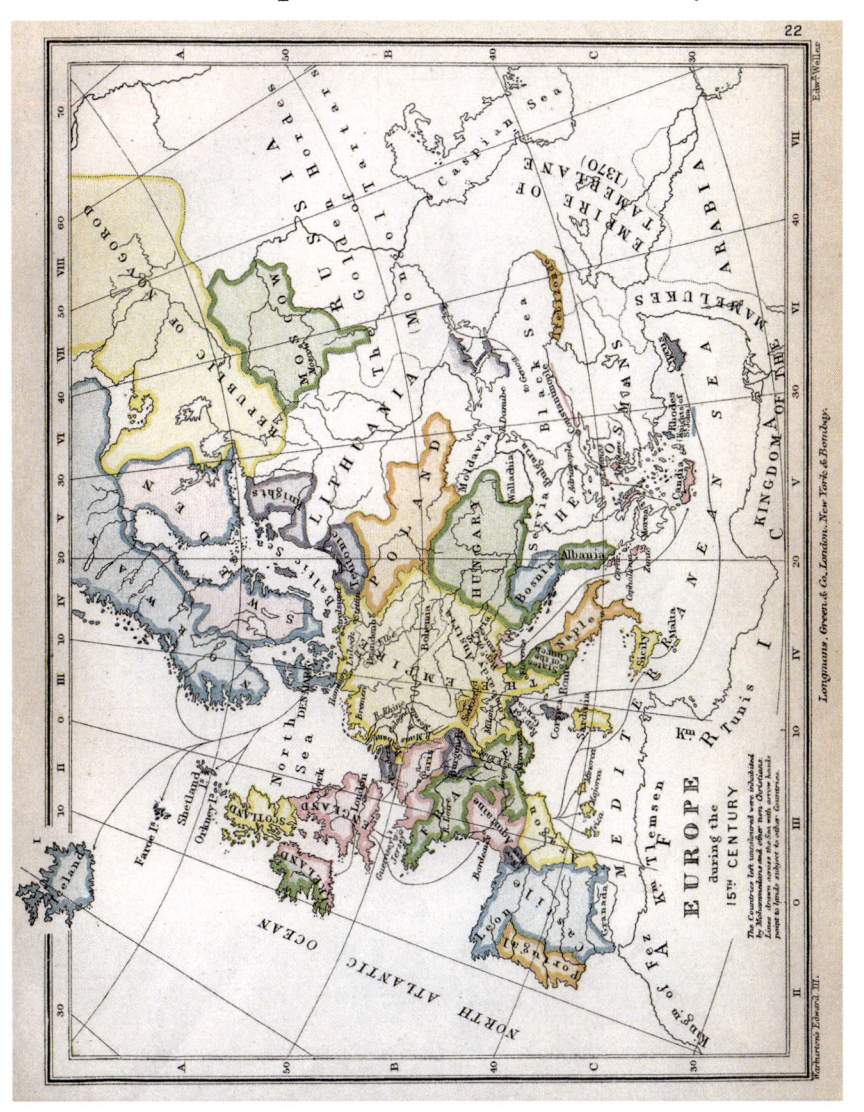

World Map

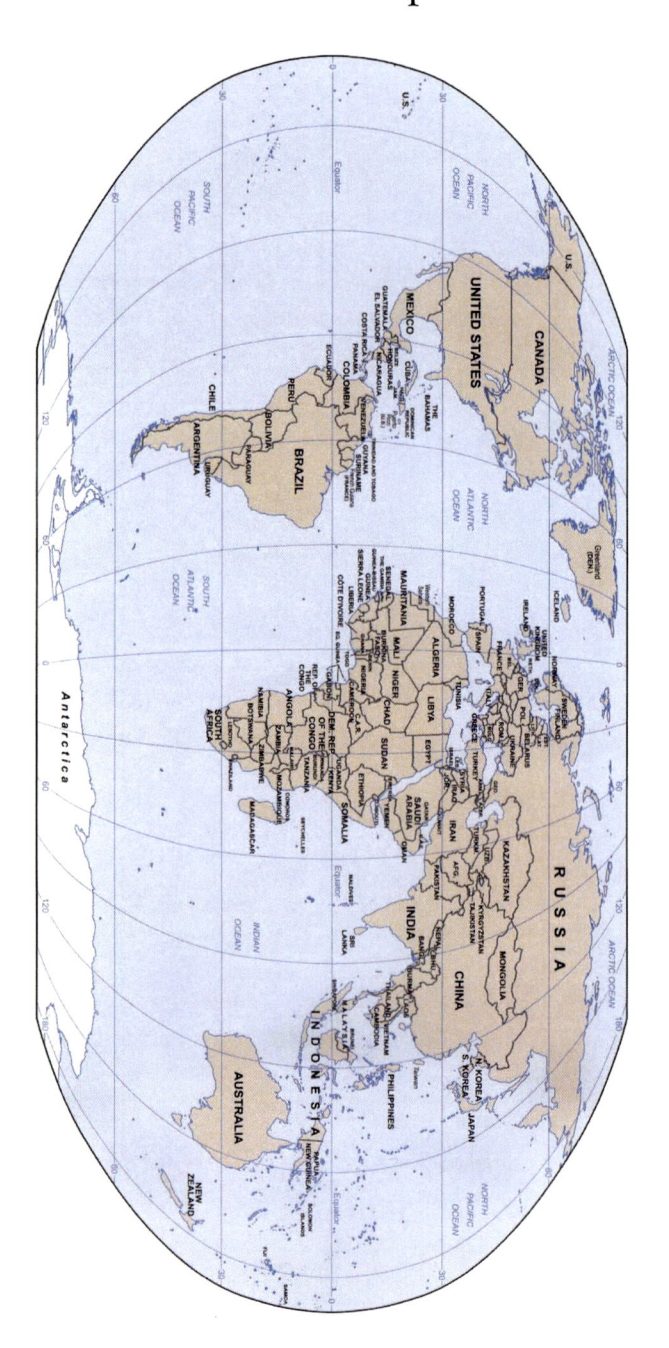

Pronunciation Guide

Aachen (AH-ken)
Abd-al-Rahman Al Ghafiqi (ABD-al-RAH-man al gah-FEE-kee)
Abu Bakr (AH-boo BECK-er)
Abu Said al-Sijzi (AH-boo SAH-eed al-SEE-ja)
aether (EE-ther)
Africanus (AH-fri-CAH-nus)
Agincourt (AH-jin-coort)
al-Andalus (AL AN-dah-LOOS)
Alaric (AL-a-rik)
Aleppo (ah-LEP-po)
Alexius (ah-LEX-ee-us)
Aristarchos of Samos (AH-ri-STAR-kus of SAH-mos)
Athelney (ATH-el-nee)
Attila (uh-TILL-uh)
Austrasia (au-STRAY-zha)
Badakhshan (bah-DAK-shun)
bakufu (bah-koo-foo)
Barbarossa (BAR-bah-ROH-sa)
Bayeux (BYE-you)
Belisarius (bell-ih-SAR-ee-us)
Bjarni Herjolfsson (BYAR-nee HER-yolf-suhn)
Bolon Tzacab (BOO-lun TSAH-cob)
Bordeaux (bore-DOH)
Borte (BORE-tuh)
Botticelli (BO-tih-CHELL-ee)
bushido (boo-shee-doh)
Byzantium (buh-ZAN-tee-um)
Calais (CAL-ay)
Cape Bojador (Cape BOH-ja-dor)
Cappadocia (cap-uh-DOH-shee-uh)
Carloman (CAR-lo-man)
Cathay (CATH-ay)
Ceuta (SAY-oot-ah)

Chaac (CHOCK)
Chararic (CHAR-uh-rick)
Charlemagne (SHAR-luh-main)
chiaroscuro (KEE-ar-ohs-COO- roh)
Childeric (CHIL-der-ick)
Cicero (SIS-er-oh)
Clotilde (cloh-TILD)
Constantinople (con-stan-tih-NO-pull)
Copernicus (cuh-PER-ni-kiss)
Cosimo (CO-see-MO)
currach (KUH-ruhk)
daimyo (die-mio)
Diocletian (die-uh-CLEE-shun)
Domenico Maria Novara da Ferrara (doh-MEN-i-CO ma-REE-ah no-VAR-uh da fer-RAH-ruh)
Eadfrith (EED-frith)
Edessa (EH-des-sa)
Einhard (INE-hard)
fief (feef)
Francesco Petrarca (fran-CHESS-ko pe-TRAR-kah)
Fushimi (foo-shee-mee)
Genghis Khan (GHEN-ghis KAHN)
Genoa (JEN-ah-wah)
Georg Rheticus (JAY-org REH-ti-kus)
Gessler (GUESS-ler)
Gil Eannes (JILL EE-ah-nays)
Giorgio Vasari (JOR-joh vah-SAH-ree)
Giotto di Bondone (JOT-toh dee bon-DOH-neh)
Giovanni Cimabue (JEE-oh-VAN-nee CHEE-mah-BOO-eh)
Gokstad (GOCK-stad)
Guinevere (GWEN-eh-veer)
Hadrian (HAY-dree-un)
Hagia Sophia (ha-GHEE-ah so-FEE-ah)
Hengist (HEN-jist)
Honorius (huh-NOR-ee-us)
Hormuz (HOR-muhz)

Horsa (HOR-sah)
Hypatius (hi-PAY-shee-us)
Itzamna (eat-SAHM-na)
Ivar (EE-var)
Jebal-tariq (JEH-bull TAR-ick)
Jerome (juh-ROHM)
Johann Tetzel (YO-han TET-sel)
Joyeuse (JWAY-oos)
Justinian (jus-TIN-ee-un)
Kaaba (KAH-bah)
Khadija (KHAH-dee-juh)
Kokachin (CO-cah-CHEEN)
Kublai Khan (KOO-blay KAHN)
Kussnacht (KOOS-nakt)
Kyoto (kyoh-toh)
Lindisfarne (LIND-es-farn)
Lutetia Parisiorum (loo-TET-see-uh pa-REE-see-or-um)
Maffeo (MAH-fay-oh)
Mainz (MINES)
Martel (mar-TELL)
Maya (MY-yuh)
Medici (MAY-dee-chee)
Medina (meh-DEE-nah)
Mercia (MER-se-ah)
Merkits (MAIR-gets)
Musa (MOO-sah)
Niccolo Polo (NEE-koh-loh POH-loh)
Nicolay Nicolaysen (NICK-oh-LIE NICK-oh-LIE-sin)
Nika (NIE-kuh)
Odin (OH-din)
Odoacer (OH-doh-AY-ser)
Ongkhan (ONG-khan)
Orleans (aw-lay-ahwn)
paizah (PIE-zuh)
Poitiers (PWAH-tee-ay)
Ptolemy (TALL-uh-mee)

quetzal (KET-sal)
Quran (kuh-RAHN)
Romulus Augustulus (ROM-yoo-lus ah-GUST-uh-lus)
Rurik (ROO-reek)
Rus (ROOS)
Rustichello (ROOS-tee-KEL-low)
Rutli (ROOT-lee)
Saladin (SAL-a-din)
samurai (sa-mur-eye)
Sassanids (suh-SAW-nids)
Schwyz (SCHWEETS)
Seljuk (SEL-jook)
Shangdu (SHANG-doo)
Sistine (SIS-teen)
Sluys (SLUHZ)
Soissons (swah-SON)
Songhai (song-HI)
Sonni Ali (SOO-nee ah-LEE)
Sosso (SO-so)
Sultan Mehmet (MEH-met)
Sundiata (SOON-dee-AH-ta)
Syagrius (si-AY-gree-uhs)
Tariq-ibn-Ziyad (TAR-ick ih-bin zee-AD)
Temujin (tay-MOO-jin)
Theodora (thee-uh-DOR-uh)
Theophanes (thee-OFF-uh-neez)
Thorvaldson, Eric (TOR-wuhl-suhn)
Tokugawa Ieyasu (toh-koo-ga-wa ee-ay-ya-soo)
Torii Mototada (to-ree mo-toh-tah-dah)
trebuchets (tray-BOO-shays)
Unterwalden (OON-ter-VAHL-den)
Uri (OOR-ee)
Valens (VAL-enz)
Valhalla (vahl-HAL-la)
Valkyrie (VAHL-keer-ee)
Valois (VAL-wah)

Varangian (vah-RAN-jee-in)
Vladimir (VLAD-ee-MEER)
Vortigern (VOR-ti-jern)
Vortimer (VOR-ti-mer)
wakizashi (wa-kee-za-shee)